"This book is infectious! Once you read it, you will want to spread the news to everyone you know who works with young ̶ true heart for evangelism, and in Outbreak, he has ̶ erful tool to help you lead the charge for effective youth ministry!"

JOSH D. MCDOWELL

"Greg has captured a great vision for God's purpose of evangelism and laid it out in an easy-to-understand format. Two of the aspects of this book that I appreciate most are its practical approach and easy application. I've never used the word 'easy' when it comes to evangelism before, but Outbreak really helps students and youth leaders clearly understand the need for 'viral evangelism' and provides them with user-friendly help. I can't wait for my youth ministry to be influenced by this material."

DOUG FIELDS
Pastor to Students
Saddleback Church
Author: *Purpose Driven Youth Ministry*

"In today's postmodern world of political correctness, it's refreshing to see that someone still believes that teenagers can win their unsaved friends to Christ. Greg Stier is not only a believer, but an enthusiastic and successful motivator and equipper of young saints who want to turn their world upside down just like the early disciples did! This book is long overdue and highly recommended!"

WAYNE RICE
Co-founder, Youth Specialties
Director, Understanding Your Teenager

"Youth leaders are in a war for our nation's teenagers, and Greg gives them practical, Bible-inspired ammunition and strategies to reach out, infect, and excite young people to a passion for God. Each chapter of this book concludes with a review statement, a challenge for the leader, and questions for the entire youth ministry team to go over, think about, and put into action."

LORI SALIERNO
CEO, Celebrate Life International

OUTBREAK

CREATING A CONTAGIOUS

YOUTH MINISTRY

THROUGH VIRAL EVANGELISM

GREG STIER

MOODY PUBLISHERS
CHICAGO

Editor: Ali Diaz
Cover Design: The DesignWorks Group, Inc., Wes Youssi

Library of Congress Cataloging-in-Publication Data

Stier, Greg.
    Outbreak : creating a contagious youth ministry through viral evangelism / Greg Stier.
        p. cm.
    Includes bibliographical references (p.).
    ISBN 0-8024-1794-9
    1. Church group work with teenagers. I. Title.
BV4447 .S695 2002
259'.23—dc21

                                                                    2001057934

ISBN: 0-8024-1794-9
ISBN-13: 978-0-8024-1794-7

We hope you enjoy this book from Moody Publishers. Our goal is to provide high-quality, thought-provoking books and products that connect truth to your real needs and challenges. For more information on other books and products written and produced from a biblical perspective, go to www.moodypublishers.com or write to:

Moody Publishers
820 N. LaSalle Boulevard
Chicago, IL 60610

1 3 5 7 9 10 8 6 4 2

Printed in the United States of America

To Doug—
Your example showed me how to go viral.

CONTENTS

HOW TO USE THIS BOOK

This book is designed to give you a hands-on guide for implementing a viral approach to evangelism through your weekly youth group meeting. After each chapter, you will find three practical helps to enable you to maximize the principles you have discovered. Red Dot Reviews, Monkey Mandates, and Staff Infection Questions will help you navigate these truths from theory to reality.

RED•DOT REVIEWS

These one-sentence summations will reinforce the point of the chapter.

MONKEY MANDATES

This section is the youth leader to-do list. It will enable you to immediately put into practice what you have learned.

STAFF INFECTION QUESTIONS

Since this book is designed to be read with your youth ministry staff (students or adults), these questions will help your team get on the same page when it comes to implementing these viral principles in your youth ministry.

I encourage you to make this a twelve-week project. Take one week for each chapter. You and your team can read the chapter and then go through the questions. On the twelfth week spend time refining your strategy. Then launch it officially in a viral kickoff in the youth group.

Have fun and go viral! ✖

ACKNOWLEDGMENTS

This book goes out with many thanks to many people. First and foremost I would like to thank my wonderful wife, Debbie, who encouraged me to go beyond what was comfortable to me, preaching behind a pulpit, and try something different, writing behind a desk. Her patience with me during my travels and writing retreats enabled me to invest in a craft that did not come as easily to me. Eric and Leslie Ludy are to be gratefully acknowledged as well. It was their insistence and persistence that encouraged me to pursue getting published. They believed in the importance of getting this vision out there and coached me along every step of the way. Thanks to the Ludys as well for the introduction to Moody Publishers.

Thanks to the wonderful staff at Dare 2 Share Ministries who tolerated an absentee president every morning from 8–11 a.m., while I worked to complete this manuscript at our local Starbucks. Lane Palmer and Debbie Bresina as staff members, your insights, ideas, and help have been tremendously influential in the crafting of this book.

Special thanks goes out to all of the youth leaders across America who have helped me to discover the principles that are represented in *Outbreak*. In addition, R. J. Koerper and Ralph "Yankee" Arnold both changed the way I define effective youth ministry. Their input into my life has infected me with a passion to see God unleash a student awakening across the world.

I would also like to thank the people and leadership of Grace Church. Although I am no longer a pastor there, I sensed the prayers of this viral congregation every step along the way while putting this book together. Special thanks to Jim Malouff, Rick Long, and Jonathan Smith, who continued to encourage, coach, challenge, and ask the hard questions.

Finally, I would like to thank the publishing team at Moody Publishers. It's been a privilege working with a team that is so godly, encouraging, and concerned about truth. Moody Publishers is truly a name you can trust. ✖

INTRODUCTION

Youth leaders are frustrated. Most of them originally got into youth ministry not because of the pay but because of the payoff. They have a deep passion to see kids come to know Jesus Christ. Youth leaders have a common purpose that drives them. "What if . . . ?" they ask. "What if God used me to touch the life of one student? What if I had the awesome privilege of being a change maker in the lives of a group of students? What if God used our youth group to set the pattern for revival of our entire church? What if God started an awakening of biblical proportions through my students?"

Youth leaders have a burning desire to see souls saved and lives changed. The problem is that as the months give way to years, the machinery of ministry and the pressure of politics often douse the hottest of flames and crush the strongest resolve.

Maybe it's the complaints about the stains in the carpets or the holes in the walls in the youth room. Perhaps it's the struggle of the juggle—that constant juggling act between parental and pastoral expectations. As a result of those difficulties and a thousand others, many youth leaders eventually give in or give up. They give in to the counterbiblical challenge to reel in their students' exuberance instead of harnessing it and focusing it. They give up on swinging for the fences. After all, it's just a job, right? The result is that youth leaders often slowly transform their roles from passionate visionary to skilled event-coordinator, from mission-driven general to sanctified babysitter, and from youth-pastor-for-life to senior-pastor-in-waiting. The struggle is not worth it. Or so it seems.

My prayer is that this book will encourage youth leaders not to give up or give in. The struggle is worth it. The battle must be won. Our kids' souls are at stake.

The purpose of this book is not to complain about the current state of youth ministry but to do something about it. The answers to the problems we are facing in the church when it comes to youth ministry are self-evident and scriptural. But they are not easy. It will take a different kind of thinking to change this paradigm. It will take men and women who are willing to pay the price, to swim against the stream of status quo thinking, and, in some cases, to even lose their jobs.

THIS BOOK IS ABOUT HOPE

I believe there is hope. Ultimately that's what this book is about. It's about hope that God will raise up a new kind of youth leader who will do what it takes to enlist fully committed disciples. It's about hope that the church will produce a new kind of student prophet who speaks forth God's Word unashamedly to their peers. It's about the hope that from the ashes of failed experiments God will create a new paradigm for effective youth ministry.

The best single piece of advice I received as I wrote this book came from Dave Rahn. Originally, I had planned to write a sociological study filled with stats and facts. After reading the original manifesto he asked me, "Greg, are you a sociologist?"

I said, "No!"

He asked, "Are you a statistician?"

I said, "No."

He asked, "What are you then?"

"I am a preacher."

He reminded me to stick with what I know best . . . the Word of God. "Sociologists and statisticians can't compete with God's Word" was his great advice. That is why you will see in this book passage after passage from the book of Acts. I am convinced that that book is the ultimate youth ministry manual. If all else fails, read the instructions. All else has failed.

In spite of the countless how-to books and training seminars available to youth leaders today, youth ministry for the most part has failed to capture the hearts and minds of the young people of the church. As a result we are losing our young.

WE HAVE EVERYTHING
WE NEED IN SCRIPTURE

Within the pages of Scripture we have everything we need to truly be successful in youth ministry. The rest is just details. The principles that brought spiritual transformation in the early New Testament church still work today. It's a matter of applying them tenaciously, wisely, and faithfully. It's a matter of calling our students to a significant mission and passionate purpose so that they will stay involved in the life of the church long after graduation. It's a matter of seeing true and lasting revival begin within us and then spread to our students.

In the book of Acts, we are reminded that awakening is messy. Souls were saved and lives were changed, but the legalists attacked, the immature complained, and the lions had a free lunch. It was messy. Revival always is. If you are going to see it happen in your youth group, get ready to stand in awe of God's awesome power. But be ready for Satan's counterattack as well.

Peruse the book of Acts, and you will see a pattern. Every single time God did His thing, Satan did his too. The Evil One is brilliant. As soon as he sees the fledgling yearnings for spiritual transformation in a group, he dispatches his cohorts to wreak havoc. He will do the same for you. It's messy. But it's worth the mess. It's worth the struggle. It's worth the fight.

THE GOSPEL AS IDEAVIRUS

This book is designed to help you go viral in your youth ministry efforts. Using the analogy of a holy epidemic, I will show you how to see Christianity as contagious and your students as "sneezers."

The idea for this book came from studying Acts, the history of spiritual awakenings, and the concepts of "viral marketing" in secular marketing and business books. I read a book called *Unleashing the Ideavirus*, by Seth Godin, and I was so impressed by the principles of a word-of-mouth-on-steroids approach to marketing that I began to compare it with the book of Acts. The similarities were astounding.

Companies that "go viral," according to Godin, are companies that turn their customers into their biggest "evangelists." Godin's bottom-line challenge for CEOs is to come up with what he calls an *ideavirus* and then unleash it like an epidemic upon the customers of the company. Originally I studied that book to get ideas on how to market my own ministry, Dare 2 Share. But as I read it, I became more and more convinced that viral marketing needs to happen with the gospel of Jesus Christ.

The epidemic of evangelism that is chronicled throughout the book of Acts isn't sweeping most churches today, let alone many youth groups. As I read Godin's marketing book and others like it, I became more and more convinced that the idea of the gospel is the best idea ever. Why? Because it wasn't developed in a boardroom of top marketing executives. Instead, it was conceptualized and planned in the secret chambers of the ultimate strategists—the Trinity! Imagine that storyboarding process in that back room of heaven! The result of that divine brainstorming session was the ultimate idea, the gospel of Jesus Christ.

When that ideavirus was unleashed in the first century, the results were amazing. Thousands upon thousands of people came to a saving knowledge of Jesus Christ. It spread so fast that the enemies of Christianity said this about Paul the apostle: "We have found this man to be a troublemaker, stirring up riots among the Jews *all over the world*" (Acts 24:5, italics added).

All over the world—that's how fast the message spread. It was only a few decades after the crucifixion and resurrection of Jesus Christ, and the message had already made a global mark. The book of Acts is a firsthand account of the spread of this evangelistic epidemic. Interestingly, the author was a doctor. Dr. Luke had seen the devastating effects of viruses upon the physical body in his years of experience as a physician. But now he was analyzing the powerful symptoms of an entirely different kind of infection—a spiritual one. Its devastating effects were inflicted upon the kingdom of darkness.

When the initial carriers of this infectious message, the apostles, died, however, something else seemed to die as well—the viral, exponential spread of the gospel message. The gospel inched forward over the next two millennia, but the church never quite ascended to the same level of viral evangelism that it had in the first century.

IT'S ALL ABOUT TO CHANGE

I think that is about to change. That's not because of the technology that is available today. It's not because of some radically new paradigm for evangelism or outreach. It is simply because of the sense of discontentment among the kids who fill our youth groups. As I travel the nation, I encounter teenagers everywhere who are sick and tired of typical church and dying instead for authentic Christianity. Students all over the nation are crying out for something real. They want a driving cause to live for and, if necessary, to die for. They are tired of the traditional. They long for the radical. The call of Christianity offers them all this and more. They must be energized, equipped, and turned loose with the life-changing, culture-transforming, world-shaking message of the gospel of Jesus Christ. No frills. No games. No wimps. Just contagious, unstoppable Christian students. It is going to take students like them and youth leaders like you to unleash this holy epidemic. That's what this book is all about! My prayer is that your youth ministry will never be the same after reading this book!

Ready to lead? Ready to charge? Ready to sneeze?✖

BAD MONKEY!

*"The single biggest threat to man's continued
dominance of the planet is the virus."*

JOSHUA LEDERBERG, PH.D., NOBEL LAUREATE

What does the word *outbreak* make you think of? Probably nothing good. You may think about the Black Plague, the AIDS virus, pandemics, or perhaps just a bad case of the flu spreading around the office.

Maybe the word conjures up memories of the now decade old movie with Rene Russo and Dustin Hoffman in virus-proof suits doing the dangerous work of seeking to contain the deadly Ebola virus. In this movie, appropriately titled *Outbreak*, African monkeys are captured and taken to America to be sold as pets. Unbeknownst to the monkey trappers, one animal is a carrier of the lethal Ebola virus.

The plot of the movie is pretty simple from there: Monkey goes to America. Monkey scratches man. Man kisses girlfriend. And so on, and so on, and so on until an entire community is infected. The rest of the movie is a battle between viral scientists (epidemiologists) and military strategists over whether or not the contaminated community should be simply contained or completely destroyed. Bad monkey!

There are two key scenes in the movie that show the velocity of the virus once an outbreak begins. One scene involves a military strategist explaining to his superiors the dangers of the virus's being unleashed upon the general populace. A computer-generated map of the United States stands behind him with a single red dot on one location. The red dot represents the point of infection. Showing how much more of the map will be engulfed with each passing hour, the military man says, "In twelve hours it will spread this far (the red dot gets bigger). In twenty-four hours it will spread this far (bigger). In thirty-six hours this far (bigger). In seventy two hours this far." By that point the map has turned completely red. The virus has become a nation killer and is well on its way to becoming a world killer. In that one short, cinematic scene, the exponential power of the virus becomes clear. It can be an unstoppable epidemic.

The next key scene depicts a man in a movie theater sneezing. The camera follows the virus out of his nose across rows and rows of packed theater seats into the open, laughing mouth of an unsuspecting movie watcher. It's kind of gross, but it makes the point. All it takes is close contact with the right person at the right time and bam! You're infected.

Throughout this book when you read the words *red dot* and *sneezers*, you will know I am referring to those two scenes.

EVANGELISM EPIDEMIC?

The word *epidemic* is usually used in a negative sense. It is associated with words like *death, plague, sickness, catastrophe, germ warfare,* and *pestilence.* But what if *epidemic* were used in a totally different context? What if the context were not death but life? What if the context were spiritual revival, not physical illness?

When you hear the word *outbreak* you probably don't think of a great, student-led, evangelistic revival spreading throughout your youth group into your adult congregation, the surrounding campuses, and the community. But that is about to change.

My premise is simple. Early Christianity was viral. It spread like an epidemic. It infected the general populace so quickly that no one was safe. In just a few years, the known world was infected by the epidemic of evangelism. It hasn't been the same since.

Today the virus has been trapped within the walls of our quarantined churches. According to George Barna, "of the 77 million American adults who are churched, born-again Christians:

- The typical churched believer will die without leading a single person to a lifesaving knowledge of and relationship with Jesus Christ.

- At any given time, a majority of believers do not have a specific person in mind for whom they are praying in the hope that the person will be saved.

- Most churched Christians believe that since they are not gifted in evangelism, such outreach is not a significant responsibility of theirs."[1]

WHY A VIRUS ANALOGY?

A virus is probably one of the most efficient forces under heaven. It is a powerful infection machine. Medical researchers are constantly studying viruses in hopes that we will soon be able to understand them better. "But fighting viruses is like fighting an enemy who keeps up with every new advancement in weapons technology; the more time they have, the more precocious and powerful they become."[2]

A virus analogy of the gospel of Jesus Christ is not meant to be disrespectful or even come close to teetering on the brink of sacrilege. In this book I am highlighting not the destructive force of a virus but its power, efficiency, and velocity. In that respect, the gospel is viral. The only thing that this virus seeks to destroy is the power of darkness. In every other aspect it is a constructive, even transformational force. It has power to change, not only individual lives but entire societies also.

THE GOSPEL AS AN IDEAVIRUS

Great ideas, under the right circumstances, with the right carriers, spread like an epidemic. These ideaviruses will transform the way we do business, according to many marketing experts. Seth Godin, author of *Unleashing the Ideavirus* and highly esteemed marketing guru, nails the power of an ideavirus when it comes to making money in the secular world in the twenty-first century:

 The first 100 years of our country's history were about who could build the biggest, most efficient farms. And the second century focused on the race to build factories. Welcome to the third century, folks. The third century is about ideas. Alas, nobody has a clue how to build a farm for ideas, or even a factory for ideas. Ideas are driving the economy, ideas are making people rich and, most important, ideas are changing the world. . . . An idea that just sits there is worthless. But an idea that moves, grows, and infects everyone it touches . . . that's an ideavirus.[3]

As I read that, I couldn't help but ask several questions. What better "carriers" than youth pastors? What better "sneezers" than students? What better "red dots" than our youth group meetings? But more than any other question, I asked what better ideavirus to infect our culture than the gospel of Jesus Christ?

The "idea" of the gospel came straight from the mind of God Himself. It is awesome, unimaginable, and amazing. After contemplating the idea of the gospel of Jesus Christ for several chapters in the book of Romans, the apostle Paul takes a break to sing with his pen in a moment of sheer worship, "Oh, the depth of the riches of the wisdom and knowledge of God! How unsearchable his judgments, and his paths beyond tracing out! 'Who has known the mind of the Lord? Or who has been his counselor?' 'Who has ever given to God, that God should repay him?' For from him and through him and to him are all things. To him be the glory forever! Amen" (Romans 11:33–36).

In the hidden councils of the Trinity in eternity past, a conspiracy of love was born. A people would be the object of God's infinite affection. They would rebel. Instead of sending them straight to hell, He would send them His own Son to live with them, teach them, and die for them. His death on the cross would provide the path for reconciliation and forgiveness, heaven and hope. All who simply trusted in Him would be restored to Him. Talk about an ideavirus that should catch on like an epidemic—the gospel is it! No idea ever conceived in the mind of man comes close to this divine conspiracy!

CHARACTERISTICS OF THE VIRUS

The virus has two defining traits. It is fast, and it is efficient. Understanding the power of those characteristics is key to understanding how the gospel will infect our youth groups.

THE VELOCITY OF THE VIRUS

Viruses move fast and infect quickly. In the movie *Outbreak* the monkey was the carrier of the virus. It infected other carriers until an entire community was infected. In the movie the virus spread so fast and so far that it was barely contained. You may be thinking, *Well, that's an exaggerated example of Hollywood fiction.* But the viral velocity of the real thing is not fiction at all. The speed of authentic viruses is documented again and again in medical history.

Viruses spread fast. Take the common cold for example. A cold can infect every member of a household in days. It can tear through an office in no time. It can spread from the infected to the infectee via a simple handshake. I know how fast a cold can spread through our little family. Jeremy to Kailey to Mommy to Daddy in nothing flat. Speed is the calling card of the virus. Once it tags you, you're it. And everybody who comes into contact with you becomes a potential victim of your virus.

Perhaps the most infamous example of the velocity of a virus in history was the Black Death in Europe in the fourteenth and fifteenth centuries. Rats, and the fleas that infested them, were the primary carriers of this dangerous virus to medieval Europeans. The crowded, unsanitary conditions of the day increased the number of rats in many populations. As a result, the virus spread so fast throughout Europe that in one year (AD 1348), 67 percent of the population died. Thirteen years later another 50 percent of the population died from the same virus.[4]

THE EFFICIENCY OF THE VIRUS

A virus is as thorough as it is fast. It fully infects its host. Once active, the virus will not stop until its task is complete. Viruses are extremely efficient. The virus has one purpose: to infect its host and dominate it completely. "When a virus attacks and infects a vulnerable living cell, it pours its own DNA and or RNA inside. Once inside, the hereditary material begins a virtual coup d'etat. It attaches itself to the cell's existing DNA and sets up a new command system."[5] A virus will not stop until it has complete control. It wants to be the sovereign of the cells.

Viruses can be irritating like a cold, dangerous like the plague, or life changing like the gospel. But there is no doubt about it: every virus is powerful and quick.

VIRAL EVANGELISM

Viral evangelism is the type of evangelism that we see again and again in the book of Acts. What are the immediate and obvious results of the unleashed virus? The first is velocity.

Did you know that every person living in the province of Asia was exposed to the virus within only two years (Acts 19:8–10)? Did you know that the gospel had infected almost the entire Roman Empire within about thirty years of Christ's resurrection? Did you know that Christianity had become the dominant religion in the Roman Empire within three hundred years?

What we see in the book of Acts and the pages of early church history is an unstoppable ideavirus that infected large groups of people at a time. It spread from person to person, life to life, mouth to ear. It spread quickly. But it was not only fast—it was efficient.

Remember that the goal of the virus is to set up a new command system in the center of the cell. Jesus desires to be sovereign of the cells, so to speak. He wants every aspect of every Christian life to be completely under His control, and He won't stop until that happens.

The process of "infection" begins at salvation and doesn't stop until the "victim" is completely under Christ's control. Philippians 1:6 demonstrates the process from beginning to end with these words: "Being confident of this, that he who began a good work in you [the initial infection] will carry it on to completion [the new command system] until the day of Christ Jesus."

SAUL TO PAUL

Take Saul for example. Ardent Pharisee, young idealist, strict legalist—those are just a few of his monikers. This focused visionary made it his goal to stop the spread of the virus of the gospel message. From his vantage point, it had already infected too many of his fellow Jews. Making it his goal to contain and destroy the virus, he went to Damascus to seek and destroy the Christian carriers. But something happened while he was on the road plotting and planning his virus-killing strategy. He himself became infected. In a split second he was transformed from virus killer to virus victim. He was so thoroughly infected that his life changed forever—as did his name. He was suddenly transformed from the esteemed Pharisee of legalistic Judaism named Saul to the despised nemesis of the kingdom of Satan named Paul. He became the primary carrier of the gospel message to the Jews and Gentiles all across the early world. Decades later, he was finally executed for spreading the virus that he once sought to kill.

Viral evangelism is the type of evangelism Paul employed. It is also the type of evangelism demonstrated again and again throughout the early New Testament church. It is fast. It is efficient. It is powerful. But these are mere descriptions. Let's get more specific with our definition.

Viral evangelism has three crucial elements: a courageous carrier, an infectious sneeze, and a contagious virus. Philippians 1:12–18 captures all three of these elements in a few short verses:

> Now I want you to know, brothers, that what has happened to me has really served to advance the gospel. As a result, it has become clear throughout the whole palace guard and to everyone else that I am in chains for Christ. Because of my chains, most of the brothers in the Lord have been encouraged to speak the word of God more courageously and fearlessly. It is true that some preach Christ out of envy and rivalry, but others out of goodwill. The latter do so in love, knowing that I am put here for the defense of the gospel. The former preach Christ out of selfish ambition, not sincerely, supposing that they can stir up trouble for me while I am in chains. But what does it matter? The important thing is that in every way, whether from false motives or true, Christ is preached. And because of this I rejoice.

In that passage we clearly see all three elements of viral evangelism:

1. A CARRIER THAT IS COURAGEOUS

Paul was a courageous carrier. He trusted the Lord and crossed the barriers in spite of overwhelming odds. He was driven to get the gospel out, no matter what the cost. In every town he entered, he unleashed it. Inevitably, a pattern developed. First, a large number of people would get infected. Then the virus killers (i.e., legalistic Jews) would have Paul arrested, beaten, imprisoned, or chased out of town. Finally, he would move on to another host, and the proclamation plague would start all over again.

Sometimes we forget what courage it took for Paul to continue to share the gospel aggressively in that often volatile and violent culture. In one painfully honest passage Paul removes his shirt and shows his scars to the Corinthians, saying, "I have . . . been in prison more frequently, been flogged more severely, and been exposed to death again and again. Five times I received from the Jews the forty lashes minus one. Three times I was beaten with rods, once I was stoned" (2 Corinthians 11:23–25). But he would not be stopped. He would run through barriers courageously with the message of truth and hope.

"So from Jerusalem all the way around to Illyricum, I have fully proclaimed the gospel of Christ. It has always been my ambition to preach the gospel where Christ was not known, so that I would not be building on someone else's foundation" (Romans 15:19–20).

Paul was driven to accomplish the mission. Push him down, and he'd get back up and continue to share the gospel. Throw him overboard, and he'd swim to shore and start a church service around a campfire. Stone him, and he'd rise from the rocks and use the pile of stones as a pulpit. Lock him in a Roman prison, and he'd share the gospel with the soldiers until the whole palace guard had heard the message of Jesus Christ. He was a courageous carrier.

To start an outbreak of biblical proportions today, we need carriers who are courageous. It will take a supernatural confidence for us to push past the barriers of embarrassment and rejection so the message can go out.

I can't think of better candidates to be courageous carriers than teenagers. We live in a student culture obsessed with adrenaline. What better rush than evangelism? Fear and trembling are prerequisites for the ultimate extreme sport—sharing your faith.

Years ago I came across a quote from Paul Borthwick in *Group Magazine* that summed up the courageous potential in teenagers:

 I've noticed something about unchurched kids in our culture—many pursue risk-taking lifestyles with religious fervor. . . . Meanwhile, our youth group kids stay locked in the safety zone. . . . Today's young people need to be called to a life of danger for the sake of following Christ. Many of them are just waiting for the church to give them something big, something significant, something risky to do.[6]

Teenagers are dying for a challenge. The proclamation of the gospel of Jesus Christ provides one. We must infect them with the gospel. Then we must call them to acts of courageousness by equipping them to infect others.

Viral evangelism requires carriers that are courageous. But it requires something more.

2. A SNEEZE THAT IS INFECTIOUS

"Because of my chains, most of the brothers in the Lord have been encouraged to speak the word of God more courageously and fearlessly" (Philippians 1:14).

Paul's sneeze was contagious. He sneezed on Mars Hill and all of Greece got sprayed. He sneezed in a Roman prison, and the whole palace guard caught a cold. But he wasn't the only sneezer. Others caught on so that "most of the brothers" were sneezing "courageously and fearlessly."

In this analogy the sneeze is the actual act of evangelism. It is the process by which others are infected with the gospel virus. Consider the physiological aspects of a sneeze. It has been described as the "involuntary violent expiration of air through the nose and mouth. It results from stimulation of the nervous system in the nose, causing sudden contraction of the muscles of expiration."[7] When someone sneezes, you can't help but know it—and sometimes feel it. The mucous that leaves the nose is traveling at one hundred miles per hour. It makes my point well: Evangelism sneezes are big, loud, and wet.

They are *big* in the sense that they are a primary focus of Christianity throughout the New Testament. The call to sneeze is not optional. It is an irrevocable mandate from the Son of God Himself. Jesus gave the Great Commission, not the good suggestion.

"Again Jesus said, 'Peace be with you! As the Father has sent me, I am sending you.' And with that he breathed on them" (John 20:21–22).

He breathed on them and in so doing commanded them to breathe on everybody else. This holy breath represented the passing on of the Holy Spirit from Jesus to the disciples. In effect, He was calling His disciples to pass on the Spirit to everyone they met, just as He had passed the Holy Spirit on to them. The process of this contagious transfer was the sneeze we call evangelism. To continue the analogy we can say that He sneezed on them and gave them the charge to sneeze on everyone else.

These sneezes are *loud* in the sense that they are meant to be heard. Evangelism is the verbal proclamation of the gospel message. As a matter of fact, the word *evangelize* means "to proclaim the good news of the victory of God's salvation."[8] Outside of Scripture the word was used to describe the joyful duty of one who was sent into a town to proclaim the good news of a military victory. In God's Word it was used to describe what the disciples and early Christians were doing all the time to everyone they met: they proclaimed the good news that Jesus had won the victory over sin and Satan through the cross. Every time *evangelism* is used both within and beyond Scripture it requires words. It requires words that clearly explain the way of salvation and the new life and purpose available in Christ. It requires words communicated with love and wisdom. But it always requires verbal proclamation of the gospel message. In *Becoming a Contagious Christian*, Bill Hybels makes this point clear:

 So can we just come out and say it? Far too many Christians have been anesthetized into thinking that if they simply live out their faith in an open and consistent fashion, the people around them will see it, want it, and somehow figure out how to get it for themselves. Or they reason that maybe these people will come and ask them what makes their life so special and, when they do, they'll seize the opportunity and explain it to them. But let's be honest: That almost never happens.

While it's a prerequisite to live a salty Christian life . . . that alone is not enough. God forbid that we stop there, because people end up in hell on that plan. It's imperative that we also put the message into clear language our friends can understand and act upon.[9]

I talk to Christian teenagers (and youth pastors) all the time who tell me, "I don't share the gospel verbally . . . I just share the gospel with my life." I tell them, "It's great to live out the message that you believe. That is vitally important. But if you don't share the gospel with your words as well, then you are not sharing the gospel at all." Evangelism requires a verbal proclamation of the gospel message. It has been said, "Preach the gospel. If necessary, use words." That quote may look good on a bumper sticker, but it's always necessary to use words when preaching the gospel. No offense St. Francis.

Evangelistic sneezes are big, loud, and *wet*. They are wet in the sense that they require contact. We must be in close proximity to people if we are going to infect them. (Gross illustration I know, but bear with me while I make my sticky point.) We must be close enough to get them wet with the sneeze. That requires premeditation. We must put ourselves and our students in positions where they are close enough to share the good news with others.

In some cases the Bible bubble must be popped. That is especially true for Christian school and homeschool students. I believe that the best thing that could happen to some of our more sheltered teenagers is to drop them off at a local mall in the middle of a group of pierced, dyed, tattooed teenagers, wish them well in their attempts to initiate relationships and spiritual conversations, and tell them you'll be back in two hours.

If we expect to start an epidemic of evangelism, we must be near the uninfected. Our students must have close contact with them. They must put themselves in situations where they can build relationships. And they must start sneezing.

Big, loud, wet sneezes should characterize the infected youth group. We should hear a constant stream of stories of changed lives and saved souls. Without sneezes, we will never see another outbreak of biblical proportions. With them, we just may see one in our lifetime.

3. A VIRUS THAT IS CONTAGIOUS

It is true that some preach Christ out of envy and rivalry, but others out of goodwill. The latter do so in love, knowing that I am put here for the defense of the gospel. The former preaches Christ out of selfish ambition, not sincerely, supposing that they can stir up trouble for me while I am in chains. But what does it matter? The important thing is that in every way, whether from false motives or true, Christ is preached. And because of this I rejoice. (Philippians 1:15–18)

Those are some amazing verses. If Paul were to preach that same message in most churches today, he would probably be stoned again (with hymnals this time). Let me give you an unscholarly paraphrase of what the great apostle is saying: "There are some guys out there preaching the gospel for the wrong motives. They think they can expedite my execution by ticking more people off about the gospel. They think that so many people will be angered by this evangelistic epidemic that it will speed up the date of my beheading. But what does it matter? The gospel is being preached. I don't care what their motives are. Either way, the gospel is being preached, and I am thrilled about that!"

That is a shocking statement. Paul was happy that the gospel was being preached even if it was being preached with wrong motives. Don't misunderstand. He was concerned with the lifestyle and motives of those who called themselves Christians. Every single one of his letters is packed full of admonitions to the believers to live out an authentic and holy faith. But what mattered most to Paul was that the pure virus of the gospel message was infecting others. He didn't care nearly as much about the motives of those perverse preachers as he did about their message. What mattered most was the message, not the lifestyle, not the relationship, not anything else.

Christians who preach the gospel with fleshly motivation miss out on the blessings of walking by the Spirit now and may miss out on some eternal rewards later. But which is more important—a believer missing out on future rewards because of wrong motives, or an unbeliever missing out on eternal life because of a silent Christian?

It is vitally important that we teach our students to live their faith out with pure motives. But it is also important that we teach them to share the pure message of the gospel with others. It is not our lives that save souls. It is the message. It is not our motives that infect others. It is the message. It is not we who are "the power of God for salvation." It is the gospel of Jesus Christ. Let's not flatter ourselves. We are nothing special apart from God's grace. We are just sinners who have already found the Savior. Now we can help others find Him too.

The sneeze of evangelism requires a carrier that is courageous, a sneeze that is infectious, and a virus that is contagious. So burn your handkerchiefs and throw your teenagers' Kleenex away! It's time to stop trying to contain our sneezes and get everyone we come into contact with drenched!

VIRAL EVANGELISM THROUGH AN ARMY OF STUDENTS

God is using students to spread the epidemic across the nation and around the world. Pockets of outbreak begin with youth leaders who are called of God and are tired of the routine. They want more than a babysitting club. They want more than a growing youth group. They want more than happy parents, satisfied students, and appeased pastoral boards. They want a movement. And they will not stop until they satisfy those insatiable spiritual ambitions that God has placed in their hearts.

Student movements are just the beginning. The more our restless twenty-first century teens move into adulthood, take over the leadership of youth groups and churches, and return to the radical Christianity of the first century, the more outbreaks we will see.

BE THE MONKEY

You are the carrier of the virus. You are the monkey who starts the outbreak. (Sorry, it was either the monkey from the movie, or the rat from the plague!) You are the host who infects your youth group with viral evangelism. If it is going to spread, it has to start with you. You must scratch and bite so that your students will sneeze and cough. You must carry the virus to every student in your youth group and find the super sneezers who will take the virus to their campuses and communities.

Think about the title *youth leader*. Are you a leader of youth? Are you worthy of your title? Are you willing to take the risk, lead the charge, and spread the message? Are you willing to deal with the parents and pastoral boards who may not like the direction in which you are taking the youth? Are you willing to demonstrate effective evangelism by example? Are you willing to shift your paradigm and transform your programs so they produce maximum evangelistic effectiveness?

This book has a single purpose: to unleash the virus in your youth group. That outbreak will be an unstoppable force. It will infect the adults in our pews and the children in our Sunday school classrooms. It will set our senior pastors ablaze with the Great Commission mindset. It will cover the map in red. My prayer is that that single red dot, the point of outbreak, will be your youth group.

So what do you say? Are you ready to scratch others and infect them with the truth? Go for it, you monkey!✖

RED·DOT REVIEW

BE THE MONKEY!

MONKEY MANDATES

MANDATE #1
Read through the book of Acts and write down all the realities that helped the gospel "go viral" that you can find.

MANDATE #2
Compare and contrast your youth ministry's spiritual climate with what you discover in Acts.

MANDATE #3
Determine, through God's strength, to do something about it.

STAFF INFECTION QUESTIONS

#1. Are the three elements of viral evangelism (courageous carriers, infectious sneezes, and a contagious virus) present in our youth group?

#2. Are we youth leaders modeling evangelism to our teens?

#3. What can we do to break the hearts of our teens for their lost friends?

"IT'S GONE AIRBORNE!"

It's the phrase that fills the heart of the virologist with terror. Once a virus escapes into the populace, it is virtually unstoppable. Recent fears that the bird flu virus will adapt, allowing for widespread transmission from person to person, find scientists and health officials issuing dire warnings. Many believe bird flu will inevitably be the next pandemic. Efforts to contain its rampant spread among bird populations have resulted in the destruction of hundreds of millions of domestic birds. But the virus continues to run rampant in migrating wild birds, spreading the disease around the globe and fueling fears that it will eventually cross into humans, go airborne, and wreak uncontainable havoc. Virologists know that it is almost inevitable that an airborne virus will become an epidemic unless the carriers are quarantined quickly and completely.

In Acts 2 the gospel went airborne, and the world never recovered.

Lives were changed, souls were saved, and a culture was transformed.

Why isn't that the norm today? The book of Acts seems to belong on the sci-fi channel instead of in the history section. In a library it could easily be misplaced in fiction. Don't get me wrong. The contents are true through and through. The Holy Spirit inspired every word. It just seems unbelievable. Could church ever have been that exciting, exhilarating, dangerous, miraculous, and, dare I say, fun?

Have you ever found yourself reading the book of Acts and imagining what it must have been like to live in Jerusalem at that time? The mind-blowing miracles, the daily conversions, the spirit of excitement and selflessness, and the powerful climate of prayer—it all combined to create an almost unbelievably electrifying atmosphere. Try reading the book of Acts sometime and then attending a typical youth group meeting on a typical Wednesday night in a typical church. Talk about a letdown!

What's changed? We live in a technologically driven world where students are obsessed with gadgets and games. Attention spans are shrinking and boredom is growing. The gospel doesn't seem as appealing to this culture. In a world of MTV, MP3s, and DVDs, has the gospel lost its sizzle? Has the iPod outmatched Our-God? Teens have too many distractions. They are too busy, too self-consumed, and too dysfunctional. There is too much competition for Christ to conquer the souls of this student culture.

Or is there? There was competition for souls in the time of the early church as well. It was not technological competition, but it was intellectual, philosophical, and spiritual.

The Greeks were obsessed with philosophy and religion. The writer of Acts describes them: "All the Athenians and the foreigners who lived there spent their time doing nothing but talking about and listening to the latest ideas" (17:21).

When Paul preached before the men on Mars Hill, he started with this line, "Men of Athens! I see that in every way you are very religious. For as I walked around and looked carefully at your objects of worship, I even found an altar with this inscription: TO AN UNKNOWN GOD" (Acts 17:22–23).

The Greeks believed in so many gods that they made an altar to the unknown god just in case they forgot one. Talk about competition for your attention. False gods and philosophies were everywhere.

The Romans were a polytheistic culture as well. There were all sorts of gods for all sorts of occasions. Like fast-food restaurants, Roman gods saturated the landscape. Whatever your mood, there was a god to go with it and fries on the side.

The competition for attention was even rampant in the camp of the monotheistic Jews. It was a battle between the liberal Sadducees, the conservative Pharisees, the radical Zealots, the communal Essenes, and others. Those battling branches of Jewish ideology passionately sought to win the minds and allegiances of their people.

It was into that competitive climate that the church was born. In that culture of spiritual and philosophical combat, the church didn't only survive; it thrived. Why? Not just because the gospel was a superior idea but because the gospel was truth and the early Christians preached it in such a culturally relevant way. Guess what? It smoked the competition. Christianity became the dominant belief system in no time. A culture was infected. It was the better idea. It was the cooler story. And it was absolutely true.

Today, instead of the church impacting our culture, our culture is impacting the church. In this postmodern society of "have it your way" theology, sharing the gospel as truth can seem obnoxious and intrusive. As a result, Christian students tend to shy away from it. No one wants to push it. "Keeping up the 'veneer of niceness' and holding to the sensible center ultimately leads many of today's believers to disavow the Gospel's claims of truth. This is how Christianity appears to be unwittingly capitulating to the culture."[1]

The result of that capitulation is usually two approaches to sharing the good news: (1) "That's cool for you. Here's what's cool for me," or (2) "This is the truth. Take it or leave it." The problem is that neither one is effective. If we want to energize our students to evangelize their world, they must know their world. And what appeals most to their world is stories. According to Mike Metzger, by the turn of the millennium, 75 percent of the West had moved to postmodern assumptions, "leaving the modernist presentation of the Gospel incoherent and implausible to the postmodern mind. Today, the postmodern world embraces stories as the universal truth, and (once again) Christians . . . are playing catch up."[2]

Because there are so many belief systems, we must present the good news about God's love through Christ as an exciting, life-altering story that just happens to be true instead of a theological treatise that cannot be false. Don't misunderstand this crucial point. The truth about salvation is a theological treatise that is absolutely true. But in our quest to "become all things to all men" we must present the gospel message to the postmodern world so that they will respond positively. That is why the most effective presentation of the gospel to this culture is through the story that just happens to be supported by the truth.

As you will see in chapter 8, Paul presented the gospel to the men on Mars Hill in the same way. It was when he used the word *proof* at the end of his talk that most of the philosophers rejected his message. Yet some responded to his message and were saved. He used the story as the bait and the truth as the hook. In the same way, when we present the gospel story to the postmodern culture, we must realize that it is when we get to the *proof* part that some will accept it and many will reject it.

New Tribes Mission uses this approach to sharing the gospel message. Missionaries from this organization tell the whole story of Christianity from creation to the cross and beyond to tribal people who have no clue as to the claims of Christianity. The narrative approach is not complicated. As a matter of fact, it is very simple. It means sharing the story of the gospel as the story of the whole Bible. When New Tribes missionaries begin to explain the gospel message to a new tribe, they don't start with the message of sin. They start with the story of creation. They lay out the message chronologically and vividly. Using skits and visual aids, they explain the beauty of the garden, the horror of the fall, and the blood of the sacrificial system. With that backdrop, the cross makes much more sense. In a lot of ways, reaching today's Western culture is like reaching a tribal people with the gospel message. Unlike a generation or two ago, people today don't immediately understand the basic tenets of sin, hell, eternity, judgment, and sacrifice. We have to go back to chapter 1. "The Bible starts with 'In the beginning . . .' and ends with a '. . . and they lived happily every after!' In a postmodern climate, which is less receptive to propositional assertions, it seems that the time is ripe for evangelicals to consider doing evangelism more as story-telling than as presenting propositions."[3]

That is exactly the approach that Paul took with the men on Mars Hill. He shared the whole story of the Bible from creation to the resurrection. He shared it as truth—truth within the context of a story. He used apologetics (the resurrection) but in the context of a story. Why? Because he knew that it took a different strategy to reach the Greeks than it did the Jews. (We'll talk more about that in chapter 8.) So too the heart of the postmodern student can be captured by the greatest story ever told.

AN AIRBORNE STRATEGY

When the gospel goes airborne, Satan shrieks. The message of the book of Acts is the story of the message spreading from town to town and country to country. We see that the strategy was simply to share the story of the gospel. Paul lets us peer into the microscope and study the simplicity of his mission in Romans 10:14: "How, then, can they call on the one they have not believed in? And how can they believe in the one of whom they have not heard? And how can they hear without someone preaching to them?"

Paul is stating the obvious: evangelism that is not communicated is not evangelism. For people to be infected with the message of the gospel they need to hear the message and believe it. Remember, the story of the gospel must be communicated with words. It is up to us to communicate those words, to share that story. We can't wait for the unbeliever to bring it up. Chuck Swindoll writes:

We have the feeling that if people want to know Christ, they will ask us. We're dreaming if we think folks are going to walk up, tap us on the shoulder, and ask, "Say, could you tell me about knowing Christ?" . . . In all my years I've seldom had anybody say to me, "You know, I've been concerned about my soul, Chuck. And I know that you are a Christian. I'd like you to help me know how to go to heaven." Are you kidding? They don't bring it up . . . we do. We initiate the contact. Christians did so all the way through the New Testament.[4]

How does that apply to your youth group? Simple. You have to bring it up with your teenagers consistently. To expect outbreak in our outreach, we must adopt this airborne strategy. Is the gospel going airborne in the context of your weekly youth group meetings? Are you consistently sharing the gospel at the end of all of your talks? If we truly believe that the gospel changes lives, then we should be presenting it consistently whenever a crowd gathers.

Building strong relationships is a great context for evangelism to happen. The evidence of a changed life is a strong witness in the courtroom of public opinion. Great games and youth group activities can attract the unchurched to attend your youth meetings. But only one thing saves—the gospel message. Give it. Give it every week. When you think that you have given it enough, give it again! Be creative as you give it, but give it. Why? Because that is the simple and effective strategy that God has given us. "How can they hear without a preacher?" You are the preacher!

I love the words of Doug Fields in *Purpose Driven Youth Ministry*: "Youth ministries that are fulfilling the purpose of evangelism are usually the ones in which the youth ministry leadership, the church staff, and the students understand and share a passion to see it expressed."[5] It takes a tribal effort for the evangelism to turn into an epidemic.

If the virus remains in the vial, there will be no outbreak. The glass must be shattered, along with all of the traditions and internal and external hesitations that stand in the way. The confining container must be broken. The words must be spoken. The message must be given.

It all sounds way too easy.

It does, doesn't it? But it is, isn't it? One would think that in this complicated culture of technological advancement, philosophical enlightenment, and spiritual choices there would be a better infection strategy than *just* sharing the gospel.

There isn't. As a matter of fact, it is the simplicity of this evangelistic strategy that gives Christianity an edge. We are not inviting people to become members of a complicated religion full of quirks and jerks, rules and regulations. We are not getting close to the unchurched expecting the truth just to ooze off of us and onto them. We are not sitting around waiting for them to say, "Hey, there is something different in your life. You must know Jesus. Please tell me about Him!" We are intentionally inviting them into a personal relationship with the God who passionately loves them. We are sharing with them the greatest story ever told. We are infecting them with a contagious and life-changing virus. That's what it means to go airborne.

Think back to when you were first infected. For me it was on June 23, 1974. I remember it as clearly as yesterday. I was eight years old at the time and thought, *Wow! That was easy!* Believing the message and receiving the gift is not complicated. It is simple. Jesus did all the work. All we must do is believe. It's that simple!

When you share the simple gospel story and equip your students to do the same, you are preparing them to go viral. God uses a simple story spoken by simple people to produce profound results.

AN AIRBORNE MESSENGER

Doug came from a broken family in the inner city. He was raised in a climate of extreme violence and dysfunction. Physical altercations between family members and absolute strangers were common in Doug's neighborhood and household.

To add to Doug's problems, he had a dangerous form of epilepsy. Grand mal seizures were a regular part of his life. Two separate times he had such severe seizures that his heart stopped and he nearly died.

Doug also struggled in school. He had a hard time learning and was a bit slow even in the most basic subjects. He tried hard, but often he just couldn't get it.

Kids can be cruel. Often they made fun of Doug. His epilepsy and learning disabilities made him an easy target. More often than not, Doug responded with his fists. He had learned the art of violence first-hand and was ready to practice it anytime, anywhere, and with any-one. As a result, suspensions from school and trouble with the law fol-lowed. Doug was walking quickly down the path of self-destruction.

One day Doug was invited to go to a Christian camp in Florida. When he went, he was challenged by speaker after speaker to make a difference with his life. Each of those powerful preachers seemed to be talking straight to him. They preached about the person of Jesus Christ and the purpose that He offers to those who follow Him. They talked about the need to tell others the good news of forgiveness through Jesus Christ so they could be saved from hopelessness now and hell later. Doug was hooked. While Doug had put his faith in Christ as a child, that week he dedicated his life to follow Jesus Christ with all of his heart and make it his life's quest to keep others out of hell.

After a few major setbacks when he arrived home, he began to live a life that was consumed for Christ. Every day was another opportu-nity to tell someone else about Jesus Christ.

At sixteen years old he didn't have a car. He didn't even own a bike. So he began to walk and talk. It was common for people driving down the street to see Doug witnessing to some person waiting at the bus stop or hitchhiking. He stuttered and stammered his way through gospel presentation after gospel presentation. The surprising thing was that more often than not, people listened. It wasn't that he was articu-late. It wasn't that he was suave. It wasn't that he was all that logical. But he reeked of a contagious authenticity that would contaminate his listeners. His smile could light up a dark room. His heart was filled with the love of Jesus Christ and the people he was talking to.

One day Doug asked me to go "soul winning" with him early on a Saturday morning. To be honest, sometimes I was embarrassed to go witnessing with him. He was too bold. Sometimes I would cringe when he tried to get a stranger's attention. But once he launched into the presentation, his sincerity attracted listeners.

That particular Saturday morning excursion was going nowhere. It was too early in the morning, and nobody was outside yet. Doug was getting frustrated. "Where is everyone?" he began to shout in frustration. "They are still in bed," I responded. Finally, we went to a tiny park near my apartment complex. About one hundred yards away, an eight- or nine-year-old boy was playing on a jungle gym. Doug jumped into action. In his excitement about finally finding someone to talk to, he began running right toward the kid, yelling, "Hey, kid! Where are you going to go when you die?" I will never forget the look of sheer terror in that child's eyes as he screamed, "Home!" and ran away as fast as he could.

Doug walked back toward me, absolutely dejected. "Doug, you scared that poor kid to death," I said. I will never forget his response. As he looked up with tears in his eyes he said, "I didn't mean to scare that kid. I just don't want to see that kid die and go to hell."

Doug saved up his money and bought a ten-speed bike. He was completely excited by his new mobile means of evangelism. He rode his bike everywhere, talking to all sorts of people—in parks, on the street, on sidewalks, and across overpasses. One day he told me the story of pulling up to a stoplight and noticing a car full of guys next to him, waiting for the red light to turn green. He thought, *Those guys are going to die and go to hell unless I tell them about Jesus.* So he knocked on the passenger side window, and one of the men tentatively rolled the window down, curious about what this teenager wanted. Doug knew that his time was short, so he blurted out the gospel message as quickly and clearly as he could. But he couldn't get it out fast enough. The light turned green.

"We gotta go!" the driver blurted out as he began to press the gas pedal and drive away. Doug couldn't let the opportunity pass. Too much was at stake. "I am going with you!" he answered as he grabbed onto the car door handle with his left hand. The car continued to accelerate, and Doug continued to share the gospel message. At twenty miles per hour Doug was still sharing. At thirty miles per hour he was almost done. Finally, at forty miles per hour Doug had finished sharing the whole story of salvation. "I hope you trust in Christ as your Savior!" he yelled as his white-knuckled fingers let go of the car handle and his ten-speed whizzed and wobbled toward the curb.

What was my response to Doug's daring story? "Doug, you are an idiot! You could have died! You could have gotten caught under the car and run over!" I will never forget his response: "It would have been worth it as long as those guys hear and believe the gospel message. I just don't want to see those guys go to hell."

Doug was one of those guys who took his Christianity seriously. He really believed in heaven and hell. It wasn't an astute faith or even a profound faith. It was a simple, childlike faith. Doug really believed. I felt convicted every time I was around him.

Sometimes when we were together I would be watching TV and he would be over in the corner reading his Bible. Every few minutes or so, he would come over to me and ask, "Greg, what does this verse mean?" I would explain it to him, and he would go back to the corner and continue studying, meticulously writing down my response and making marks and notes in his Bible margins. He studied because he wanted to be a better witness for Jesus Christ.

Finally, at the age of nineteen, Doug graduated from high school. With diploma in hand he went off to the army. Once again he struggled to fit in with those around him. He marched left foot forward when everyone else was starting with the right. He just couldn't get it. But he could give it . . . the gospel, that is. I remember the letters he would send me from time to time sharing the opportunities that God had given him to share with his fellow soldiers and commanding officers. Soon Doug was honorably discharged by an army that appreciated his efforts but knew that life wasn't for him.

When Doug came back home, he met a girl who was a waitress at a local restaurant. He witnessed to her, and she trusted in Christ. He thought she was cute, so he asked her out. She said yes. When he asked her to marry him on their second date, she said yes again.

Doug has never stopped sharing his faith. Today he is a custodian at a high school in Ankeny, Iowa. Every week or so, he calls me. We talk about his family, his job, his church, and his life. We also talk about the people he has been witnessing to. Twenty-five years after his decision to become a soul winner at a camp in Florida, Doug is still winning souls.

One day at the judgment seat of Christ, Doug's name will be called. On that day I believe thousands will stand and applaud this epileptic, socially challenged, struggling custodian for the impact he made on their lives.

I will be one of them. Doug is my big brother. He is seven years older than I am. I remember the old Doug before he got serious about Christ. I remember the new Doug after he got infected. He had every excuse to keep quiet. But he refused to be excused.

One of the reasons I do what I do today, traveling and training teenagers to share their faith, is because of that one loner teenager who shared his faith relentlessly, courageously, and consistently. I know that if my brother Doug could do it as a struggling teen, your kids can as well.

AN AIRBORNE MODEL

When the gospel goes viral, the results are mind-boggling. History has proved that to be true again and again. For example, John Wesley created an airborne model that spanned two countries—England and America.

 The Methodist movement became epidemic in England and North America, tipping from 20,000 to 90,000 followers in the U.S. in the space of five or six years in the 1780's. . . . [Methodism's founder, John Wesley] realized that if you wanted to bring about a fundamental change in people's belief and behavior, a change that would persist and serve as an example to others, you needed to create a community around them, where those new beliefs could be practiced and expressed and nurtured.[6]

A STUDY IN VIRAL EVANGELISM

I thank God for my youth ministry ancestry. Back in the late seventies and early eighties I spent my teenage years in a national youth movement called the Christian Youth Ranch. To be honest, I have no idea why they called those youth outreach meetings *youth ranches.* They had nothing to do with actual ranches (although my last name is pronounced "Steer") but everything to do with youth. A small army of churches across the nation adopted this outreach model for their main youth group evangelism strategy.

The plan was simple. There was a Thursday night outreach meeting —fun, exciting, and friendly. Students were told to invite as many teenagers as possible every single week. Once there, teens participated in exciting games, great worship, and a strong Bible message. The gospel was not only presented, but students were also given the opportunity to respond right away. The new believers were encouraged to get involved in a Bible study where they could grow deeper in their newfound faith. This strategy was pretty basic. But basic strategies that are executed prayerfully and relentlessly have a way of being effective.

I remember being one of the hundreds of youth ranch teens from the Denver area. There were game nights, roller skating nights, 100-foot banana split nights—you name it, we did it. Youth ranch was well planned, user-friendly, and a blast. The skits were hilarious, the students were friendly, and the atmosphere was electric. It was a safe place to connect. It was a fun place to be. And at the end of every meeting you knew the gospel would be given. You banked on it. You brought your friends to hear it. And once they began a relationship with Christ, they brought their friends to hear it.

The youth ranch meetings were done with excellence. Although the leadership didn't have a large budget, they poured creative energy and hard work into every meeting. We teenagers weren't embarrassed to bring our friends. A lot of the group didn't really know how to share their faith. But we knew the night would be a great time, and, most important, we knew the gospel would be given by the youth leader.

I can't remember a week in all of my teen years where at least one person didn't trust Christ as Savior during the youth ranch meetings. Think about that for a moment. When's the last time a teenager trusted Christ as his or her Savior during one of your youth group meetings? I honestly can't recall a single week when it didn't happen from seventh grade through my senior year of high school. Pretty amazing stuff.

You peeked during the every-eye-closed invitation if you brought a friend. You could almost feel the corporate prayers of the roomful of Christian students as they prayed for their unsaved friends to respond to the invitation to accept Christ. At its highest point, the youth ranch I attended numbered more than five hundred students consistently. The most we ever had at one event was around eight hundred kids! That was especially impressive when you realize there were only a few hundred adults attending that church on Sunday morning. At one point, youth ranch grew so big that the leadership decided to break it up into five different youth groups across the Denver area. Other teenagers, barely out of high school themselves, led some of those youth ranches.

That was when I got my first taste of viral evangelism. I saw it firsthand. I wanted more. At the age of fifteen I began traveling and training other Christian teenagers and youth groups in the Denver area to unleash the virus. Deep in my heart of hearts I knew that if teenagers and youth leaders from other denominations adopted the youth ranch paradigm, there would be an outbreak of biblical proportions. But that philosophy didn't fly in our church. We were expected to stay put and work in our own youth ministry. I did it anyway. God placed a vision in my mind and a fire in my heart that would not go away—a vision for an evangelism epidemic led by the youth leaders and students in every church across America.

ROOTS OF AN AIRBORNE MOVEMENT

The Christian youth ranch movement is a study in viral evangelism. It began in Miami, Florida, in the early fifties with a believer named Ray Stanford. While piloting a B-24 in World War II, Ray had two engines shut down and was forced to crash-land his plane. At that point, Ray promised God that if He spared Ray's life, then he would witness to his crew. God answered his prayer and spared his life, but Ray didn't share his faith with his crew.

Back home while in the Air Force Reserves, Ray was flying a twin-engine plane, and again both engines quit! When that happened, God brought to mind Ray's earlier promise. This time Ray kept it! He eventually shared his faith with his entire former crew and squadron at a military reunion. In fact, he began sharing his faith with anybody who would listen. Eventually he became a senior salesman in the National Cash Register Company and made a very good living. He used all of the powers of his entrepreneurial soul and focused them on reaching the prospects that would be most likely respond to the message of Christ . . . teenagers. As a successful salesman, he knew how to persuade. He used those skills to clearly communicate the gospel message with student after student.

As more and more teenagers trusted in Christ as their Savior, they had questions. Ray didn't know a whole lot about Christianity, so he told them that he would find the answers for them in the Bible. His knowledge of the Scriptures grew deeper and deeper. He became more and more effective at evangelizing and discipling teenagers.

Starting with a small outreach-centered Bible study in his house, Ray began a mission to unleash the virus. It worked. The small group of teens grew and grew. Teenagers were stacked on top of each other in his kitchen, living room, hallways, and even bathroom. Finally they moved to a bigger location.

Eventually parents began showing up too to find out about the exciting brand of Christianity that was so intriguing to their formerly irreligious kids. So Ray started a church. He thought the adults would be a good asset to help fund the youth movement. And that is exactly what took place. Grove Community Church became the breeding ground for the virus to spread across south Florida. The more it spread, the more Ray's vision of the viral potential of the gospel grew. As a result, the youth ranch phenomenon began.

Ray quit his high profile job and launched out in faith into full-time Christian work. He believed that when the clear gospel of grace was unleashed through an army of students, it would make a world-wide impact.

Over the next few years, however, Ray and the leadership of the youth ranch movement began to notice a disturbing pattern. Students would come to Christ through Christian youth ranch, grow in their faith, reach their friends for Christ, then graduate, and go off to college. When they came back, often they had changed. Many of them were caught up into the lure of the world or, in some cases, in the web of false doctrine. Ray decided to start a Bible college to stop that terrible trend.

Florida Bible College grew fast. The Christian youth ranch movement created a huge reservoir of potential students. The college mushroomed to more than one thousand students within just a few years. Those students were trained to do youth ministry. Their assignment: share the gospel and help out the Christian youth ranch movement. Every major at FBC was streamlined toward evangelism in one way or another.

The graduates took the virus back home. Youth ranches began to pop up all over Florida and Georgia and other states. The outbreak spread across the nation and finally reached Colorado through one infected Georgia-bred preacher affectionately known as "Yankee" Arnold. That was my first encounter with the power of an evangelistic epidemic. I have never recovered.

I could share story after story of how the viral truth from the Christian youth ranch movement infected my entire family and transformed them from a group of body-building, skull-cracking fighters into a group of Bible-wielding, gospel-sharing preachers. One by one my family was infected and absolutely transformed by the truth. One of my uncles even went to Florida Bible College as a result. That transformation had a deep impact on me as a child. I saw firsthand the power of the gospel virus. It taught me that once that message goes airborne, not only people but also entire families and communities are affected.

Although the youth ranch movement has since died out, the virus has not. It has merely been contained, waiting to be unleashed in your youth group.

WILL YOU GO VIRAL
WITH YOUR YOUTH GROUP?

The principles you learn in this book will prepare you to give your youth group a Great Commission mind-set. If you apply the principles in the following chapters, you will get to the point where you expect many students to trust Christ through your youth ministry efforts. As a matter of fact, you will be surprised if a week goes by and nobody becomes a Christian.

Shouldn't that be the norm? Isn't that what we see throughout the book of Acts? We have the same God, the same message, and the same mandate as the early disciples. We must now apply the same strategy.✖

GO AIRBORNE EVERY WEEK!

MANDATE
Promise to give the gospel
every week in your regular
youth group meeting.

STAFF
INFECTION
QUESTIONS

#1. What are the advantages and
disadvantages of giving the
gospel every week?

#2. What are some creative ways
to bypass the disadvantages?

#3. How can we maximize the
advantages?

#4. Evaluate the Christian youth
ranch model compared to
your current youth ministry
model.

#5. How can we glean the benefits of the Christian youth
ranch model without forsak-
ing the uniqueness of your
own youth ministry culture?

STUDENT SUPER SNEEZERS

God loves to use teenagers. I don't know why. Those hormone-filled, hyper, messy, societal aberrations have always been underrated and scorned by the culture around them . . . even in the pages of biblical history. Yet God consistently chooses the underdog. He used a teenage girl named Esther to rescue His people from annihilation. He even used a young buck named Daniel to save a legion of wise men in Babylon from the sword of a bloodthirsty king. Something about teenagers motivates God to do the impossible through the improbable.

In the history of awakening you see a pattern. God uses student super sneezers again and again to cause spiritual outbreak. Maybe it's because they are tired of the hypocrisy. Perhaps it's because their idealism drives them—they truly think that changing the world is possible. Maybe it's because of their childlike faith. Whatever the reason, in the history of revival God inevitably raises up an army of teenaged carriers to spread the message. Study the revivals of Moody, Spurgeon, Finney, Taylor, Whitefield, and Wesley, and you will see this undeniable reality. Because students have been on the leading edge of every major awakening, I am confident that God will use them once again to shake a nation and eventually a world with the power of the gospel of Jesus Christ.

STUDENTS BEING USED
IN POLITICAL MOVEMENTS

By the time Douglas Hyde wrote *Dedication and Leadership* more than forty years ago, he had converted to Catholicism after spending twenty years in the Communist Party. He wrote the book as a challenge to his Catholic colleagues to apply the same tenacity and tactics that the Communists did in their recruiting and training of new converts. In writing about those tactics, Hyde communicated the vast, untapped opportunity Catholics had in calling teenagers to acts of heroism in spiritual quests, just as the Communists had challenged students to the same kind of acts in political quests. He wrote these words that still ring true today:

 Youth is a period of idealism. The Communists attract young people by appealing directly to that idealism. Too often, others have failed either to appeal to it or to use it and they are the losers as a consequence. We have no cause to complain if, having neglected the idealism of youth, we see others come along, take it, use it and harness it to their cause—and against our own.[1]

Those young Communists were idealistic and unrealistic, but they made an impact on those around them. Douglas Hyde continues:

Young people have always dreamed of better worlds and we must hope that they always will. The day we lose our dreams all progress will cease. Idealistic young people will want to change the world and will pursue their own idealistic course in any case. If their idealism is not appealed to and canalized within the circles in which they have grown up they will seek elsewhere for an outlet. . . . The Communists' appeal to idealism is direct and audacious. They say that if you make mean little demands upon people, you will get a mean little response which is all you deserve, but, if you make big demands on them, you will get a heroic response.

Indeed, if any political movement can utilize teenagers for a global cause, why can't every religious movement?

STUDENTS BEING USED IN RELIGIOUS MOVEMENTS

The fastest growing religions and cults uncork the bottled-up energy of teenagers and expect an explosion of changed lives. From Muslims to Mormons, students are viewed not as a liability to be babysat but as a resource to be utilized.

THE INTERNATIONAL CHURCHES OF CHRIST

The International Churches of Christ (or the Boston Movement) know what they are doing when it comes to multiplying their recruitment effectiveness through young people, specifically college students. Kip McKean, the founding evangelist and pastor of the Boston Movement, popularized "Campus Advance" principles in the early eighties. He trained his followers to evangelize college campuses aggressively and then immerse new believers into a radical, authoritarian style of discipleship. Using these principles, his church grew from thirty to a thousand in just a few years. Today they have churches on every continent.

However, the International Churches of Christ preach a gospel that centers on a requirement of water baptism in their church and a strict adherence to God's commands for salvation. They also practice an intensive form of "discipleship" process that borders on mind control. College students, who are often weak Christians, are susceptible to such a persuasive and apparently loving approach. But the deeper one gets, the tighter the reins get. I personally witnessed one friend get tangled in that winsome web of deception and manipulation. Young people are easy targets for false doctrine, so perpetrators seize the opportunity.

THE CHURCH OF JESUS CHRIST
OF LATTER-DAY SAINTS

Whereas the International Churches of Christ focus on recruiting young people from outside their church to be members, the Church of Jesus Christ of Latter-Day Saints (the Mormons) focuses on energizing and equipping its own young people. Although I disagree with Mormon theology, I have tremendous respect for their tenacious and strategic approach to youth ministry. They know what they are doing when it comes to reaching and recruiting students. Mormons provide an intensive and extensive training program for young people that begins when they are children and continues past their high school years.

In the book *Mormon America*, Richard and Joan Ostling chronicle the Mormon approach to unleashing the tremendous potential in their own young people. In the following words the writers provide a taste of the grueling two-year mission Mormon students are asked to invest in the church. "They will continue their work, with an hour out for dinner, until 9:30 p.m. Their day began at 6:00 a.m. with prayers and study and will end at 10:30 p.m. after more of the same." But those demanding hours are only the beginning. "They are not permitted to communicate with family and friends by fax or e-mail and are allowed only two telephone calls home each year, on Christmas and Mother's Day. Collect."[2]

After attending a four- to nine-week boot camp (depending on whether or not they have an English-speaking assignment or must learn a foreign language), young Mormon missionaries are turned loose to recruit others for the cause. *Boot camp* is an appropriate term because those sincere young Mormons are being trained to do battle for souls. Their goal is to invade and persuade. They do both effectively. But the biggest result is the change that takes place in them during this two-year period. They leave as boys. They come back as men. They know what they believe and why they believe it. Their theology has been hammered out on doorsteps. Their resolve has been tested and strengthened by thousands of slammed doors, barking dogs, rainy days, and mocking looks. They have passed through the fire and have been purified for the cause of Mormonism. For the rest of their lives being a model witness is no problem. The saying "Once a Marine, always a Marine" seems to hold true for Mormons too. Long before the recruit ever enters boot camp, he has been readied through years of systematic preparation:

 The universal lay priesthood, including the emphasis on two-year missionary assignments, is no doubt a major reason why LDS [Latter-Day Saint] children remain loyal and involved through adolescence and young adulthood. Every boy from age twelve is incorporated into the system with special status. . . . A boy is ordained into the lower of two priesthood levels, the Aaronic priesthood, at age twelve and progresses through three subcategories. As a deacon, he distributes the sacrament, collects fast offerings, cares for the building and grounds, and helps otherwise by assisting the elderly, acting as a messenger, and so forth. The major program for deacons consists of church-sponsored Boy Scout troops. Between the ages of fourteen and sixteen he becomes a teacher. He can now perform all deacon functions and ordain deacons, and also prepares the sacrament, ushers, is allowed to speak at church meetings, and participates in "home teaching" (the monthly visit to each ward household for spiritual strengthening). Finally, he becomes a priest between the ages of sixteen and eighteen. He can teach and exhort during home teaching sessions, baptize, administer the sacrament, and ordain teachers and deacons to the priesthood.[3]

Mormons know youth ministry. Although there are not as many female missionaries in the field, there are some. These young women work just as diligently for the cause as the young men. Mormon leaders know how to harness the passions of adolescents and point it toward a mission. Meanwhile, the church of Jesus Christ that proclaims the one true Word struggles to get kids to attend a weekly Sunday school class. Something is amiss.

STUDENTS BEING USED
IN SPIRITUAL AWAKENINGS

In a chapter titled "The Zeal of Youth: The Role of Students in the History of Spiritual Awakening," Alvin L. Reid writes, "The purpose of this chapter is to isolate and emphasize the vital but often overlooked role of students in the history of spiritual awakening. Specifically the author will argue that students have played a larger role in the origin, continuity, and effects of revival than has generally been recognized."[4]

Reid goes on to document how the Moravian missionary movement began as a youth movement. He also shows the prominent role young people played in the First Great Awakening under Jonathan Edwards. Edwards wrote, "The work has been chiefly amongst the young; and comparatively but few others have been made partakers of it. And indeed it has commonly been so, when God has begun any great work for the revival of his church; he has taken the young people, and has cast off the old and stiff-necked generation."[5]

Reid argues that the same kind of youth awakening led the way in the Second Great Awakening. "At the turn of the nineteenth century, the Second Great Awakening instilled a fresh passion for God in the emerging nation. A major precipitating factor in this movement was the outbreak of revival on college campuses."[6]

He demonstrates in exacting detail how students led the charge in the Second Great Awakening. Finally, he provides examples of student-led awakenings in the nineteenth and twentieth centuries as well. He makes a convincing case that students were not just on the fringes of these revivals; they were at the epicenter.

Clearly God has used student super sneezers throughout church history to spread the virus. In the annals of the Old Testament we have glaring examples as well.

THE FIRST TEENAGED SUPER SNEEZER

The classic story of David and Goliath is a stellar example of how God can use one young person to win a war, shock a nation, and change the course of history. The parallels between how God used a young Israeli then and how He is using young students today are astounding.

You remember the scene, don't you? The Israelite army is facing off against the Philistine army. The battle lines are drawn. Both armies are in place. But nobody wants to jump-start this thing, so the Philistines send out their biggest, their baddest, and their best to challenge the Jews. They send Goliath.

He was nine feet, six inches tall. That's nearly two feet taller than the tallest players in NBA history, Manute Bol and Gheorghe Muresan (both seven feet, seven inches). Goliath was probably a lean four or five hundred pounds of sheer warrior muscle. His suit of armor weighed one hundred twenty-five pounds—maybe more than David himself. When Goliath came out from behind the battle lines, I imagine the scene from *Jurassic Park* when the footsteps of the approaching T. rex shake a cup of water sitting on the dashboard of the tiny car like a distant sonic boom.

When Goliath came, the Israelites went. They ran in sheer terror when they saw him approaching. I can't say I blame them. That guy was a champion among the Philistines. He bore the battle scars on his body. He had killed hundreds, maybe thousands, in the throes of battle. Defeat was as foreign to him as the Philistines were to the Israelites.

At first, the Israelite battle lines were quiet in true and trembling fear. But then David sneezed, and all the armies of Israel caught the cold. His singular act of heroism sparked the army to valor. When they saw the giant fall, they clawed and crawled their way out of their fox-holes and charged the enemy.

That is the same pattern I see in churches with thriving youth ministries across the nation. A handful of students in one dead church can remind the adults of what this Christianity thing is all about. Passionate evangelism burning in the hearts of on-fire teens can set a whole congregation ablaze. David's heroic act reminded the men of Israel's army of the power of their God. The same can happen with the adults in our churches when an awakening like that in the book of Acts is manifest in the lives of students.

THE GOD WHO LOVES LEFTOVERS

David was a leftover. He was actually a looked-over. When Samuel went to the house of Jesse to anoint a king, David's own father forgot about him. He asked every single one of his older brothers to pass by Samuel, but old Sammy never got the divine confirmation that any of them was the one God had chosen as future king.

The older brothers were tall, dark, and handsome. By the world's standards they had it all. But God had a different set of standards. After seeing manly and handsome Eliab, Samuel thought, *This has to be the guy right here.* But God whispered in Samuel's ear, "Do not consider his appearance or his height, for I have rejected him. The LORD does not look at the things man looks at. Man looks at the outward appearance, but the LORD looks at the heart" (1 Samuel 16:7).

Finally Samuel asked if there was anyone else. It was almost as if Jesse said, "Oh yeah! I guess there is one more. But he is the youngest, and he is out wandering around with the sheep." But David was the one whom God had chosen to be king. David, the left*over*, the looked-*over*, had won *over* the heart of God, not with his external appearance but with his internal character.

God loves leftovers who have nothing going for them but Him. The story of David and Goliath emphasizes this point. Instead of using the physically impressive Saul or one of the thousands of well-trained Israeli soldiers to defeat Goliath, God used David.

David's sneeze, his singular act of heroism, triggered a national victory. Just look at these four parallels between the story of the original young super sneezer and the potential army of them today in our youth groups.

THE GIANT GOT BIGGER

Goliath was big. But the giant—no, the *giants*—our students face today are even bigger. Just as the Israelites cowered behind the lines when Goliath roared out his threats, our students are trembling in the trenches. You know the giants. You know the statistics. Let me remind you of how desperate the situation is today. Crime is up. Morals are out. Hope is over. Sin is in.

SUICIDE

According to statistics from the Center for Disease Control and Prevention, in 2003 nearly a quarter of female high school students seriously contemplated suicide and 12 percent made a suicide attempt (females are nearly twice more likely than males to seriously contemplate and/or attempt suicide).[7]

ADOLESCENT VIOLENCE

Statistics show that the current adolescent violence wave began to a large degree between the mid-eighties and mid-nineties. During that decade, adolescent violence took an unprecedented leap and set the pace for the Columbine era of suburban student crime. Unfortunately, teens in this millennium aren't beyond the reach of violence either. In 2003:

 One out of three high schoolers admitted to physical fighting. One out of every eleven high school students was a victim of dating violence. Twenty-seven percent of high school males carried weapons to school. Twelve percent of twelve to eighteen year olds reported being targets of hate-related words at school.[8]

DRUG USE

Findings from a 2004 report by the *Partnership for a Drug-Free America* show that at least 8.7 million teens (37 percent) have tried marijuana. And a new category of substance abuse has emerged—37 percent of teens say they have close friends who have abused prescription painkillers like Vicodin, OxyContin, and Tylox.[9]

Although those drug, violence, and suicide statistics for young people may not be at their record highs, that does not mean they are not problems for teens today. The bottom line is that teen-America today is substantially different from teen-America just a generation ago. The current generation is in desperate need of Jesus Christ. Goliath is on steroids.

CHURCH EVACUATION

Perhaps the most disturbing statistic concerning teenagers is not outside the church but inside it. Teenagers are evacuating the church after graduation. When the tassel is moved at the conclusion of that important ceremony, so are they—right out of the body of Christ into the workforce, college dorm, or party zone. According to George Barna in his report *Third Millennium Teens*:

 Perhaps the most direct indication of the brewing trouble comes from the response to a question concerning how likely teens say they are to attend church once they are independent. After they graduate from high school or move away from home, just two out of five teens contend it is "very likely" that they will attend a Christian church on a regular basis, and another two out of five say it is "somewhat likely." What makes these figures most alarming is that questions of this type typically produce an overestimate of future behavior. If we apply a "correction factor" to these responses, we would estimate that about one out of three teenagers is likely to actually attend a Christian church after they leave home.[10]

We are losing our young at a record pace. The giants have sur-
rounded them, and they are not hesitating to attack. But it is against
the backdrop of utter hopelessness where God does His best work. It
was true in David's time. It is still true today.

In the midst of bad news, it is good to remember that the giants
are no match for the virus. God designed His contagious message to
destroy the power of sin and topple the strongest of opponents.

GOD LOVES TO USE UNLIKELY HEROES

David was the most unlikely of heroes. He was too young, too
unknown, too misunderstood, and too inexperienced. Yet God used
him to save an entire nation.

HE WAS TOO YOUNG

David was the youngest of the eight children of Jesse. His three
oldest brothers were fighting in Saul's army. David spent most of his
time in the fields with the sheep he was tending. But on one particular occasion David was sent on an errand to take his brothers and their
leader some cheese and crackers. He was an errand boy delivering gro-
ceries, not a warrior. He was a kid with snack packs, not a soldier with
weapons. He seemed too young to be a fighter. But God didn't think so.

How many times do youth leaders hear similar words?

"Teenagers are too young to sing in the choir or go on a missions
trip to Mexico or go out to share their faith."

"Once they get a little older, then they will be able to make a difference. Until then just keep them out of our hair. Entertain them.
Dazzle them with games and pizza nights and laser tag. Once they get
old enough, they will have the maturity to do something of importance. But they are too young right now."

That's bad theology. God loves to use those who are too young, too
poor, and too bad to do that which is too extreme, too outrageous, and
too crazy.

HE WAS TOO UNKNOWN

David was a shepherd boy. He was not a national icon, a well-known warrior, or a political leader. He tended sheep. That's all. Being a shepherd in his culture put him on the lowest rung of the vocational ladder. It was like being a trash collector in our society. It was a lonely job with few contacts with the outside world. A shepherd was known only by his sheep. Contact with people was rare. The sky was his roof. The sheep were his companions. The Lord was his guide.

HE WAS TOO MISUNDERSTOOD

David's own family misunderstood him. The young David was not asking questions about Goliath to show off in front of the Israeli warriors; he was genuinely interested in why that loud-mouthed giant was getting away with his ravings against the true God.

In the same way, adults often misunderstand the true motives of our students.

- We call them "hyper and easily distracted." Maybe they are just excited about life.
- We call them "bored with church and youth group." Maybe we are just boring.
- We call them "dangerous and volatile." Maybe they are just waiting for a bigger challenge.
- We call them "disrespectful and self-centered." Maybe we haven't given them a reason to respect and serve.
- We call them "reckless and foolish." Maybe they are willing to be reckless for the kingdom and fools for Christ's sake if we just give them the chance.

I have made the same mistake. Sometimes I've grossly underestimated teenagers. Kids whom I wrote off as too quiet, too shy, too loud, too obnoxious, too shallow, or too immature have managed to surprise me again and again.

HE WAS TOO INEXPERIENCED

David had no fighting experience. He was green—a rookie. He had never been through the Bethlehem Boot Camp for aspiring warriors. He didn't know anything about hand-to-hand combat. The closest he had come was taking out a lion and a bear that were pestering his flock of sheep. He hadn't a clue about military tactics and strategies. He was a shepherd. He knew more about manure than maneuvers! But God chose to use him anyway.

Our students are also too inexperienced. They don't know what life is all about yet. They think they do, but they don't. It is the stage of their lives where they are testing boundaries and trying to find their niche, their personality, their friends, and their passions. More often than not, that quest is messy and frustrating for parent, student, and youth leader. Like David, they are not ready to do battle with the big issues of life. But God chooses to use them anyway.

I can't count how many times I have heard youth leaders tell me that their kids aren't ready to take the lead, do the missions trip, or participate in the outreach project. "Our kids are too inexperienced," they tell me. Baloney. That is just where God wants them. It is in the position of utter inexperience where one can be utterly dependent on God. It is that absolute trust that gets God excited about using the unusable to accomplish the unthinkable.

He loves to use the most unlikely heroes. Think of some of the surprising choices He has used throughout biblical history to be the instruments of transformation.

He chose:
. . . a novice boatbuilder named Noah
. . . an elderly patriarch named Abraham
. . . a patient ex-con named Joseph
. . . a stuttering shepherd named Moses
. . . a confident senior citizen named Caleb
. . . a God-fearing prostitute named Rahab
. . . a terrified Benjamite named Gideon
. . . a frisky warrior named Samson

    . . . a prejudiced preacher named Jonah
    . . . a fig-picking prophet named Amos
    . . . a young dreamer named Daniel
    . . . a reluctant queen named Esther
    . . . a determined cupbearer named Nehemiah
    . . . a converted tax collector named Matthew
    . . . a cricket-eating, camel-fur wearing, water-drenched
       baptizer named John

Maybe the secret of why God loves to use the unusable, the outcasts, the off-putting, and the unlikely is tucked away in 1 Corinthians 1:26–29:

Brothers, think of what you were when you were called. Not many of you were wise by human standards; not many were influential; not many were of noble birth. But God chose the foolish things of the world to shame the wise; God chose the weak things of the world to shame the strong. He chose the lowly things of this world and the despised things—and the things that are not—to nullify the things that are, so that no one may boast before him.

Notice the phrase "so that no one may boast before him." The reason God chooses to use the unusable is simply because they are unusable. In other words, the glory goes to the User, not to the used. God receives maximum honor with minimum vessels. That is why I am absolutely convinced that He desires to use the teenagers of today to initiate a revival of biblical proportions. They are the most unlikely. They are the ones who stain the carpets of our churches and mess up the hymnals in our pews. But if God could use a shepherd boy named David to save a nation, He can use our students to initiate an awakening! He loves to use unlikely heroes.

A PASSION FOR GOD IS MORE
IMPORTANT THAN THE WEAPONS OF WAR

"Then Saul dressed David in his own tunic. He put a coat of armor on him and a bronze helmet on his head. David fastened on his sword over the tunic and tried walking around" (1 Samuel 17:38–39).

What a sight to see David clanking around in Saul's armor. First Samuel 9:2 says that Saul was head and shoulders above the men of Israel, and here is a teenaged boy named David trying to navigate Saul's tent to no avail. Finally he removed the borrowed armor. David knew that if he was going to win against the giant, he was going to win with the meager tools that God had given him.

Meanwhile, Goliath had the latest greatest defensive protection and offensive weapons available at the time. The Philistines were on the cutting edge of military technology. Goliath had an incomparable track record. He had never lost a fight. He was the Philistine's national champion. Goliath had a sword without equal (1 Samuel 21:9), a spear, and a javelin sharpened and ready for fresh Israeli blood, and a man-sized shield for protection from enemy arrows.

Goliath had it all. All David had was a passion for God and a slingshot. That was all he needed. More than any other words in the Old Testament, I love David's unflinching proclamation to his enemy:

> *"You come against me with sword and spear and javelin, but I come against you in the name of the LORD Almighty, the God of the armies of Israel, whom you have defied. This day the LORD will hand you over to me, and I'll strike you down and cut off your head. Today I will give the carcasses of the Philistine army to the birds of the air and the beasts of the earth, and the whole world will know that there is a God in Israel. All those gathered here will know that it is not by sword or spear that the LORD saves; for the battle is the LORD's, and he will give all of you into our hands."* (1 Samuel 17:45–47)

Now those are fighting words. Those are faith-filled words. And they come from nothing more than a teenager.

What does that have to do with the coming student awakening? Everything! The enemy has got it all. From a franchise on Internet pornography to a stranglehold on evangelical apathy, to a nation steeped in moral compromise, Satan has aligned a formidable array of weapons against the kingdom of God. Wouldn't it be just like our God to use an army of students to defeat the ultimate enemy?

Give me David and a slingshot. Give me a teenager with a heart for God and the most basic of training. Give me a nerdy student with a passion for the kingdom over the coolest leadership kid who is all head and no heart. Give me unruly, messy kids who just happen to love Jesus any day of the week and twice on Wednesday night. That's what revival is made of.

Tools are important. The latest evangelistic Web sites, the sharpest outreach programs, and the best student-equipping events are all part and parcel of effectively helping students to change this culture. But more important than any tool, more essential than any weapon against the wicked one is a passion for the Lord Jesus Christ.

Give me David and a slingshot. Give me your unusable teenager.

IT ONLY TAKES ONE
(THE REST WILL FOLLOW)

It only took one teen to take the lead, and the army of jaw-hung soldiers got the point. That's all it takes in your church . . . one teen-ager. As a preaching pastor for over ten years, I have seen the power of youth groups on fire for the Lord Jesus Christ. The adults of our congregation were constantly challenged by reports from the youth department of the latest student-led community outreach. A steady stream of new teen converts reenergized the whole congregation. It reminded us of what "the Church" was all about. It challenged us not to settle for anything less than true evangelistic impact. Often such community outreaches were led by a single teen.

That's one of the reasons I think you should ask your senior pastor to read this book when you are finished with it. It's the lead pastor at a church who can lead the way for this to take place. I'm convinced that pastors can unleash this outbreak in their entire congregation by using the youth ministry as the "infection point."

One of the most powerful catalysts for the adults in a church is to witness a life-changing, soul-reaching youth group in action. Down deep inside most Christian adults love to see teens transformed and long to see the entire church infected with their kind of passionate enthusiasm. Sure there are some who may complain, but the majority in a healthy church body will rejoice at seeing these young people changed by the power of Christ.

Many senior pastors were, at one time, youth leaders themselves and most understand the need to train, equip, and unleash young people for a Great Commission cause. Those pastors who do not, they need to be gently reminded.

Can you imagine your youth group going viral and as a result infecting the adults at your church with this same outreach outbreak? Believe it or not it can happen. I've seen it firsthand.

As the president of Dare 2 Share Ministries, which is an organization that exists to "energize and equip teenagers to know, own, live, and share their faith in Jesus," I have heard countless stories from students, youth leaders, parents, and pastors whose students have led the way for the whole church evangelistically.

I will never forget the story from one Episcopal youth leader who brought his youth group to one of our weekend training events. He told me how one of the shyest girls in the youth group came to the conference and was deeply influenced by the call to evangelize. She went out to share her faith with the rest of the group and came back pumped up. The next day she was slated to share a testimony to the rest of the church. She didn't. She preached a sermon instead. I will never forget the excitement of that youth leader as he told me how that girl communicated to her liturgical congregation that she had surrendered herself fully to the call to proclaim Christ. She told them that she had not once seen a person come to Christ in their congregation. She then went on to say that as a youth group they were going to lead the way evangelistically, with or without the adults. Her shocking sermon was met with applause. God used one young Israeli boy to defeat a giant and one young, quiet girl to defeat another. The same can happen in your youth group. It only takes one; the rest will follow.

David's defeat of Goliath sparked a military victory and led to the beginning of a viral revival across the nation. Young David's passion for God was infectious. For most of his years as leader of Israel he unleashed a spiritual outbreak of biblical proportions. But it all began when he was a ragged, unknown, teenage shepherd boy. Perhaps God will raise up an army of ragged teenagers today to topple the giants in our land. Let the outbreak begin!✖

RED·DOT REVIEW

IT TAKES STUDENT SUPER SNEEZERS TO GO VIRAL!

MONKEY MANDATES

MANDATE #1
Pray for God's help in identifying giants and unleashing your Davids.

MANDATE #2
Write out your answers to these two questions:

1. Do I really believe God is going to unleash a revival through an army of students? Why or why not?
2. What do these students look like?

S STAFF INFECTION QUESTIONS

#1. What three giants are students in our youth group currently facing?

#2. How can we help our students defeat them?

#3. Do we tend to focus more on the weapons of warfare (youth ministry tools, techniques, and programs) than on a passion for God? If so, how can we improve?

CREATING A CONTAGIOUS YOUTH MINISTRY

"I think I'm coming down with something."

We've all said it. Those hours leading up to the onset of a viral infection can be miserable. You know something is brewing under the surface. You can almost feel the battle for the domination of your body as the soldiers of your immune system give way to the territory-devouring enemy called *the virus*. Sooner or later the front lines of protection collapse, and the sneeze or the cough—or worse—takes over.

So how can you tell when your youth group is coming down with something spiritual and spectacular? What are the symptoms of a viral happening in your youth group? What are the signs that your youth group is developing a contagious environment? What actions do we need to take to create an atmosphere that is conducive to outbreak? How can we do something catchy and infectious? The Word of God holds the answers.

Nobody said it would be easy. Building a Great Commission culture that is contagious is no simple task. It takes a total investment. Your leaders, your kids, and you must be fully committed to transforming the atmosphere from typical to supernatural. That catchy atmosphere should undergird every youth group meeting. Beyond the games, the music, and the teaching should be an unmistakable sense of God's presence that is overpowering and undeniable.

This chapter centers on four actions taken from four passages in the New Testament. Each of these Scriptures holds a key to help us do something viral in our youth groups.

KNOW WHERE YOUR RED DOT IS

"But you will receive power when the Holy Spirit comes on you; and you will be my witnesses in Jerusalem, and in all Judea and Samaria, and to the ends of the earth" (Acts 1:8).

There is a key scene in the movie *Outbreak* where the top military strategists are looking at a computer-generated map with a few red dots on it. The viral expert is explaining the velocity of the viral outbreak to the leaders. He shows how far and fast the virus could spread over the course of the next twelve, twenty-four, and then thirty-six hours if left unchecked. Eventually the map is transformed from a picture with a few red dots scattered across it to one completely drenched in red. The virus has done its job. It has become a world killer.

Every virus has an infection point . . . the red dot. It is the entry point into a particular population that launches the epidemic. That's where the outbreak begins. For the early New Testament church the red dot was Jerusalem. Jesus told His disciples that the City of David was where the infection would begin. That prophecy was fulfilled as the message engulfed the Jews of Jerusalem (Acts 1–7). The gospel message was either accepted or rejected in that growing climate of turbulent truth. It could not be ignored.

After Acts 8–12 the red dot gets bigger—much bigger. It spread out to Judea and Samaria. Jesus told His disciples that it would spread from Jerusalem to "all Judea and Samaria" (Acts 1:8). That is exactly what took place. Persecution spurred it on and spread it out. Infected people fleeing the scene of the outbreak brought the virus into formerly uninfected areas. Dr. Luke records the symptoms in his report to Theophilus.

After Acts 13, the gospel went viral throughout much of the civilized world. In about thirty years the message of Christianity had turned the map of the Roman Empire red.

WHERE'S THE RED DOT IN YOUTH MINISTRY?

Some in youth ministry today have said that the red dot is the school campus. Youth leaders who spend time every day with kids on campus know the challenges that come with a solely campus-centered approach to youth ministry. We can't possibly reach every student on every campus by ourselves. It is becoming increasingly difficult for youth leaders to even be permitted on public campuses in many parts of the country. The "separation of church and state" debate has caused many public schools to tighten their rules regarding the presence of a youth minister on public property. In addition, finding time to visit school campuses is tough for most youth pastors because there are so many other things to do. Youth group meetings, camps, retreats, leadership training, and Sunday school must all be planned, administrated, and executed. Many youth groups represent several different high schools, which means the youth leader must visit several in order to simply get to the red dots represented in his or her own group. As a result, those who view the campus as their red dot may get burned out by the sheer time it takes to do it right.

While I am a firm believer in campus ministry, I am convinced that the best red dot for the youth leader is the weekly youth group meeting. First, it is a consistent meeting place. It can be the best opportunity to infect the lost friends of the students in the youth group. From there it can spread to the campus and community and, then, go global.

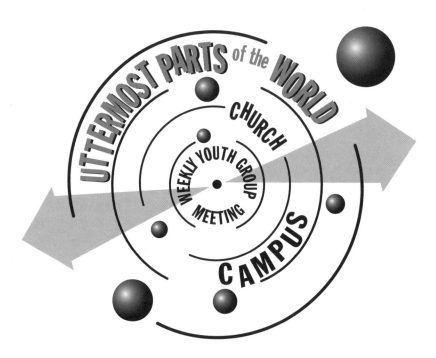

When youth leaders begin to teach their teens in the youth group setting how to go back to their campuses, the virus begins to spread. Those students become the carriers of the viral message into uncharted territories. And it all starts with your red dot, the youth group.

SYNAGOGUES WERE RED DOTS

When Paul entered a new city on his missionary journeys he headed straight for the synagogue. He knew that it was one of the best places to reach people with the message of God's grace. What made it such a fertile ground for evangelism?

First of all, Paul expected lost people to be there. He knew that most of the people in attendance hadn't heard the story of Christianity. He would open the Old Testament scrolls and begin proving to his listeners that Jesus was the Messiah for whom they had been waiting.

Second, those who came to the synagogue expected to hear a message from the Scriptures. Paul gave them what they wanted—a relevant sermon. He also gave them more than what they asked for—they got a revolutionary message of grace.

Third, synagogues were all over the world. Thanks to the dispersion of the Jews, synagogues were almost everywhere in the Roman Empire. Jews and God-fearing Gentiles attended every Sabbath. It was a consistent meeting place at a consistent meeting time (like your youth group meeting). "The establishment of synagogues wherever the Jews were found in sufficient numbers helped greatly to keep alive Israel's hope of the coming of the Messiah, and to prepare the way for the spread of the gospel in other lands."[1] As a result, the synagogue meeting became Paul's red dot, his primary infection point, in almost every city he visited on his missionary journeys.

Do you see the parallels? There were lost people in the synagogue. They were a fertile ground for Paul's evangelistic efforts. There are also lost kids in our youth groups. According to George Barna, "The data shows that half of the kids who call themselves Christian and participate in youth groups in a typical month are not born again—a pool of more than 7 million unsaved kids who journey to the church on a regular basis."[2] The best place to kick off your evangelistic efforts is your own youth group. You may be surprised at the number of students who do not genuinely know Christ!

WHY YOUR YOUTH GROUP MEETING IS YOUR BEST RED DOT

Paul chose the infection point from which to spread the virus of the gospel of Jesus Christ. We should do the same. Here are five more reasons why your youth group meeting is the best place to go viral.

1. IT'S THERE.

It's already established. Your weekly youth group meeting is a constant. If you run a quality, highly relational, fun youth ministry, most of your students are probably pretty consistent in their attendance. That consistency can become a conduit to effective evangelism. The better the quality of your youth ministry, the more students will come. The more they come, the more they will be exposed to the contagious message of Christianity. Attending youth group is already programmed into the students' weekly routine, so why not transform the typical Wednesday night youth group meeting into a phenomenal outreach tool?

2. TEENS ARE A GREAT MISSION FIELD.

The vast majority of those who come to Christ do so before the age of eighteen. The teenage years are a transitional phase of life that is exciting, confusing, depressing, and exhilarating. Kids ask questions—hard ones. They think about the "whys" and the "why nots" of life. What a great time for evangelism! Christianity holds all of the answers to all of their questions and all of the solutions to all of their problems!

3. INVITATIONAL EVANGELISM STILL WORKS.

Nine out of ten unchurched teens say they would go to church if they were invited by a friend.[3] That means that 90 percent of your youth group members' friends are just waiting to be invited to attend! That statistic doesn't necessarily mean that they will come after the first invitation. As I encounter youth groups across America that are exploding evangelistically, I find that their teenagers don't give up and they don't let up. It is not surprising that students who invite friends on almost a daily basis are the most successful in peer-to-peer evangelism.[4]

What does the nine out of ten statistic mean for your youth group? Let's say you have thirty teenagers in your youth group. If each of them has ten non-Christian friends and invites them consistently to youth group, 270 students would eventually come to your youth group and hear the gospel message! And it doesn't stop there. If those who become believers are discipled and trained, then you will reach their circles of influence as well. It is exponential!

4. IT DOESN'T TAKE A WHOLE LOT MORE EFFORT.

This is a huge selling point with youth leaders. This strategy doesn't take another night of the week. It doesn't require a huge budget. The initial work involves training your students in an invitational strategy (which I will describe later in this chapter) and unleashing a team of students to lead the way. The ongoing work requires increasing the quality of your weekly youth group meeting incrementally, reminding students to invite their friends, and taking a few minutes at the end of every youth group meeting to give a short gospel presentation and invitation.

5. DISCIPLESHIP IS A NO-BRAINER.

The toughest part about campus-based evangelism strategies and street evangelism is getting the new believers plugged into a church. That problem is almost completely solved by a youth-group-based, invitational approach to evangelism. Once students have been in your church building, the chance of their coming back again and again goes way up. Of course their return depends upon a few other obvious factors: (1) whether they had a pleasant experience; (2) whether they connected with other kids; and (3) whether someone invites them back and follows up with them right away. Of course there is fallout. Some kids will show an initial interest, but they don't ever come back. But even they weren't a waste. A seed was planted that may sprout weeks, months, years, or even decades later. Our job is to keep chucking seeds and cultivating the sprouts with our best discipleship efforts. But there will always be some fallout. Expect it. There has been fallout since the early church. As the parable of the sower reminds us, we go with the growers and pray for the others!

UNLEASH YOUR SUPER SNEEZERS

One of the great misnomers of Acts evangelism is that it centered on a few carriers like the apostle Paul. But if you take a close look at the New Testament, you will see that while evangelism was often triggered by a carrier like Paul, it was actually often carried out by an army of super sneezers. Someone like Paul would blast into town, gain an initial group of believers, equip them, and then turn them loose for ongoing evangelism after he was gone.

Paul expected Timothy to do not only the work of an evangelist but to train "reliable men who will also be qualified to teach others" (2 Timothy 2:2). When Paul left Thessalonica after only three weeks of ministry, he had already equipped believers there for ongoing evangelistic effectiveness. He wrote to those relatively new converts, "The Lord's message rang out from you not only in Macedonia and Achaia— your faith in God has become known everywhere" (1 Thessalonians 1:8).

The new believers were strategic evangelists. That was not an accident. It was all part of Paul's strategy, which was Christ's strategy in the passage we know as the Great Commission.

One passage in particular gives us a glimpse into the Pauline plan for proclamation. It demonstrates the importance of equipping the super sneezers in your youth group.

Paul entered the synagogue and spoke boldly there for three months, arguing persuasively about the kingdom of God. But some of them became obstinate; they refused to believe and publicly maligned the Way. So Paul left them. He took the disciples with him and had discussions daily in the lecture hall of Tyrannus. This went on for two years, so that all the Jews and Greeks who lived in the province of Asia heard the word of the Lord. (Acts 19:8–10)

Paul's strategy is clear in that passage. He started with evangelism. He led some people to Christ after three months of preaching in the synagogue week after week. He then discipled the new believers. He went down the road to the local community college, rented a classroom, and taught them the Word of God. Evangelism and discipleship were the obvious parts of his plan. But there is another more hidden agenda that most of us miss in our strategies: equipping for evangelism.

Look closely at this phrase: "So that all the Jews and Greeks who lived in the province of Asia heard the word of the Lord." How could that be possible? Did all the Jews and all the Greeks in the province of Asia go to the school of Tyrannus to hear Paul preach? That doesn't seem likely. Did Paul go to every Jew and Greek in the province of Asia? How could he have done that while he was having daily training sessions? The only viable scenario is that those who heard him were equipped to evangelize. The synagogue was the red dot. Paul was the carrier. His students were the super sneezers. He trained them and equipped them, not only in basic doctrine and the Christian life but also in how to share their faith. He then turned them loose to do it. By the time they were done, everybody in the province of Asia had heard the gospel . . . everybody! Paul understood the power of multiplication.

Think about how many thousands of teenagers are within one square mile of you right now. Unless you live in a rural area, it would be impossible for you to reach every student by yourself over the course of the next few years. But if you train and equip your teenagers who rub shoulders with other teenagers who rub shoulders with other teenagers to share their faith, the potential is mind-boggling.

According to John Maxwell, "Even the shyest of people will influence at least 10,000 others during their lifetime."[5] Think about that. Every one of your students could fill a large arena with the people he or she will touch in one way or another over the course of a lifetime. That means that every single student, no matter how shy, is a potential crusade evangelist.

Just as Paul equipped his super sneezers, you must do the same. Find the students in your youth group who have the PGI factor.

"P" STANDS FOR PASSION FOR EVANGELISM

Which students in your youth group are the most on fire to share Christ with their friends? If you have a hard time identifying them, it's time to start breaking hearts. Shatter their complacency with a picture of their friends hanging over the abyss of present hopelessness and future hell.

One of the defining characteristics of every true spiritual awakening in history has been a driving sense of passion and urgency. Study the writings of Spurgeon, Moody, Whitefield, and Wesley, and you will see this recurring theme. The glory of heaven, the fury of hell, the imminence of Christ's return, and the brevity and fragility of life are all subplots in the sermons of the pulpiteers of the past.

Are you cultivating a passion for evangelism in your students? The only way to do that is to do what Jesus did. Paint a picture for them. When Jesus wanted to break the hearts of His disciples for the souls of the lost, He described the reality of the grim darkness of eternal torment in vivid, horrifying detail. Check out the story of the rich man and Lazarus in Luke 16:19–31. In this terrifyingly descriptive passage Jesus pulls back the veil of hell. From that moment on, His followers never viewed the pain of the afterlife the same way. Now they imagined real people suffering real torment for a real eternity. *Real* is the operative word. If we are going to fan the flames of passion in the hearts of our kids, the fire of hell must be real to them.

I will never forget the challenge from one of my youth leaders when I was in junior high school. He asked me to go to a local, busy shopping mall and find a place to sit where the crowd would be thick and bustling. Then I was to watch people for thirty minutes. But I was to watch them with an eternal perspective. He wanted me to put an imaginary tag on their foreheads that read "Bound for hell." At first it seemed kind of weird. But pretty soon I could see nothing but little "Bound for hell" signs on every forehead. When those thirty minutes were over, my face was wet with tears, and my perspective was transformed forever. It helped me to see people differently. It broke my heart.

The Lord used my youth leader to give me a new set of lenses to wear. Those lenses help me to see people not as they are but as they will be someday. The Lord wants to use you to help your teens to see people differently as well.

If you think the theology of hell is an archaic, outdated scare tactic that is a culturally irrelevant, biblically inferior, psychologically damaging motivation to evangelization, then think again. Jesus spoke more about hell than about heaven. He wasn't afraid to use it to scare unbelievers to repent or to motivate true believers to proclaim Him as Lord.

Personally, I believe that the eternal flames have a singular purpose for us as believers. They should drive us to tears. What better tool to rip through the self-centeredness of the typical youth grouper than the pending flames of hell for their friends who don't know Christ?

When was the last time you spoke about hell to your kids? If we want kids to be passionate about evangelism, we need to give them a reason to be passionate. Hell is definitely a reason! The kids in your group who are most passionate about evangelism are great candidates to become super sneezers.

"G" STANDS FOR GIFTING IN EVANGELISM

"It was he who gave some to be apostles, some to be prophets, some to be *evangelists*, and some to be pastors and teachers, to prepare God's people for works of service, so that the body of Christ may be built up" (Ephesians 4:11–12, italics added).

God has given you a gift in your youth group when it comes to evangelism. He has gifted one or more of your kids with the supernatural ability to evangelize. Some of your kids are supernaturally anointed evangelists. Their primary purpose is to evangelize and "prepare God's people for works of service." These gifted evangelists are called to energize other teens to evangelize. That point is often missed when it comes to understanding the real purpose of the gift of evangelism. Christians tend to think that evangelists are the ones who have to do all of the witnessing. But that is only half of the equation. Evangelists are called to evangelize and to equip others to follow their example.

My job as an evangelist is to raise up other evangelists. It is my duty to reproduce reproducers. Perhaps one of the reasons we haven't seen the scale of awakening that we see in the book of Acts is because we tend to relegate evangelism to the evangelist. But the true evangelist's job is to relegate evangelism to the rest of us. He or she is to model it personally and equip others publicly.

Which of the students and adult sponsors in your youth group are gifted in evangelism? Have you identified them and turned them loose to equip others? For many youth leaders the only way to find out who is gifted in evangelism is to do evangelistic projects. Such outreaches show us who thrives when it comes to evangelism and who doesn't. Once the gifted are identified, they must be equipped to equip other students.

"I" STANDS FOR
INFLUENCE TOWARD EVANGELISM

In his book *The Tipping Point*, Malcolm Gladwell identifies the importance of finding those who are influential to lead the charge in our endeavors to get the Word out to as many people as possible. Evangelism falls under this category. Gladwell compares the midnight ride of Paul Revere to the midnight ride of William Dawes. Ever heard of the second guy? Probably not. The reason that virtually every red-blooded American knows of Paul Revere's ride and none but a handful of history buffs know about William Dawes's is because of the result of each ride. One succeeded powerfully where the other failed miserably. Gladwell writes:

 At the same time that Revere began his ride north and west of Boston, a fellow revolutionary—a tanner by the name of William Dawes—set out on the same urgent errand, working his way to Lexington via the towns west of Boston. He was carrying the identical message, through just as many towns over just as many miles as Paul Revere. But Dawes' ride didn't set the countryside afire. The local militia leaders weren't alerted. In fact, so few men from one of the main towns he rode through—Waltham—fought the following day that some subsequent historians concluded that it must have been a strongly pro-British community. It wasn't. The people of Waltham just didn't find out the British were coming until it was too late. If it were only the news itself that mattered in a word-of-mouth epidemic, Dawes would now be as famous as Paul Revere. He isn't. So why did Revere succeed where Dawes failed?

The answer is that the success of any kind of social epidemic is heavily dependent on the involvement of people with a particular and rare set of social gifts. Revere's news tipped and Dawes' didn't because of the differences between the two men.[6]

Gladwell goes on to chronicle the differences between William Dawes and Paul Revere. The famous Revere was a fisherman and a hunter, a card player and a theater lover, a frequenter of pubs and a successful businessman. He was a member of several select social clubs. When Paul Revere came into a town, "he would have known exactly whose door to knock on, who the local militia leader was, who the key players in town were. He had met most of them before. And they knew and respected him as well." On the other hand, "Dawes was in all likelihood a man with a normal social circle, which means that—like most of us—once he left his hometown he probably wouldn't have known whose door to knock on."[7]

What does that have to do with evangelism and your students? A lot. When you find the students in your group who are passionate, gifted, and influential in the area of evangelism, you have found the Paul Reveres in your youth group. They will "ride" from student to student and motivate them to be active in sharing their faith. These leadership-level kids are well connected and well respected. They are the movers and the shakers.

Find those students in your youth group who have the PGI factor. Passion, Gifting, and Influence are all a part of the job description for the on-site student super sneezers.

THE E-PLAN: PRAY-PURSUE-PERSUADE

If you want to start an evangelistic epidemic in your youth ministry, it must be simple and effective. The more complicated it is, the more chance you have for failure. The simpler it is, the more chance you and your teens can execute it with effectiveness. This e-plan is simple. It starts with motivating your teens to pray for their friends. It continues with equipping them to pursue their friends on a spiritual level. It culminates with training your teens to persuade their friends to come to your youth group meeting and to Jesus. Let's look a little deeper into each of these key parts of your e-plan.

PRAY

Want to see your students get their hearts broken for their friends who don't know Jesus? Get them to pray consistently for these friends and family members. I am not talking about casual prayer once a week in a youth group setting. I am talking about intense, intentional, intercessory prayer every day.

Sometimes we forget the power of prayer to save a soul. As I travel and train teenagers all across America, I am asked the same question over and over again: "I have this friend whom I have witnessed to, but he is not open to the gospel. What do I do?" My response is always the same: "Keep sharing the gospel with love and keep praying. Only God can save his soul."

The best strategy without prayer is like the fastest car without fuel. I don't remember who said it, but it's a quote I heard as a teenager: "Satan laughs at our plans. He mocks our strategies. But he trembles when we pray." Teach your teens to pray with passion for the souls of their friends who don't know Christ. And make your own list!

PURSUE

Once you get your teens to start praying for their unreached friends get them to start pursuing them on a deeper level, a spiritual level. What does this mean? Simply equipping your teenagers to turn everyday conversations toward Jesus. Any subject can be turned toward spiritual subjects with a little practice and prayer.

Jesus gave us many great examples of this, like in John 4 with the Samaritan woman at the well. In no time, He'd turned a conversation about a drink of water to the subject of getting her spiritual thirst quenched by Him. But how does a teenager learn to make these "salvation segues" toward Jesus?

Let's say one of your students is talking to a friend about some movie they both have seen. Maybe it's a supernatural thriller that has demons or ghosts or whatever spooky thing. This conversation can be easily turned with a simple question, "What do you believe about the supernatural world? Do you believe in demons? Angels? God?" Or maybe they are talking to their friend about a recent death. This becomes an easy transition to what happens after a person dies. There are countless ways to naturally turn conversations toward spiritual subjects and, ultimately, to the gospel itself. Practice this with your teens so they can help point others toward Christ.

PERSUADE

Once teens bring the subject of spiritual truth up, they have a goal for their friends, to persuade them to go A–E:

Attend the youth group meeting
Believe in Christ
Connect to a tribe
Develop spiritually
Evangelize others

Let's take a look at each of these key stops along the journey to salvation and spiritual growth.

ATTEND THE YOUTH GROUP MEETING

There is no more powerful witness than the body of Christ being the body of Christ. As your teens bring unreached friends to youth group and these unbelievers witness your group worshipping, praying, connecting, and loving, something amazing can take place: their souls are convicted and connected at the same time. They are connected to the group through the love they feel and are convicted by the Word and Spirit of God as each does their work in the hearts of the teens.

This means training your teens to become talking billboards for your youth group meeting. I can't count how many times I have heard testimonies like this one:

My friend Sherri invited me out to youth group like twenty times. I finally gave in. I told her that I would go once just to get her off my back. To be honest I just didn't want to go. Church didn't sound fun at all. Boy, was I wrong. I mean, it was fun and stuff and everybody was friendly. But the thing that got me most was the message. I have never heard anything like that before. That night after youth group Sherri asked me what I thought about it. I told her that I became a Christian that night. Now I am always inviting all my friends out to youth group too.

Train your teens to invite their unreached friends to youth group all the time. Assure your students again and again that the gospel will be presented every week. Once it catches on, evangelism will go viral through your youth group.

BELIEVE IN CHRIST

When students participate in the group meeting it's much easier to bring the gospel up with them. Here's how it works. Lets say one of your students invites their friend Jordan to attend the youth group. Afterward your youth group member simply asks the question, "Hey, Jordan, what did you think of what the youth leader said?" This simple question becomes a wide open door for a conversation about the gospel message.

Note: Your teens don't have to wait to share Jesus with their friends until they attend your student ministry. Maybe as they go deeper in the spiritual conversation the gospel message comes up and comes out. GREAT! As a matter of fact, the more effective you become at equipping your students to share their faith, the more effective they will become when it comes to leading teens to Christ before they even get to your meeting. The sooner the better!

CONNECT TO A TRIBE

When members of your student ministry bring their friends to the youth ministry, it is vital that they search for a tribe to connect them to on a personal level. This current culture of teenagers connects to anywhere from three to six teens as part of their inner circle of friends. Encouraging them to create this inner circle of friendship in your student ministry vastly increases the chances of them coming back and staying. The visitor is not emotionally invested into the youth group until he or she has at least two friends to relate and connect to on a deeper level. Each friend becomes a wall of emotional safety that protects the newcomer from feeling overwhelmed by the crowd. It ensures a safe place in the rowdy and raucous student ministry setting.

While the whole idea of teens being connected to a tribe may sound insignificant, it is vitally important. It was a tribe that Solomon was talking about in Ecclesiastes 4:12,"Though one may be overpowered, two can defend themselves. A cord of three strands is not quickly broken."

What's true of a cord of three strands is also true of your teenagers. Once they unite with at least two others, they form an emotional bond that is hard to break. It is these kinds of relationships that will cause teens to come back to youth group again and again.

The job is not done until every visitor is connected with a like tribe. This means that your youth group members have to have their senses attuned to who would be the best third party to connect to. This may take a little trial and error, but once a newcomer finds the right tribe, it will be obvious.

DEVELOP SPIRITUALLY

Once a teenager puts her faith in Christ it is time to help her develop spiritually. This can be done by getting her in some kind of Christianity 101 class, small group, or "tribal" study where she can learn more about her newfound faith in Christ.

Here's a principle that may help you in this process: the teen who invites the newcomer to attend the youth group to begin with is the best one to initiate the discipleship process as well. Why? Because of the relationship!

Spiritual development (aka discipleship) is crucial for new believers. Jesus didn't command us to go and make converts but disciples. This entails teaching and modeling truth in understandable and practical ways. It involves making sure that every new family member in the body of Christ understands the basics of who God is; what the gospel is all about; the reliability of God's Word; the deity of Christ; how to commune with God through prayer, Bible study, and meditation; and the importance of the local church. The list goes on but these are some of the basics.

One way to help your teens (both new believers and others) to grow deeper in their faith is to get them to sign up for Soul Fuel on www.capturetheirhearts.com. Soul Fuel is a weekly e-mail blast that presents core biblical truth in a relevant and compelling way. You can also sign up to receive FREE youth leader curriculum on this site that will help you take your teens deeper into the Soul Fuel core truth of the week.

EVANGELIZE OTHERS

The final step in this process is equipping these new believers to reach out to others with the gospel of Jesus. How? Train them to pray, pursue, and persuade. Something special takes place when these new believers are trained to share their faith. Sharing the love of Jesus with others becomes a part of their spiritual DNA, and oftentimes it's these teens who become the spark for ongoing outreach in the youth ministry.

THE E-TEAM

While everybody in your student ministry should be exercising the e-plan with their friends (Pray-Pursue-Persuade), there is a team of super sneezers that should be leading the way for viral evangelism well beyond just their friends. This team of elite epidemic launchers is what I call the e-team.

An e-team (or evangelism team) is a group of students in your youth group who are passionate about evangelism and are willing to take the lead when it comes to infecting the rest of your youth group with a Great Commission mind-set. These students model, mentor, and manage the movement on a peer level.

This team of teens is not necessarily developing the program, acting in the drama team, or teaching up front. What they are doing is setting the pace for outreach. They are leading others to Christ. They are inviting unchurched kids to the youth group. They are equipping other students to share their faith. They are leading the charge for follow-up.

When students see other students sharing their faith, evangelism becomes contagious. The authors of *Contagious Faith* cite one national study on the impact of peer evangelism: "Students who saw other students lead peers to Christ were dramatically more effective in their own evangelism efforts than those who didn't benefit from such examples."[8] When your teenagers see you sharing your faith, they think, *That's cool, but that's what he gets paid for.* When they see other students sharing their faith, they think, *If they can do it, I can do it too.*

The e-team is more than just an evangelism team. It is a team of students committed to the big picture of the Great Commission. The e-team is the trigger for the evangelism explosion and spiritual revival in your youth group, church, and community. Their primary goal is not merely addition but spiritual multiplication. Replicating an Acts-like culture of spiritual transformation is what drives the e-team. It's about much more than just witnessing. It's about awakening.

JERUSALEM, JUDEA, SAMARIA, AND THE UTTERMOST PARTS

Jesus told his disciples in Acts 1:8 that they would be his witnesses starting with their peers in their own hometown of Jerusalem, expanding outward to their region of Judea, outside their comfort zone with people they normally didn't like in Samaria, and finally to the outer edges of the known world.

The early disciples became the e-team of the first century that led the way for this outer expansion of the gospel message. Your e-team leads the way in their own version of this same expansion. Jerusalem can represent each teenager's own circle of closest friends; Judea could represent all the teenagers at their school; maybe Samaria represents a demographic or neighborhood that your teens wouldn't be "caught dead in." And obviously the uttermost parts of the world are still the same.

PURSUE RELATIONSHIPS IN JERUSALEM AND JUDEA

The e-team does more than just pursue the friends who reside inside their own sphere of influence. They make new friends. They are pushing the boundaries of their friendships outside their "Jerusalem" (their comfortable friends) into their "Samaria" (acquaintances and strangers). The e-team members are always on the lookout for those who are willing to talk or are open to at least build a casual friendship.

The goal is to create a new set of glasses that e-team members view their classmates through, a kind of spiritual night-vision goggles where they can see through the darkness of teen confusion to those who are willing to engage or just talk. Oftentimes this means that e-team members are on alert to find teens who are sitting by themselves in the school cafeteria or who just moved into town or just went through something traumatic. They go and begin to pursue relationships with these people and introduce them to Christ, invite them to the group, and connect them to a tribe as soon as possible.

But it doesn't stop there. The e-team is involved in reaching every teen on their campus for Christ. They are seeking to build relationships in a natural and loving way with teen after teen. Regardless whether a contact comes to youth group or trusts in Christ, these teens seek to continue the friendship if the other person is open. This may lead to several miniature e-teams where small groups of e-team members from the same church and school identify teenagers to build relationships with together. This "infection strategy" brings a whole different feel to going to school. No longer is it just an educational exercise—it is a mission field.

While the whole student ministry is executing the e-plan (Pray-Pursue-Persuade), the e-team is going a step further with PR (not public relations, but pursuing relationships). They are taking the initiative to build relationships with teenagers at their school. But it doesn't stop there.

PR IN SAMARIA

This is when teenagers begin to reach out as an e-team to a neighborhood, perhaps one very different from their own. Maybe your e-team adopts a neighborhood of twenty-five houses for a year and once every two months goes there to serve and share. The purpose of this is to build new friendships with teens and families in that neighborhood with the ultimate goal of getting them to A–E at either your church or a closer church. Of course there are safety issues: teens should always go in tribes on these kinds of projects, have adult supervision, etc., but the goal is to build good will, serve the community, build new relationships, share Jesus, and transform lives.

Maybe this Samaritan outreach is working together with a local rescue mission to collect canned food in the neighborhood around your church, asking neighbors to let you come back every two months, taking prayer requests in the process and then, maybe the third time around getting into a spiritual conversation with your new friends. The list of possibilities is endless. But the goal is to get teens outside of their normal worlds to build new relationships.

PR TO THE UTTERMOST

Why wouldn't the e-team be leading the whole missions trip effort for your student ministry? It could be the annual push for every e-team to drive the mission trip for that year. But missions trips aren't the only way that your team of super sneezers can infect the uttermost.

What about getting teenagers in chatrooms where they can engage with other students from other countries about spiritual subjects? Although there needs to be coaching and accountability about safety and boundaries, there is huge opportunity for online evangelism and pursuing cyber relationships where the gospel of Christ can be shared in love.

What about training your e-team to befriend foreign exchange students at their own school so they can start doing foreign missions without ever leaving the country?

What about getting your e-team to sponsor a child or two with Compassion International? Through the Compassion organization, every child hears the gospel, is trained in the basics of God's Word, and is taken care of on a physical, emotional, and educational level. Imagine having your whole e-team going on a missions trip to visit their sponsored child and serving the child's family (every Compassion host church runs a center called a "project" where children are taught, fed, and loved).

Whatever you do to PR to the uttermost, your e-team can lead the way!

UNLEASH THE VIRUS EVERY WEEK

"For I resolved to know nothing while I was with you except Jesus Christ and him crucified" (1 Corinthians 2:2).

When I was a preaching pastor, I received criticism from time to time that I preached the gospel too much. It was our policy at Grace Church that whenever an expository or topical sermon was preached on Sunday morning, there would be a short gospel presentation and invitation at the end. Some people got tired of hearing the gospel every week, and they told me so. I never understood that rebuke. How can you preach the gospel too much? How can we ever hear too much of the cross or the gift of eternal life made available through the shed blood of Jesus Christ? How could we ever get tired of the salvation story? One thing is for sure. Paul the apostle never got tired of preaching it. He reminded the Corinthians that when he was with them he had one message: "Jesus Christ and him crucified."

Paul preached the gospel all the time—in and out of the pulpit. Sir Winston Churchill once said, "A fanatic is someone who won't change his mind and won't change the subject." Paul was a fanatic about the gospel. He preached it again and again in every town he visited until it sank in. Once it sank in, he preached it some more. Every letter he ever wrote reeks of it. Every sermon he ever preached was anchored by it. Again and again he pounded home the message and implications of the gospel message to his audience.

Look at the apostle Paul's famous letter to the Romans. Every chapter has as its epicenter the gospel message:

- In chapters 1–3 he proves the need for the gospel by exposing our sinfulness.

- In chapters 4–5 he explains the simplicity of the gospel by demonstrating that salvation is by faith alone apart from our good deeds.

- In chapters 6–8 he shows the power of the gospel to transform a believer's life.

- In chapters 9–11 he demonstrates the sovereignty of God in the gospel and how it takes a divine act of God to regenerate the lost.

- In chapters 12–16 he unveils the practical implications of the gospel in the daily life of the believer.

Are you, like Paul, a fanatic about preaching the gospel message? Do you present it at the end of every youth group meeting? Do you unleash the virus weekly?

More often than not, youth leaders and pastors are guilty of committing the sin of assumption. We assume that every person present in our youth group has heard the gospel. We assume that because most of our kids have heard it, that they have responded in faith to it. That assumption is wrong. The vast majority of youth groups across America have kids who don't trust Christ in them.

I will never forget being invited to speak at a meeting for Christian students on a large university campus. The woman who invited me to speak gave me some clear instructions before the meeting started. She told me that everybody attending the meeting was already a Christian and that she would prefer me to stick to a message geared toward believers. I assured her that the bulk of my message would be geared toward that audience. But I also made clear that it is my policy to present the gospel at the end of every talk at every event. I explained that we could never assume that every Christian gathering has only Christians present. Furthermore, I explained that we could never take salvation for granted. She was not happy with my response. She reiterated, this time more intensely, that she did not want me to give the gospel at all. I repeated just as fervently that that was not an option. I wasn't there for the honorarium. I was there for the opportunity. Finally in disgust she gave up trying to convince me otherwise.

That night after sharing an encouraging message to the believers,

I concluded by saying, "Maybe you are here tonight and all this stuff doesn't make a bit of sense to you because you are not sure if you are a Christian." As I began my gospel presentation I could see her countenance change. She was clearly angry that I had dared to defy her prime directive. I am sure that in her mind it was a complete waste of time to go through the gospel with that group of people who were most assuredly already believers.

When I finished I asked the audience to bow their heads and close their eyes. When I asked that anyone who was trusting in Christ as Savior for the first time that night raise his or her hand, I noticed that the woman had cupped her hand over her face and was peeking through her fingers to see if anyone was going to actually raise a hand.

Two hands went up. They belonged to the girl directly to her right and the girl directly to her left. Both girls trusted in Christ as their Savior that night. I could see the surprise in her eyes when she saw those two hands go up. Then I could see the embarrassment on her face as she turned and looked up at me. I tried to restrain myself, but I couldn't help it as my left eyebrow moved up in a crooked rebuke. She knew that one eyebrow was screaming out, "I told you so!"

There are at least four compelling reasons to give the gospel every week in your youth group meeting:

1. IT WILL MAKE A STATEMENT.

Your students will know that anytime they bring a lost person to youth group he or she will hear the gospel. That knowledge is psychologically invaluable when it comes to the typical teenager in the typical youth group. The typical teenager is uncomfortable bringing up the gospel and sharing the message with his or her friend. So instead of risking the embarrassment of messing up, they shut up. But if that same teenager knows that every single week the gospel will be presented in the youth group setting, there is a strong likelihood that, with some prodding, he or she will invite unchurched friends to youth group.

As a teenager in youth ranch I saw literally thousands of friends of friends come to Christ throughout my junior and senior high years. All of us knew that every week the gospel would be given, so we invited everybody we knew to invite everyone they knew every single week. We knew we could bring the gospel up after youth group by simply asking, "What did you think of what the youth leader was saying about going to heaven and stuff?" It worked.

At Grace Church the people know that the weekly presentation of the gospel is nonnegotiable. It started with a promise I made on March 12, 1989, to the twenty members of Grace Church at the time. I vowed that the gospel would be clearly presented at the end of every service. Rick Long is the preaching pastor now, and he faithfully gives the gospel every week. And every week people come to Christ, and the church grows. At this writing, the church has about 2,300 members and approximately 65 percent of our congregation came to Christ at our church.

On a typical Sunday at Grace there is a welcoming atmosphere, great worship, and a sermon laced with plenty of humor and illustrations. At the end Rick gives the gospel. He may start by saying, "Now some of this stuff doesn't make sense to some of you because you don't know for sure that you are going to heaven when you die. I'm going to tell you in the next two minutes how you can know for sure." The people of Grace are riveted in rapt attention, not because they haven't heard it before (they hear it every week) but because they know that most likely there are people in the room who are about to come to Christ. You can almost feel the prayers going up as the message is going out. Finally, Rick asks everybody to bow their heads and close their eyes as he gives the invitation. He says something like, "With your heads bowed and your eyes closed, would you raise your hand and put it right back down if that made sense and you are trusting in Jesus Christ as your Savior this morning?" Fred the factory worker is watching to see if his friend Joe will raise his hand. He does. Fred gets a chill. After the service Fred begins, "What did you think about what Pastor Rick was talking about?" The reproduction process begins when Joe starts to make a mental list of people he is going to invite to Grace to hear this great news. This same process should be happening in your youth group every single week.

Giving the gospel every week in the context of your regular youth group meeting makes a definite statement to your teens. It tells them that you are serious about the Great Commission. It reminds them that every time they bring visitors, they will be exposed to the virus in a contagious context. But there are other reasons you should give the gospel every week.

2. IT WILL ENGAGE YOUR STUDENTS IN SPIRITUAL WARFARE.

When students bring lost friends to youth group they get a new perspective. All of a sudden they are rooting for you to pull off a good lesson, praying for you to give a clear presentation of the gospel, and asking God to do a mighty work in the lives of their friends. In other words, it engages your students in spiritual warfare.

An unseen battle takes place in your youth room every time you present the gospel. Satan dispatches his soldiers of darkness to deceive, distract, and destroy the attention spans of the visiting students. The counterattack that youth leaders and students must employ is prayer. As you train your students to pray (with their eyes open) while you are presenting the gospel every week, you will get more and more of a sense of that bloodless battle for the souls of the unsaved teens by the invisible forces of darkness in your youth room.

On a practical note, train your students not to put their Bibles away while you are giving the gospel (as it usually signifies the end of the youth meeting). Train them instead to be riveted to you. The psychological effect on visiting students is amazing. What your teens are focused on they will focus on. If your teens are distracted, the visitors will be too.

Even more important than where they are looking is what they are praying. Remind them constantly of the importance of praying during the gospel presentation for the students in the room who don't know Christ. At that point you are asking them to join with you in the quest for souls to accept Christ as Savior. It is a dangerous partnership . . . dangerous to the kingdom of darkness, that is.

3. IT WILL TRAIN THEM
HOW TO SHARE THE GOSPEL.

One of the side benefits of giving the gospel every week is that it trains your students how to share the gospel. As they hear you give it every week, it reminds them of the basic truth of "Jesus Christ and him crucified" and how to communicate that message in a compelling way.

4. IT WILL REMIND THEM WHAT THEY BELIEVE.

Your presentation also becomes a catechism of sorts for your students. Catechisms have lost their groove in many evangelical churches. If you were to interview the typical youth pastor in the typical evangelical church and ask for a definition of the word *catechism*, many would reply with a blank stare and the question, "Isn't that something the Catholics do?"

Webster defines a catechism as "a summary of religious doctrine often in the form of questions and answers." A creed is defined as "a brief authoritative formula of religious belief." Catechisms and creeds are almost as old as the church. They were used to indoctrinate new believers and children into the basic belief systems of the church. Yet creeds and catechisms are almost unheard of today in evangelical churches. As a result, students lack a systematic structure of basic beliefs to cling to.

More than ever our teens need a catechism and a creed. They need to understand the basic tenets of Christian belief. That will become their only ammunition when they are unleashed into the world outside of their youth group. It will give them a strong anchor for their souls in a culture that will assault their belief system like a series of tsunamis.

When you give the gospel every week at the end of your talk, you are taking your teens back through a catechism of sorts. You are reminding them of the basic building blocks of their faith. That weekly reminder ingrains their belief systems deeper. In the words of my country-bred pastor when I was growing up, "The more mud you throw against the wall, the more it's going to stick."

THE PLEDGE

I am asking you to make a pledge right now to give the gospel every week at the end of every youth group meeting. It only takes a few minutes but has eternal ramifications. The more you do it, the better you will get at it and the more your kids will know you are serious about it.

How about it? Will you take the pledge right now? Raise your right hand and repeat these words:

"I _____ on this _____ day of _____, do hereby promise in the presence of God to give the gospel at the end of every youth group meeting from now on."

That wasn't so hard, was it? Now do it.

IT TAKES TENACITY

Applying the four main steps outlined in this chapter in the context of a youth group setting takes tenacity. It is a little like competing in a triathlon. Anybody who has participated in such a race knows the temptation to quit. Barriers must be broken through by sheer tenacity and perseverance. The first barrier is indecision. You must get past the hesitations and insecurities that whisper in your ear, "You can't do this. It will never work."

3 Stages of the Race

1. HESITANCE	INDECISION BARRIER	2. ACCEPTANCE	IMPATIENCE BARRIER	3. EXPECTANCE
*Kids **never** trust Christ in my youth group.*		*Kids **sometimes** trust Christ in my youth group.*		*Kids **always** trust Christ in my youth group.*
Make a decision "We will change."		**Encourage the participants** "Don't give up!"		**Adjust your strategy** "Let's be creative!"
Lead the way "I will start!"		**Engage the on-lookers** "Come join us!"		**Accomplish your mission** "Let's think big!"

The second barrier is impatience. Get ready for complaints. It takes time for your students to understand the strategy, to get used to a weekly gospel presentation, and to start seeing the need to bring their unsaved friends to youth group. It takes patience for you to learn how to present the gospel message in a clear and concise way and to give an invitation that works effectively. Until kids begin trusting in Christ as their Savior on a regular basis in your youth group, many of your Christian teens will get tired of hearing the gospel at the end of every one of your lessons. But once you break through this barrier, your youth group will experience evangelism critical mass. Don't stop until you go viral. Pretty soon, your problem will be how to plug in all of the new believers into a discipleship program. What a great problem to have.

DON'T FORGET ABOUT QUALITY

Have you ever walked into a restaurant and been immediately turned off? Maybe you wait for a few minutes to be seated and nobody helps you. Perhaps there is food on the floor or rude wait staff or misspelled words on the menu. Whatever it is, the lack of quality automatically predisposes you to a bad experience. It is no different in a youth group setting.

If you want to have a highly contagious youth group, it must be a truly quality experience for current and visiting students. In business you can have the best marketing plan in the world, but if the product doesn't deliver, then it is only a matter of time before word spreads and sales drop.

Is your youth ministry done with absolute excellence? Do you spend plenty of time planning, organizing, and praying for your youth meeting, or do you fly by the seat of your pants? Do you hear a steady stream of complaints from parents and teens that the youth ministry is disorganized? Are your lessons well prepared, well transitioned, and well illustrated? Do you unleash the spiritual gifts and talents of your students in an organized way during youth group through testimonials, singing, drama, and prayer? Is your youth group a setting where your teenagers are comfortable inviting their unchurched friends because they are sure of your commitment to excellence?

Don't hide behind the small budget excuse. What you lack in budget, make up for in hard work, prayer, and creativity.

Applying the four steps takes a commitment to quality and an attitude of tenacity. If you work hard, think big, and stick with it, you will see God do amazing things through your highly contagious youth group.✖

RED·DOT REVIEW

UNLEASH YOUR E-TEAM WITH
A PRAY-PURSUE-PERSUADE CHALLENGE!

MONKEY MANDATES

MANDATE #1
Go to www.dare2share.org and register your e-team right away and get some free resources to help you launch the outbreak in your youth group with effectiveness.

MANDATE #2
Pick a launch date for the e-team strategy.

STAFF INFECTION QUESTIONS

#1. Who are the students in our youth group who are the most passionate, gifted, and influential toward evangelism?

#2. What are we going to do right away to get our student ministry to do the e-plan?

#3. How will we train all of our students in the Pray-Pursue-Persuade strategy? How will we begin to unleash our e-team to PR (pursue relationships) in their Jerusalem, Judea, Samaria and uttermost parts of the world?

INCREASING THE VELOCITY OF THE VIRUS

*"So the churches were strengthened
in the faith and grew daily in numbers."*

—ACTS 16:5

They are scattered throughout the book of Acts. Once you recognize their presence, they seem to jump off the page at you. They point to the triggering of a viral event. What are they? Outbreak indicators.

Outbreak indicators are the passages that point to an action in the church that exponentially accelerated the spread of the gospel message. Those triggering actions can be re-created in the context of our youth groups to accelerate the spread of the gospel.

Here is a list of the outbreak indicators in the book of Acts:

Those who accepted his message were baptized, and about three thousand were added to their number that day. (Acts 2:41)

And the Lord added to their number daily those who were being saved. (Acts 2:47)

But many who heard the message believed, and the number of men grew to about five thousand. (Acts 4:4)

Nevertheless, more and more men and women believed in the Lord and were added to their number. (Acts 5:14)

So the word of God spread. The number of disciples in Jerusalem increased rapidly, and a large number of priests became obedient to the faith. (Acts 6:7)

But the word of God continued to increase and spread. (Acts 12:24)

The word of the Lord spread through the whole region. (Acts 13:49)

The word of the Lord spread widely and grew in power. (Acts 19:20)

When the triggering actions that precede each of those passages are replicated in the context of our youth group meetings, an outbreak of outreach can take place. I have narrowed these triggering actions down to seven. As you apply them to your youth ministry you will see explosive results.

OUTBREAK INDICATOR #1
SEIZE EVERY OPPORTUNITY
TO SHARE THE GOSPEL

"Those who accepted his message were baptized, and about three thousand were added to their number that day" (Acts 2:41).

On that day the church was born. On the day of Pentecost, Jews had gathered from all over the known world for a celebration of the festival of harvest. The celebration was held fifty days after the Passover celebration. That event occurred less than two months after the resurrection of Jesus Christ and a mere ten days after His ascension. Since the ascension of Jesus, the disciples had been praying passionately for the promised Spirit of God to come upon them. Their prayers were about to be answered.

> *Suddenly, a sound like the blowing of a violent wind came from heaven and filled the whole house where they were sitting. They saw what seemed to be tongues of fire that separated and came to rest on each of them. All of them were filled with the Holy Spirit and began to speak in other tongues as the Spirit enabled them. Now there were staying in Jerusalem God-fearing Jews from every nation under heaven. When they heard this sound, a crowd came together in bewilderment. (Acts 2:2–6)*

The NIV Study Bible text notes read, "Jews from different parts of the world would understand the Aramaic of their homeland. Also the Greek language was common to all parts of the world. But more than this was occurring; they heard the apostles speak in languages native to the different places represented."[1]

Imagine the moment. The Spirit of God came upon the apostles, and they began speaking in other languages fluently. I believe that each apostle was speaking in all of the different languages, one after another. That was the miracle. They were mostly blue-collar followers of Jesus, and suddenly they were fluent in several different languages. That symphonic display of the power of the Spirit drew a crowd. Each person there recognized his or her native language being spoken by one apostle, then another, then another. That merry-go-round proclamation of God's truth shocked and bewildered the crowd. So Peter seized the opportunity to preach the gospel. "Then Peter stood up with the Eleven, raised his voice and addressed the crowd" (Acts 2:14).

Peter could have just flexed his miracle muscles and let the crowd "ooh" and "ah," but he didn't. He understood that God's plan was to gather a crowd so that he could share the gospel with them.

That's the pattern throughout the New Testament. Wherever a crowd gathered, God's spokesmen seized the opportunity to preach the gospel. Whether it was a group of angry Judaizers (Acts 7), a mob (Acts

21:30–40), or a gathering of rulers, political officials, and kings (Acts 25:23–26:1), whenever those heroic preachers had an opportunity to share the gospel they seized it. The only time that didn't happen was when a crowd gathered in Ephesus to protest Christianity. Yet even then, "Paul wanted to appear before the crowd, but the disciples would not let him" (Acts 19:30).

What does that teach us about viral evangelism in our youth groups? Whenever a crowd gathers and there is even the remotest possibility that people who don't know Christ are present, we should seize the opportunity to give the gospel. Once again, do you give the gospel in every youth group meeting? It may seem redundant. But revival is worth redundancy.

The result of Peter's proclamation of the gospel was the addition of three thousand members to the newly born church. For you it may mean the addition of three. But one transformed soul is worth the effort.

OUTBREAK INDICATOR #2
CREATE A COMMUNITY THAT IS CONTAGIOUS

The second outbreak indicator occurs in Acts 2:42–47:

They devoted themselves to the apostles' teaching and to the fellowship, to the breaking of bread and to prayer. Everyone was filled with awe, and many wonders and miraculous signs were done by the apostles. All the believers were together and had everything in common. Selling their possessions and goods, they gave to anyone as he had need. Every day they continued to meet together in the temple courts. They broke bread in their homes and ate together with glad and sincere hearts, praising God and enjoying the favor of all the people. And the Lord added to their number daily those who were being saved.

Wow! Sounds like a blast, doesn't it? There is a reason for that—it was! This entity called the church was vibrant, exciting, and contagious.

The short celebration of God's blessing on the Jewish crops was suddenly transformed to a lifelong celebration of God's blessing on the Jewish souls. The gospel was the seed. Eternal life was the harvest. The church was the festival of celebration.

"Everyone was filled with awe" (Acts 2:43). Before we get into the nuts and bolts of this powerful text, I want to point out what word I think best describes what was going on here—*fun*. That's right, fun! I think that youth group should be the most fun place in the world. I am not talking about games. I am talking about a climate. When God's Word is preached with power, worship becomes exciting, ministry occurs with excellence, and church is a blast.

Are your teens having fun in youth group? Do they look forward to it? Are they constantly inviting their friends to experience it? If not, you have neglected a basic element to a viral event—a contagious community.

What does this community look like? You will see at least three descriptions of this contagious climate in these verses.

ABSOLUTE ACCEPTANCE

Jews had gathered from all over the early world to experience the festival of the harvest. The newly converted Jews were from "every nation under heaven," but there was not a hint of prejudice or pride. Instead there was a climate of absolute acceptance.

The youth ministries that are the most effective when it comes to reaching people for Jesus Christ go the extra mile to make visiting students feel welcomed and loved. From the moment visiting students get out of their cars to walk into the building, they must feel loved. A few teens need to be assigned to greet and meet every single visitor. The visitor should be introduced to other students, the youth leader, and other adults.

In a society where cliques rule, the youth group should stand out as a glaring exception. It should be a blast of fresh air in a cultural climate too often polluted with prejudice. The atmosphere should seem almost surreal to them. Visitors should ask, "What kind of place is this? Are these people for real?" And that's a huge part of it—it needs to be for real. "Hi, I'm ____. What's your name?" can come across more genuine to some than a loud and hyper barrage of information and questions. Teens have great perception about whether people genuinely care or if they're being fake nice or overly enthusiastic. While students should greet, there will be even more opportunities to prove that they really do care in the days after the initial introduction. As the defining characteristic of the early believers was consistent love, that should define our students as well.

ABSOLUTE SELFLESSNESS

"All the believers were together and had everything in common. Selling their possessions and goods, they gave to anyone as he had need" (Acts 2:44–45).

Here is where it gets really good. The party continued. As the days gave way to weeks and the weeks to months, those newly converted party animals from all over the world didn't want to go home! They were learning and growing and thriving.

But there was one problem. They were running out of financial and material resources. The bank accounts were drying up. So what happened? Many of the believers sold their possessions and pooled the money with other self-sacrificing Christians to support those who were struggling financially. That communal atmosphere was a phenomenon. They didn't want the party to stop, so they pulled out the stops to keep it going.

How does that apply to your youth group? A student should never miss an event because of a lack of finances. Special offerings, anonymous gifts, and absolute selflessness describe the viral youth group. Newcomers sense it. It is an inescapable, unavoidable atmosphere of sheer servanthood.

ABSOLUTE EXPECTANCE

"And the Lord added to their number daily those who were being saved" (Acts 2:47).

Daily. Every day. Every twenty-four-hour period. Once every rotation of the earth. Every single day people got saved and were immersed into the body life of the early New Testament church!

Can you imagine being a part of a church where you absolutely expected people to come to Christ every single day? In today's Christian culture that is almost unimaginable. To us, evangelism is a slow, meticulous process where someone is finally added to the church. No wonder we have lost the air of anticipation in our churches and youth groups. In the early church, "everyone was filled with awe" because of all the changed lives. In today's church everyone is filled with awe when someone actually comes to Christ!

When the outbreak comes to your youth group, expectance will be one of the most obvious signs. Your teens will begin to expect other teens to come to Christ every single week! They will expect to hear consistent testimonies of powerful conversions, not from some camp speaker once a year but every single week in youth group!

In *Contagious Faith*, Dave Rahn and Terry Linhart make this point well. Referring to the most evangelistically effective groups in their study, they write:

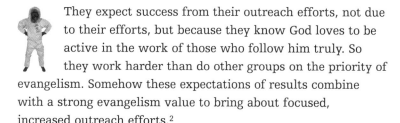

They expect success from their outreach efforts, not due to their efforts, but because they know God loves to be active in the work of those who follow him truly. So they work harder than do other groups on the priority of evangelism. Somehow these expectations of results combine with a strong evangelism value to bring about focused, increased outreach efforts.[2]

In the Christian youth ranch movement I expected teens to come to Christ every single week. And students came to Christ in droves. Why? Because the leadership had cultivated a climate of absolute expectance.

OUTBREAK INDICATOR #3
CAPITALIZE ON THE RESULTS
OF INEVITABLE PERSECUTION

"They hung me up across an iron gate, then they yanked open the gate and my whole body lifted until my chest nearly split in two. I hung like that for four hours."[3] That is how Peter Xu Yongze described his treatment during one of five jail sentences on account of his belief in Christianity. "Despite all the persecution and suffering, God is calling more and more people in China," he said.

That sounds backward. Persecution seems like a setback, not a step forward. We tend to think of persecution as Satan's way of squashing the virus. But throughout church history it has proved again and again to be God's instrument for increasing the velocity of the virus.

When persecution in China broke out against the church in the late 1940s, all of Christianity held its breath. Communists had come into power, and as a result, churches were closed, missionaries expelled, and Christianity became a forbidden religion. Pessimistic prophets made dire predictions that the church in China would become extinct. When missionaries were expelled from China in 1949, it is estimated that there were approximately 1.8 million Christians living there. Today in China, estimates vary between 40 million to 70 million Protestants, only 10 million of whom are registered members of government churches. They meet in unofficial buildings or even each others' homes risking fines, imprisonment, torture, and even death. Peter Xu Yongze said that while he was in jail, he saw several people being killed for their faith:

 "A believer was praying, so a jailer made other prisoners lift him up to the ceiling and drop him to the ground many times until he died. . . . [In China] They say you can believe, but you can't evangelise. But that is a natural act for Christians. The Bible commands us to preach the gospel."

Imagine, in the face of horrible persecution in China, the church doesn't just stay alive, it advances! Why? Because persecution precedes progress when it comes to the body of Christ.

Throughout the book of Acts that pattern is clear—the bigger the persecution, the bigger the outbreak that followed. Let's look at the big, bigger, and biggest persecution of the church in the first part of the book of Acts and the big, bigger, and biggest results that followed.

A BIG PERSECUTION

The priests and the captain of the temple guard and the Sadducees came up to Peter and John while they were speaking to the people. They were greatly disturbed because the apostles were teaching the people and proclaiming in Jesus the resurrection of the dead. They seized Peter and John, and because it was evening, they put them in jail until the next day. (Acts 4:1–3)

The arrest of two apostles was the beginning of a pattern that would escalate to a full-blown persecution. Peter and John were arrested, then rebuked and released. What were the big results? The early church capitalized on the results of persecution. "But many who heard the message believed, and the number of men grew to about five thousand" (Acts 4:4).

A BIGGER PERSECUTION

"They called the apostles in and had them flogged. Then they ordered them not to speak in the name of Jesus, and let them go" (Acts 5:40).

Now the persecution is intensifying. It went from a simple arrest to a terrible beating. Flogging is a horrible punishment. Some died from it. But the apostles didn't. It became a battle scar to rejoice over. It became a badge of honor—a trigger for a bigger outbreak.

"The apostles left the Sanhedrin, rejoicing because they had been counted worthy of suffering disgrace for the Name. Day after day, in the temple courts and from house to house, they never stopped teaching and proclaiming the good news that Jesus is the Christ" (Acts 5:41–42).

Think about that for a moment: The disciples had been given an executive directive not to share the message of Jesus Christ anymore. They were then flogged. What did they do next? They got some tracts to pass out at the temple. They bought a map of Jerusalem to plot their door-to-door strategy. They started witnessing before the blood on their robes had time to dry!

That is equivalent to being arrested for sharing your faith, being thrown in jail, standing before the Supreme Court, and being commanded not to share the gospel anymore. Just for kicks the Court has you pummeled before you are released. Would you go back and witness? The apostles didn't flinch in the face of persecution.

THE BIGGEST PERSECUTION

"On that day a great persecution broke out against the church at Jerusalem, and all except the apostles were scattered throughout Judea and Samaria" (Acts 8:1).

Tempers had been flaring among the legalists concerning this Christian movement that some had nicknamed "the Way." Arguments, debates, and disputes were the order of the day. Anger gauges were buried in the red, and a full-scale war against Christianity was about to erupt. That's when Stephen showed up and pushed the legalists over the edge with his unflinching stand for truth.

"Heroes needed. Wimps need not apply." If God were to write a want ad for His representatives, that's how it might read. God is looking for heroes. Like us, the early Christians were too. That's exactly what they found in Stephen. Stephen had been falsely accused of speaking blasphemy against God and Moses (Acts 6–7). He stood before the Sanhedrin to defend himself. As he did, he gave what may be the most powerful and brilliant apologetic in Christian history.

In a few short moments he had that angry crowd of legalists yelling "amen" in the aisles. Using Jewish history as his sermon subject, he took his audience down memory lane. Starting with Abraham and concluding with Solomon, Stephen recounted the glory years of Judaism. His audience loved their roots. They loved the stories. And Stephen had them hooked. Suddenly they were thinking, *This guy doesn't look so bad.* He knew his history. He respected their roots. He loved his God. He won the crowd over. He set them up.

Throughout his sermon he used phrases like, "But our fathers refused to obey him." He consistently pointed back to the disobedience of their Jewish ancestors. And then he gave the punch line: "You stiff-necked people, with uncircumcised hearts and ears! You are just like your fathers: You always resist the Holy Spirit! Was there ever a prophet your fathers did not persecute! They even killed those who predicted the coming of the Righteous One. And now you have betrayed and murdered him" (Acts 7:51–52).

Their reaction? "They were furious and gnashed their teeth at him. . . . They covered their ears and, yelling at the top of their voices, they all rushed at him, dragged him out of the city and began to stone him" (vv. 54, 57).

Hoping to crush this Christian thing once and for all, the angry young men under the authority of the stodgy old Pharisees unleashed a full persecution against "the Way." On that day all hell broke loose against the church. Those legalistic Jews had had enough of this "sect" called Christianity. The virus had to be stopped, no matter what the cost.

But the results of this full-scale attack were not what they expected. In their efforts to stomp out the virus, something went wrong. They chased the carriers out of their city and into others. Thousands of Christian carriers invaded the surrounding cities, communities, and nations. The outbreak was airborne. Here's how Luke describes it: "Those who had been scattered preached the word wherever they went" (Acts 8:4).

A martyr was dead. A hero was born. His name was Stephen. Some had been beaten for their faith in Christ, others had been imprisoned for it, but Stephen died for it. Word spread. Instead of squelching the revival, Stephen's death became the kerosene on the flames. Suddenly the bar had been raised. The church needed a martyr, a rallying point, and a clarion call for the ultimate self-sacrifice. They had that in Jesus, but now they also had a fellow sinner-saint who, like Jesus, died for the holy cause as well.

Every cause needs a rallying point. The death of Stephen became the rallying point for the early believers of the first century. In the fourteenth century the death of William Wallace became the rallying point for his people, the Scots. His life represented the unswerving drive to be free from English rule. His death called his people to action. His execution triggered a series of events that eventually led to the independence of Scotland.

Throughout the centuries every worthy cause has had a rallying point. This is still true in the twenty-first century. Your kids need a cause. They need to fight against persecution, to stand for truth. They need someone to rally behind. It doesn't have to be a stoning incident! But they do need a rallying point.

You may be thinking, *Persecution? My kids don't endure persecution for sharing their faith! I mean, come on, we don't live in the burning-at-the-stake, boil-you-in-oil, cut-off-your-head kind of times. My kids are just not persecuted!*

Think again.

Persecution comes in all shapes and sizes. Every time your teens suffer for sharing Christ, they are being persecuted. It may be the passive persecution of avoidance. Their friends may avoid your teens in the hallways at school because of their witness for Jesus Christ. It may be the snide persecution of sarcasm where your students receive biting remarks from a classmate, teacher, or friend. As intolerance for the mention of God's absolute truth (which is also seen as intolerant) escalates, we see more and more examples of psychological persecution. Our students have been told in one way or another that it is not okay to communicate the gospel as truth. They are accused of being narrow-minded. Someday this psychological persecution may turn physical. That may be the trigger necessary for an outbreak of biblical proportions.

As your teens grow bolder in sharing their faith, others will grow bolder in their stand against them. Their stories must be shared in the context of the youth group meeting. These students must be championed. They are the rallying points for the rest of your youth group. They become the modern-day martyrs and heroes. Wimps need not apply.

CASSIE

She has become the modern-day martyr for the twenty-first century Christian community of teenagers. Just as the last words of patriots and prophets have became rallying points for nations under siege of tyranny, the last words of this young girl became a clarion call to the young people today under siege of Satan. "Yes, I believe in God" has become a rallying point for Christian teens all across America. Cassie has become their martyr. And rightfully so.

Her mother said it this way: "According to the dictionary, the Greek *martyria* means 'witness' and refers to someone who refuses, in the face of terror and torture, to deny his or her faith. By that definition it's not at all inaccurate to call Cassie a martyr."[4]

Cassie wasn't perfect. She battled with the same adolescent problems that most teenagers struggle with. But she was willing to die for her faith at that critical moment. That willingness to stand in the face of death rallied many in this generation of passive Christian students to choose a side.

I will never forget that day. On April 20, 1999, at 8:00 a.m., I was being interviewed at a local radio station a mere ten minutes away from Columbine High School. The interview was to promote our newest conference series at Dare 2 Share Ministries. The theme of the upcoming conference was spiritual warfare, and it was based on Ephesians 6:10–20. The tour was entitled the "When all hell breaks loose . . ." tour. Little did I know that just a few hours later, all hell would break loose just ten minutes down the road.

At 11:30 that morning I was meeting with a group of youth pastors promoting the conference tour when a pastor burst in with the news . . . a shooting was taking place at Columbine High School. A chill went down my spine as I looked down at the promotional flyer in my hand with the words "When all hell breaks loose" scrawled across the front of it. I knew many of the students at Columbine High School. I lived about thirty minutes away, and over the years I had trained scores of students from Columbine school at conferences, retreats, youth group meetings, and camps.

As the days passed and the details of that bloody morning became clear to a watching nation, the story of Cassie Bernall made national headlines. That Christian girl was shot for her belief in God. You might think that would make believing teens more tentative about their faith. But it had the completely opposite effect. Her story became a rallying point for Christian teenagers, not only at Columbine High School but also across the nation.

Who but God can know the thousands upon thousands who have been influenced for Jesus Christ because of Cassie's courageous story? One teenager's untimely death became a viral event. The church in America has yet to recover.

PERSECUTION UNIVERSITY

At the Dare 2 Share conferences we train thousands of students to share their faith. We then turn them loose to go put it into practice. Students go door-to-door and mall-to-mall lovingly sharing the message of Jesus Christ with complete strangers. Most students get slammed at some point during the witnessing experience. Some are cussed at, chased out, or even pushed over. You might think that the climate in the auditorium is solemn or sullen after these teens return from their first taste of persecution for Christianity.

It isn't. Kids are pumped. Those who get slammed will graduate from what we call "P. U.," or "Persecution University." We tell them that Jesus was the first graduate and the disciples soon followed. We remind them that it is a privilege to suffer for the sake of Jesus Christ. When they give their testimonies and exclaim to the crowd, "Today I graduated from P. U.," they get a standing ovation. Those students often begin to look forward to persecution. It becomes the holy badge of honor instead of the scarlet letter of disgrace.

How does that transfer to the youth group setting? As your students are slammed for sharing their faith, heroize them! Make them martyrs. Ask them to share their stories with the rest of the group. For the really good testimonials, ask the pastor for a few minutes on Sunday morning, so the student can share with the adults. Transform them into rallying points for the rest of the youth group and the church. The more intense the persecution, the more rapidly the virus spreads.

GET TOUGH

Persecution has another effect. It toughens youth groups. The students, youth leaders, and youth groups that I have encountered over the years who are most effective in evangelism are also the most galvanized toward resistance. Persecution becomes a rite of passage from weakness to strength. Trial by fire toughens them and prepares them for other challenges in life.

I remember being recruited as a teenager to go out with the other little "fundies" (fundamentalists) on a venture appropriately entitled "Friday night soul winning." Scores of students scattered from our youth group all across the Denver metropolitan area and invaded every mall with the gospel of Jesus Christ. Our target was other teenagers. I was scared to death—and rightfully so. Throughout those years I was yelled at, thrown out, picked up, pushed, and hit for sharing my faith. It wasn't that I enjoyed the persecution, but I did become immune to it over the years. That immunity to rejection prepared me for life (especially the dating years!). It toughened me.

"Hell week" in SEALs training does the same thing. The first few days of hell week are so intense and so difficult that many drop out. From sleeplessness to intense physical challenges, to being plunged in and out of the cold water for hours on end, those young warriors undergo preparations for battle through the ultimate preplanned persecution program. According to those who survive the first few days, there comes a point where soldiers retreat to the inner sanctum of their minds and become almost oblivious to the pain. It is at that point where the victory is won. Those who don't make it to that level of galvanization don't make it through the week.

Maybe what we need is a "hell week" for Christian students when it comes to evangelism. The week of intensive evangelism would prepare them for the war on the souls of their friends.

That is why we take kids out to share their faith at every Dare 2 Share conference. We want them to experience the thrill of victory and the agony of defeat. We want them to taste both acceptance and rejection. We want them to graduate from P. U., to be toughened in the process, and to be prepared to go back and tell their friends.

Why not take your students out to witness at a local mall this week? It could prepare them to reach their friends for Christ more effectively than any book or seminar.

OUTBREAK INDICATOR #4
ORGANIZE YOUR MINISTRY FOR EXCELLENCE

The organism needed organization. Because of the explosive growth of the early church in Jerusalem, problems were starting to rear their ugly heads. The food closet ministry was in shambles. Although the Jewish widows were receiving gifts of food, the Gentile widows were not. People were starting to talk. Gossip was starting to spread. Problems were starting to mount. The apostles were getting distracted. Instead of preaching the Word, they were refereeing arguments. Instead of praying for awakening, they were facilitating a food fight. So they took immediate and decisive action.

"So the Twelve gathered all the disciples together and said, 'It would not be right for us to neglect the ministry of the word of God in order to wait on tables. Brothers, choose seven men from among you who are known to be full of the Spirit and wisdom. We will turn this responsibility over to them and will give our attention to prayer and the ministry of the word" (Acts 6:2–4).

The results of this apostolic delegation? "So the word of God spread. The number of disciples in Jerusalem increased rapidly, and a large number of priests became obedient to the faith" (Acts 6:7).

How often do we get distracted from the task at hand as youth leaders? Instead of giving "our attention to prayer and the ministry of the word," are we refereeing childish conflicts between teenagers and sometimes between parents and even pastors? As a result, our youth group may seem more like a crisis management center than an infection point for a spiritual outbreak.

What is the answer to this problem? The recruitment, training, and establishment of godly adult leadership. I wholeheartedly believe that one of the most important duties of a youth leader is to find godly adults to help lead the youth ministry. I use the word *find* intentionally. There must be an active recruitment of targeted adults, not a passive "whosoever will may come" approach. Enough with the bulletin announcements and pulpit pleadings for adults to volunteer to teach Sunday school to teenagers. If your youth ministry is going to have an outbreak, you need more than one carrier of the virus. You need adults who are contagious to work with your youth group.

Think of the most godly, passionate, authentic adults in your church and start praying for and planning to recruit them into youth ministry. Cast the vision to them. Let them see the power and potential of student ministry. Invite them to a camp, retreat, or conference as a spectator. Let them see the Spirit of God in and through your teens. Give them specific stories of transformed lives. Define your standards for youth ministry adult leaders for them. Then ask them for a commitment. If they say no, don't be discouraged. Keep lovingly prodding them to join a team that can make an eternal difference. Don't settle for warm bodies. Look for blazing souls. Let these blazing souls be the "deacons" of your ministry. They can invest not only spiritually in the teens, but they can referee the food fights as well.

What do you do? You pray. You teach. You plan. In other words, you lead.

MOSES COULD HAVE BEEN A YOUTH MINISTER

If Moses were on earth today he could get rich promoting the "Leadership—the Moses Way" conferences. He could travel the circuit of corporate venues and make a killing lecturing on leadership. Think about it. He was the sole leader of more than two million discontented followers.

At one point in his ministry he became the ultimate crisis manager. All those people depended on him to fix their problems. He tried. But as skilled as Moses was, he was no match for the problems of an entire nation of people. What were the results of his hearty efforts?

"Moses took his seat to serve as judge for the people, and they stood around him from morning till evening" (Exodus 18:13). Moses was the center of attention. He was the definite leader. But that one-man show wasn't enough. His father-in-law, Jethro, who was visiting from out of town, saw what was taking place and gave him some much-needed advice:

> "What you are doing is not good. You and these people who come to you will only wear yourselves out. The work is too heavy for you; you cannot handle it alone. Listen now to me and I will give you some advice, and may God be with you. You must be the people's representative before God and bring their disputes to him. Teach them the decrees and laws, and show them the way to live and the duties they are to perform. But select capable men from all the people—men who fear God . . . and appoint them as officials over thousands, hundreds, fifties and tens. Have them serve as judges for the people at all times, but have them bring every difficult case to you. . . . That will make your load lighter, because they will share it with you. If you do this and God so commands, you will be able to stand the strain, and all these people will go home satisfied." (Exodus 18:17–23)

Moses was getting distracted from his primary duties of leading, praying, and teaching God's Word. (Those are the same prime directives that youth leaders have.) In the process, he was wearing himself out and his people as well. We do the same things with our youth groups when we try to be the center of attention and run everything. Like Moses, we need godly leaders to shepherd the smaller groups of souls in our youth groups. Without them we will wear ourselves out. With them we create an atmosphere that is ripe for an outbreak.

Once again, do not settle for anyone. Seek out the most godly, authentic, on-fire adults in your congregation and infect them with the vision of viral evangelism through an army of student super sneezers. Once they are recruited, organize your youth ministry around them for explosive growth.

It almost doesn't matter what your programming bent is when it comes to organizing your youth ministry. You may use cell groups, a traditional midweek meeting model, Sunday school, or a combo package. What matters most is that you have godly leadership to shepherd the smaller groups, put out the smaller fires, and mentor your students on a more personal basis than you have time for.

Dave Rahn and Terry Linhart share some pointed conclusions about the type of adults we must recruit if we want to have an organized and effective approach to evangelism. These conclusions come from their extensive study of effective evangelistic youth ministries. They evaluated twenty-two different youth ministries across the nation. Their conclusions regarding the type of adult leadership that energizes students to evangelize most effectively are as follows:

- Adults should model evangelism-related behavior.

- Adults should provide dependable programs of quality.

- Adults should make themselves available to talk with spiritually curious teenagers.

- Adults should teach the Bible.

- Adults should organize student-leader development and evangelism opportunities.

- Adults should train student leaders in evangelism skills.

- Adults should meet at least weekly for accountability with student leaders.[5]

Once the apostles learned the vital importance of delegation and organization, the early church exploded numerically. Once Moses learned that lesson, he saved himself and the people of Israel a lot of grief. The same thing happens when we apply the principle of delegation and organization to our youth ministry endeavors.

OUTBREAK INDICATOR #5
LEARN TO PRAY WITH EXPECTANCE

When's the last time you witnessed a miracle? I am not talking about the cheap, dime-store stuff. I am not referring to the slap-'em-on-the-head, sleight of hand, silly "miracles" of some big-haired, polyester preachers who flood our cable channels. I am talking about the real thing.

I am absolutely convinced that we should be witnessing miracles in our churches and youth groups on a regular basis. Every time a life is changed, a soul is saved, and a prayer is answered, we witness a jaw-dropping display of flexed heavenly muscle. That should be the rule, not the exception.

That is exactly what living in the early church was like. Miracles were expected. When people prayed, they actually expected results. They expected God to act. And He did—again and again, in unimaginable and unanticipated ways.

The fifth outbreak indicator of the book of Acts is expectant prayer. It is clearly seen in chapter 12. King Herod had had enough of the Christian movement. It was time to put a stop to all of the nonsense. The virus was infecting too many people. The apostolic carriers had gone too far with their monkey business. What better way to stop it than to kill the carriers themselves? After executing James, he set his sights on the main leader of the early church, Peter. "After arresting him, he put him in prison, handing him over to be guarded by four squads of four soldiers each. Herod intended to bring him out for public trial after the Passover" (Acts 12:4).

When the cold steel of the prison door shut behind him, hope seemed gone. With the click of the prison lock Peter was probably reminded of Jesus' prediction of Peter's death. It looked as if that prophecy by the Sea of Tiberius after the resurrection of Christ was about to be fulfilled.

What was the response of the early church? "The church was earnestly praying to God for him" (v. 5). That body of believers had seen God's mighty hand work again and again in miraculous ways. And now they asked God to do it again. He did. As a matter of fact, He did much more than they even asked for.

In Acts 12:6–19, Peter is miraculously released from prison by an angel in the middle of the night. That is especially amazing when you realize that Peter was sleeping in between two well-trained Roman guards and bound with two well-forged chains.

In verses 20–23 God goes above and beyond the prayers that the church had prayed. He kills Herod. Rather than Herod killing Peter, the puppet king of the Jewish people dies instead. That leads to the third answer to prayer.

"But the word of God continued to increase and spread" (v. 24). The outbreak is clearly linked to the expectant prayer of God's people. It was the result of bended knees and broken hearts.

There is a direct link between expectant prayer and church growth throughout history. Jonathan Edwards, powerful preacher of the Great Awakening, said, "When God has something very great to accomplish for His church, it is His will that there should precede it, the extraordinary prayers of His people."[6]

Extraordinary prayers have extraordinary results. Ordinary prayers have ordinary results. Wimpy prayers have wimpy results. Which kinds of prayers are being prayed in your youth group? Do your students expect to see miracles take place weekly? Do you? How is your prayer life? Is it a quick rush through a list each day, or is it an ongoing dialogue with the God of heaven and earth? Are you praying for big things from a big God? Or have you underestimated His miraculous powers?

THE ULTIMATE MIRACLE

Remember that the biggest miracles your students will see from week to week are changed lives and saved souls. Once the disease of sin is cured through the cross, other miracles fade by comparison.

The creation of the universe, the parting of the Red Sea, and the healing of the ten lepers are all nothing compared to the redemption of just one soul. In the moment a person trusts in Christ as Savior the angels in heaven rejoice, and the demons in hell shriek. Sins recorded in God's ledger are erased, and a name is recorded in the Lamb's Book of Life that can never be erased. That person is immersed in the body of Christ, and the Spirit of Christ is immersed in that person. The death of the old self is eclipsed by the spiritual birth of the new self. The power of sin is broken, and the penalty of sin is paid. In that millisecond of trust, a transformation takes place that is unimaginable and almost indescribable.

If students are coming to Christ on a weekly basis in your youth group setting, then your students are seeing the grandest scale of miracle on a regular basis. Other miracles pale next to the experience of salvation.

How does that apply to the youth group setting? Simple. Is it your students' experience to pray for the ultimate miracle of salvation when they attend church? In my opinion every single student in your youth group should have at least one other person for whom he is praying to come to Christ. It only takes a few minutes, but what a potential impact! Maybe you hold this miniprayer service during Sunday school or in small groups. Whatever the setting, it is absolutely the most important step you will take in immersing your students into an expectant attitude of passionate prayer. Soon they will be expecting miracles every week.

OUTBREAK INDICATOR #6
TEACH YOUR STUDENTS THE GRACE OF GOD

I realize this point may sound like a stretch. The teaching and preaching of doctrine may not seem like an evangelistic aphrodisiac.

But according to the book of Acts, it is a pivotal reason why the early church grew. It is the sixth outbreak indicator in Luke's historical essay on the first-century body of believers.

George Barna writes the following:

 When pressed to identify the single, most important reason why they attend youth group . . . it turns out that relationships bring the kids to the place, but they will not return unless the church delivers the goods. What are they looking for? Substance. Learning practical and credible insights about God was listed twice as often as anything else as the most important reason for returning. The fellowship, the games, the music, the casual and friendly atmosphere—all of those elements are important to getting kids in the door—the first time. Getting them there the second time demands those things plus solid teaching.[7]

Do you find that surprising? We shouldn't. If truth from God's Word is taught accurately, passionately, and practically, there is no more exciting thing. It intrigues, even excites, the lost. They want answers, and God's Word provides those answers. What better truth than the grace of God? This powerful doctrine is the foundation of Christian living and evangelism. The amazing grace of God should be a recurring theme in all of our teaching. It was in the book of Acts.

SOMETHING TO FIGHT FOR

The first big internal theological conflict of the early church is recorded in Acts 15. They were arguing over the grace of God. A group of legalists in the early church were stirring things up. They did not like all those Gentiles who were flooding the early church. They wanted to add circumcision and adherence to the law as prerequisites to salvation (more about this in chapter 7). I am sure that many new believers were thrown into confusion over this new stipulation to the free gift of salvation. Paul and Barnabas had a fit over it.

"This brought Paul and Barnabas into sharp dispute and debate with them" (15:2). The apostles met in a theological summit to discuss the emerging heresy. What was their conclusion?

> *The apostles and elders met to consider this question. After much discussion, Peter got up and addressed them: "Brothers, you know that some time ago God made a choice among you that the Gentiles might hear from my lips the message of the gospel and believe. God, who knows the heart, showed that he accepted them by giving the Holy Spirit to them, just as he did to us. He made no distinction between us and them, for he purified their hearts by faith. Now then, why do you try to test God by putting on the necks of the disciples a yoke that neither we nor our fathers have been able to bear? No! We believe it is through the grace of our Lord Jesus that we are saved, just as they are." (Acts 15:6–11)*

The conclusion was clear. External acts of devotion such as circumcision and adherence to the law had nothing to do with the reception of salvation among the Gentiles or the Jews. The grace of God had everything to do with it.

Later Paul and Silas went out across Asia and Galatia sharing the results of this summit with the churches that had already been established through Paul's first missionary journey. The results were amazing.

"As they traveled from town to town, they delivered the decisions reached by the apostles and elders in Jerusalem for the people to obey. So the churches were strengthened in the faith and grew daily in numbers" (Acts 16:4–5). The more the early church grasped the grace of God, the more it grew. The same is true of our youth groups.

Students today live in a culture that is performance driven. From competitive sports teams, to dating, to education, teenagers know firsthand the need to accomplish, to prove, to perform. If they don't, they will be cut, dumped, or held back. Many students who fail to perform up to expectations enter into a lifestyle that becomes a downward spiral of despondency or decadence. They can't reach the standards, so they ditch them completely.

The grace of God was completely foreign to the performance-driven world of the legalists in the first century. Nothing has changed in the twenty-first. The legalists still expect and inspect. Anything short of the bar fails to qualify. The rest are losers.

The problem is that the early church, just like the church of today, was filled with losers. It was composed of failures who continued to miss the mark of God's standards again and again. Five of the seven churches in Revelation 2–3 were losers. Think of the Corinthians. They were getting plastered at the Communion tables, excusing immorality, and bickering with each other. Think of the great apostle Paul himself: "I know that nothing good lives in me, that is, in my sinful nature. For I have the desire to do what is good, but I cannot carry it out. For what I do is not the good I want to do; no, the evil I do not want to do—this I keep on doing" (Romans 7:18–19).

At times like that the apostle would scream out with his pen to his readers, "Hey! I am a loser too! I struggle just like you do! I fail! I sin! I lust! I trip! I fall!"

You see, the early church was made up of losers. But they were losers who were loved by God. They were losers who had freedom to fail. They were losers who fell again and again and again (just like us, just like our kids). But they were losers who failed forward. They limped their way to godliness through countless trials. They were losers who knew that the grace of God would catch them in His net of grace every time they fell off the tightrope of expectation. That freedom to fail became the impetus to perform, but for an entirely different reason than the legalists. They had the freedom to fail, so they took the risk of obedience.

Do your kids know the grace of God? The degree to which they hear it from you and experience it themselves will be the degree in which they grow and their youth group grows. When kids are learning and experiencing the unconditional grace of God for losers, they will bring their friends. They won't be able to help themselves.

Phillip Yancey shares some profound words in *What's So Amazing About Grace?* "The world runs by ungrace. Everything depends on what I do. I have to make the shot. Jesus' kingdom calls us to another way, one that depends on not our performance but his own. We do not have to achieve but merely follow. He has already earned for us the costly victory of God's acceptance."[8]

I believe with all of my heart that the message of grace should be woven throughout every talk that we give, every devotional that we share, and every sermon we preach. Why? Because God's grace reflects in full measure the hope we have in Christ. Hope is a scarce commodity in the community of adolescence.

Are you teaching your teens about the unconditional grace of God on a consistent basis? Do they truly know that He loves them no matter what? Are they serving to be accepted or because they have been accepted?

The early believers in the first churches were in awe of the message of God's grace. It was so unlike anything they had ever heard that it took their souls by storm, and they never recovered. The same thing should be happening in our youth groups every week. Amazing grace —how sweet the sound.

OUTBREAK INDICATOR #7
CALL YOUR STUDENTS TO HOLINESS

Holiness and youth ministry are terms that don't seem to go together. One reeks of stained glass, dusty pews, and choir robes; the other of sweaty students.

There are two major purifying events in the book of Acts. Both are followed by an immediate jump in evangelistic effectiveness. The first is the classic story of Ananias and Sapphira. The early church was in a giving spree. People were selling off their lands and donating the money to the church so that the ministry could keep rolling on.

That lakefront property outside Galilee that was going to be used one day to build a nice house for retirement wasn't nearly as important as the need for the gospel message to go out in power. Imagine the excitement as person after person cashed in land assets and brought them to the disciples. Ananias and Sapphira had some extra property, so they decided to sell it and give most of the profits to the church growth program. The only problem was that they didn't bother to tell anyone else that they were not giving all of the profits. The church was still getting a truckload of much-needed capital. But they held back a little bit for themselves—not enough for the disciples to notice, just enough to pad their pockets a bit.

Keeping back some of the profits was not the problem. Pretending that they were giving away everything was. They were lying with their actions. God knew it. So did Ananias and Sapphira. He struck them dead. Word spread. Numbers grew. Lesson learned. The outbreak indicator makes that clear.

"Great fear seized the whole church and all who heard about these events. . . . Nevertheless, more and more men and women believed in the Lord and were added to their number" (Acts 5:11, 14).

What was the lesson? Don't lie to God. The Lord will not tolerate duplicity. Nothing makes Him sicker than those who claim to be Christians but live a lie. The early believers took note. Like the Israelites in the Promised Land, the people of God needed a wake-up call. Their modern-day Achan was Ananias. The church learned from the burn. Nothing gets attention like death.

The second purifying event is found in Acts 19:13–14: "Some Jews who went around driving out evil spirits tried to invoke the name of the Lord Jesus over those who were demon-possessed. They would say, 'In the name of Jesus, whom Paul preaches, I command you to come out.' Seven sons of Sceva, a Jewish chief priest, were doing this."

Exorcism had become fashionable among some of the Jews. Because the followers of Christ had so much success with exorcisms, the seven sons of Sceva decided to use the name of Jesus as kind of a magic dust to ensure that their exorcisms would work. The problem was, they really didn't believe in Jesus. They just wanted to use His name for effect. One day they tried using the name of Christ on the wrong demon.

The inhabiting demon replied with a stinging fallen-angel come-back: "Jesus I know, and I know about Paul, but who are you?" (v. 15). That formidable one-liner (that sounds like it came out of an old Clint Eastwood western) summed up the problem. "He gave them such a beating that they ran out of the house naked and bleeding" (v. 16). Not only were the brothers beaten, but they were de-pantsed and disgraced by one demon-possessed madman.

What was the result of this event?

When this became known to the Jews and Greeks living in Ephesus, they were all seized with fear, and the name of the Lord Jesus was held in high honor. Many of those who believed now came and openly confessed their evil deeds. A number who had practiced sorcery brought their scrolls together and burned them publicly. When they calculated the value of the scrolls, the total came to fifty thousand drachmas. In this way the word of the Lord spread widely and grew in power. (Acts 19:17–20)

That is an amazing aftermath! The lost Jews and Greeks in Ephesus took note and stopped misusing the name of Christ. What is even more shocking is what happened in the church community. "Many of those who believed now came and openly confessed their evil deeds. A number who had practiced sorcery brought their scrolls together and burned them publicly" (vv. 18–19).

It seems there were not only unbelievers who had been misusing the name of Christ in Ephesus, but some believers were still dabbling in sorcery. Ephesus, a center for witchcraft and idolatry, still had a powerful hold on many of the Ephesians who had converted to Christianity. It's hard to imagine, but many of those who were sitting under the teaching of the great apostle Paul week in and week out had secrets locked away in their closets. Many in the church of Ephesus were still holding on to their magic books, The Witchcraft Guide for Dummies and the how-to-be Harry Potter books.

That purifying event jolted double-minded believers into an instant pursuit of holiness. The bonfire ensued. They burned fifty thousand drachmas' worth of books. A drachma was a silver coin that was worth about a day's wages. At a $100/day rate the scrolls would have been worth $5 million today. That's a lot of money. That's a lot of books. That's a lot of secret sins. That's a lot of revival.

It may be hard for us to relate to this example at first glance. I mean, come on, how many of the kids in our youth group are steeped in witchcraft? Probably not many (but maybe more than you think). At the same time, many of our kids are steeped in sexual sin and spiritual rebellion. Many of our kids honor celebrities more than Jesus Christ. Many would rather watch a movie than go to church. Many are more vocal about their favorite band than about their personal faith.

We need another bonfire. I am not talking about a literal book burning. I am talking about a personal bonfire in the heart of each of our kids. Standing before the flames of sacrifice, they must make a choice to clean out the closet of their hearts and throw the trash into the blaze.

What was the result of the purification in Ephesus? "The word of the Lord spread widely and grew in power" (Acts 19:20).

The final outbreak indicator points to the power of purity for increasing the velocity of the virus through our youth groups. It teaches us that true viral awakening is ultimately the work of God's hands. But He will not unleash the reservoirs of revival on an impure people. God demands holiness. Sin must be confronted head-on and not swept under the carpet of convenience. Your teenagers who are engaged in evil must be confronted.

I believe that one of the reasons we have not seen a sweeping student awakening in America in the last century or so is because the church has refused to deal with her own. We tend to wink at sin instead of rebuke it. We view confrontation of sin as a thing of the past in our enlightened age of self-help, self-centered theology of prosperity.

The old relic of church discipline must be dusted off, polished, sharpened, and wielded once again in our youth groups. That may sound extreme, but that is because church discipline is so unused in the twenty-first century that we tend to relegate it to the cruel days of the Inquisition. *Discipline* sounds unsophisticated and mean. But it is really an act of love. If we don't purify our youth groups, we putrefy our teenagers. Failure to deal with sin in the lives of our students is more cruel than actually dealing with those sins. Not dealing with them leads to a rotting of the core. A rotting of the core leads to a youth group that is dangerously close to losing the power of God's presence.

Think about the seven churches in Revelation 2–3. Jesus warns the Ephesian church to purify their presence and return to their first love or, in His words, "I will come to you and remove your lampstand from its place." What did that mean? It meant the fire of His burning presence would be extinguished. It meant the blaze of revival would be doused. It meant the explosive spiritual growth would be stopped. It meant the outbreak would be contained. The same is true of our youth groups.

Modern youth ministry tends to cater to the carnal. As a result, many youth group meetings tend to tantalize the taste buds of the tawdry instead of prodding the piety of the passionate. Too often we are afraid to confront a sinning student because we fear offending the parents or, worse, losing our cool factor with the kids. We look the other way—sometimes we even run the other way. We think there is too much at stake.

What is really at stake? The spiritual blessing of God on your youth group? When God's hand was removed from the Israelites because of Achan's sin, Israel tasted the bitter bile of defeat for the first time in battle. When God's hand is removed from our youth groups, we too will taste ultimate defeat.

How do we confront sin in the lives of our students? We do it humbly. We do it in love. We do it with the hope of repentance and restoration. But we do it unflinchingly, not because we want to but because we must.

What if they refuse to repent? Take them through the proper steps of confrontation. The final step is expulsion. If you have done everything in your power to reconcile students to Christ and they still refuse to repent, they must be shown the door. Parents may get angry. Pastors may plead their case. But you must stand firm. Your kids will know you are serious about sanctification in the youth group setting . . . and so will God.

Those seven outbreak indicators in the book of Acts are as relevant today as they were two thousand years ago. Apply them to your youth group and you may get grief, but you will definitely get results. The questions you must ask yourself are these: How much do you want awakening, and are you willing to pay the price? I think you are. Otherwise you wouldn't be reading this book.✖

RED·DOT REVIEW

LOOK FOR THE OUTBREAK
INDICATORS IN YOUR YOUTH GROUP!

MONKEY MANDATE

S STAFF INFECTION QUESTIONS

MANDATE

Post this prayer in your office as a reminder: "Lord, make us contagious. Enable us to be infected with Your truth and contagious in our Christianity. Use our e-team to spread the viral message of Jesus Christ. May it start in our youth group and spread to the campuses and the community around us. May it spread across our state, our nation, and our world. Keep us from the contamination of sin and legalism. Fill us with Your infectious grace and love. Make us contagious, O God."

#1. Are we seizing every opportunity to give the gospel personally and as a youth ministry? Why or why not?

#2. Which of the following are the weakest in our community—acceptance, selflessness, or expectance of God's power? What can we do to strengthen those areas?

#3. In what ways is our youth group being persecuted, and how can we capitalize on it?

#4. How can we make our ministry more organized for excellence? How do we apply the Jethro principle in recruiting and leading adult sponsors?

#5. How can we learn to pray
with more expectancy as a
youth ministry staff?

#6. How can we better teach and
model the grace of God to our
students?

#7. Are there any teens in our
youth ministry who may be
blocking the blessing of God
because of sin issues? If so,
how should we lovingly and
boldly deal with it?

DON'T TAKE YOUR ANTIBIOTICS!

Antibiotics, which act against bacteria, have no power over viruses, be they HIV or the common cold. Nonetheless, many people expect their doctors to prescribe medicine for whatever ails them. Overuse and misuse of antibiotics is a major factor in the evolution of new strains of drug-resistant bacteria. The paradox . . . is that these powerful drugs have given rise to more powerful bacteria, the so-called superbugs that are invulnerable to many of the more than 100 antibiotics now on market.[1]

ow many times have you gone to the doctor with a horrible cough and terrible symptoms only to have him or her tell you that what you had was viral and there was nothing that could be done about it? You simply had to wait it out. You might be offered some medication to treat the symptoms, but the viral infection would have to run its course. Treating viral infections with an antibiotic does absolutely no good. Antibiotics are designed to stop bacterial, not viral, strains. As a matter of fact, the overuse of antibiotics is actually making us increasingly immune to immunity. Overuse of antibiotics creates bacterial superbugs that are invulnerable and dangerous.

In the same way some evangelistic antibiotics are not directly effective against the viral message of the gospel, but they can affect us as carriers. These antibiotics weaken our evangelistic immune system, and we become more susceptible to the superbug of silence.

What are these evangelistic antibiotics? They are the reasons, rationale, and rantings against viral evangelism that we battle internally, externally, and supernaturally. The doctor who provides these invisible, immunity-killing drugs to our souls is none other than Satan himself. His pharmacy is full of lies coated in easy-to-swallow gel caplets called excuses.

Let's look at three of the main antibodies that are making our youth groups immune to the Great Commission.

CHURCH MEMBER HESITATION

"We don't want those kind of kids in our youth group."
"Too many youth outreaches leave the church a mess."
"Teens aren't mature enough yet for that kind of challenge."
"My kids aren't ready for that step yet."

When blue hairs collide with each other, things can get red quickly. Your radically saved, former-rave, currently blue-haired kid named Josh meets "I've been saved for fifty years," Sunday school teaching, "never miss a service" blue-haired charter member Mrs. Smith. As they pass each other in the church foyer, they have one thought in common: *Things have got to change around here!*

Those collisions begin to occur as the epidemic of evangelism invades and pervades your youth ministry. Grumblings and rumblings will reverberate throughout the hallways and foyer. People will start to complain. Some of that hesitation is natural. The stained carpets, damaged sound systems, broken windows, and emptied budgets that inevitably follow a Great Commission mind-set youth ministries can understandably upset the applecart of the typical church.

But there can be a supernatural element as well. Satan can use those natural issues to his devilish advantage. He can use natural complaints as a way to shut down the youth ministry from the top down.

One well-placed criticism from one well-respected church member can bring the revival in your youth ministry to a screeching halt.

What can we do to prevent viral shutdown? How can we turn church member hesitation into church member applause for our efforts? How can we make the blue hairs embrace each other? Here are a few things to remember.

IT'S NATURAL TO RESIST CHANGE

Most of us are at least somewhat resistant to change. The older you are, the truer that maxim is. If we are realistic, we must expect resistance from the adults in our congregation to a purpose-driven approach, and we must plan accordingly.

Resistance to change is not always bad. It is resistance to change that keeps us guarding the heritage of orthodox truths delivered to us by the apostles two thousand years ago. It is resistance to change that keeps us from rushing into foolish decisions. But sometimes resistance to change goes too far. When it starts shutting down evangelism in a church or youth ministry, it gets flat-out dangerous.

IT TAKES WISDOM AND LOVE TO CHANGE MINDS

George Whitefield, magnificent pulpiteer of the First Great Awakening, used to pray that God would give him the gentleness of a lamb and the courage of a lion before entering into potentially volatile situations. His goal was to be strong in his convictions yet meek in his attitude. We must do the same as we deal with the adults in our congregations who are hesitant to embrace raw, unchurched students.

Part of wisdom is helping them understand the vision. Most old-time church members resonate with words like *revival* and *salvation* and *missions*. Many get misty-eyed when they think back to the days when Billy Graham thundered from the pulpit in cities all across America, and they wonder why those days can't be resurrected. Now you can tell them the great news—those days are back! But this time the crusade is in your own youth group. And the students roaming the hallways of your church are truly walking the sawdust trail of transformation.

MISSIONS BEGINS IN THE FOYER

There are hidden dangers in the missionary map in the foyer of your church. The type of thinking that views missions as "out there" in the Peruvian mountains, the African plain, or the Indian jungle is dangerous. True missions starts in our own backyard, our own Jerusalem, and then extends to the uttermost parts of the earth. Kevin was a blue hair. Dyed, pierced, and rebellious, he came to church Sunday after Sunday because Mom and Dad made him. Although he had trusted in Christ as a kid, he rebelled against the God of his youth and embraced the skater culture of punk rock and cynical living. He sat with a scowl every Sunday. His eyes were dead, and his fire was out. Every Sunday I could feel him staring through me as I preached. He was one of those kids who elicited stares from the old folks and visiting families.

As a church we patiently prayed for Kevin and gently prodded him to get serious about Jesus. Then one day it happened. I will never forget it. He came up to me after a not-so-spectacular sermon and said simply, "I want to be a disciple now." It wasn't a sermon or event or a dynamic worship encounter that transformed him. It was the slow steady movement of God's Spirit through His people that made Kevin snap. Today he works with teenagers in our youth group, and he especially gravitates toward the scowling ones. Missions starts in the foyer. We must lovingly help our church members embrace that fact.

PERSUASION WORKS BETTER THAN POLITICS

The art of persuasion is infinitely more effective than the perversion of politics. Perhaps the greatest tool to use in convincing those key church or board members who are antagonistic toward the invasion of unchurched students into the church community is not your tongue but your ears. It has been said, "Seek first to understand, then to be understood."[2] When you listen to their point of view and seek to empathize with their concerns, when you ask questions to clarify exactly what they are saying, and when you truly try to understand them, those efforts have a magnificent effect. Once a person feels understood, he or she is much more likely to be open to your point of view.

Listen to this powerful analogy from Steven Covey's classic book *The 7 Habits of Highly Effective People*, which illustrates how listening first can be an effective persuasion tool:

 This principle worked powerfully for one executive who shared with me the following experience, "I was working with a small company that was in the process of negotiating a contract with a large national banking institution. This institution flew in their lawyers from San Francisco, their negotiator from Ohio, and presidents of two of their large banks to create an eight-person negotiating team. The company I worked with . . . wanted to significantly increase the level of service and the cost, but they had been almost overwhelmed with the demands of this large financial institution. The president of our company sat across the negotiating table and told them, 'We would like for you to write the contract the way you want it so that we can make sure we understand your needs and your concerns. We will respond to those needs and concerns. Then we can talk about pricing.'

"The members of the negotiating team were overwhelmed. They were astounded that they were going to have the opportunity to write the contract. They took three days to come up with the deal.

"When they presented it, the president said, 'Now let's make sure we understand what you want.' And he went down the contract, rephrasing the content, reflecting the feeling, until he was sure and they were sure he understood what was important to them. . . .

"When he thoroughly understood their perspective, he proceeded to explain some concerns from his perspective . . . and they listened. They were ready to listen. . . . What had started out as a very formal, low-trust, almost hostile atmosphere had turned into a fertile environment for synergy.

"At the conclusion of the discussions, the members of the negotiating team basically said, 'We want to work with you. We want to do this deal. Just let us know what the price is and we'll sign.'"[3]

God created us as creatures who long to be deeply understood. When we are, it is amazing how flexible and understanding we can be with others. When we aren't, it is shocking how quickly irreconcilable differences can rear their ugly heads.

Veteran youth ministry leader Ridge Burns put it this way, "Sometimes 'political' people just want to be heard; they don't necessarily need to have action taken on the issues they're raising. So it's very important that I provide them with forums where they can express themselves."[4] Ask questions. Understand. Only then share your vision with others.

A TIME TO QUIT

Once in a while a youth leader is involved in a church body that incapacitates him or her to do real ministry. Believe it or not, some youth leaders face constant demands that they stop challenging students to reach their friends for Christ. If you are in such a situation, I beg you to do everything you can to persuade and encourage the key leaders in your congregation to reconsider their stance against evangelism. Listen to them, love them, pray for them, and share with them. But if you have done your best to listen to them and love them and they still are vehemently against your outreach efforts—then resign.

Why stay involved in a youth ministry where you are handicapped to do real ministry? The need for young people to hear the message of hope through Jesus Christ is too urgent to be thwarted.

STUDENT INTIMIDATION

"What if I don't know what to say?"

"I could lose all of my friends!"

"How do I even bring it up?"

"What if they ask me questions that I don't have the answers to?"

One of the biggest mistakes we make when it comes to motivating students to share their faith is to focus on their fears. Why is that a mistake? Because they are already focusing on them! Most teenagers are absolutely terrified to communicate the gospel of Jesus Christ to their peers. Instead of focusing on their fears, we need to give them a bigger motivation that will help burst through the barriers of intimidation.

One of my favorite movie scenes is in *Braveheart* when William Wallace rides up to the battlefront where the English and the Scots are squaring off. The ragtag Scottish army is outmatched and vastly outnumbered, and they are starting to leave the battlefront in paralyzing fear. The nearly impossible odds have overwhelmed them. As the battle force is falling apart, the incomparable Wallace rides up with his scarred crew of battle-hardened warriors. He addresses the crowd:

Wallace: I am William Wallace, and I see a whole army of my countrymen here in defiance of tyranny. You have come to fight as freemen, and freemen you are. What will you do without freedom? Will you fight?

Soldier: Against that? No, we will run, and we will live.

Wallace: Aye, fight and you may die. Run and you'll live. At least a while. And dying in your beds many years from now, would you be willing to trade all your days, from this day to that, to tell our enemies that they may take our lives, but they can never take our freedom!

That powerful speech inspired the Scots to take the long-term perspective. Wallace called them to rise above their fears of pending death and to look instead at the big picture. In response, the army united to fight in an absolute display of unshakeable confidence . . . and won the day.

In the same way, our students face a terrifying foe when it comes to sharing Christ with their friends. They are facing off against the possibility of rejection, humiliation, and defeat. What do we do? We give them the Wallace speech. We help them rise above their fears and see the big picture. We paint a picture of the souls of their friends dangling between heaven and hell. That eternal perspective will "incourage" your students. It will instill courage in their hearts and give them the boldness to do battle with the Evil One for the souls of their lost friends.

"DO NOT BE AFRAID"

Usually those words are spoken by a heavenly being to a trembling human. Our natural reaction to the unknown is fear. God's supernatural reaction is to calm those fears. That is the same soothing reminder we must give to the students under our care. Natural fears desperately need supernatural comfort.

The question is how do we deliver that divine message without being condescending and trite? I believe that one of the best things that we can do is to give them a bigger "Yes!" to quench their "No!"

Doing teen evangelism training conferences for more than a decade has given me a unique perspective on this powerful truth. The opening night of each conference is designed to shatter inhibitions. We design the evening to be a heart-wrenching ride down the roller coaster of truth that students will never forget. The goal is to paint a picture that is so graphic, so intense, and so dramatic that the students will never forget it. Whether the drama deals with a letter from hell sent by a friend who died without ever hearing the gospel message, or an illustration of someone standing before the judgment seat of Christ after living a life of mediocre impact, the opening night is designed to reach through their rib cage and grab their heart. In other words, we give them a bigger "Yes!" Instead of focusing on their fears, we rivet their attention to a gigantic motivating force. That approach has helped countless students to overcome the fears that rattle around in their minds. You can do the same in your youth group.

GENERATION NEXT

In their insightful book *Millennials Rising*, authors Neil Howe and William Strauss uncover something special about the current generation of teenagers. Describing them as the next "hero" generation, they paint a picture of young people filled with power, potential, and positivism.

 When you think of today's young people . . . you cannot help but rivet on their potential for power—organized power, legal power, official power. As the oldest Millennials reach their twenties, they will fill colleges, move beyond parental control, and begin making up their own minds about their nation and the world. What they will say, and especially what they will do, could shock and disturb many of today's adults who have spent most of their lives cultivating individualism and an instinctive distrust for power. But power, when harnessed, can be a force for good. "Change the world" was a fine youth slogan back in the 1960s, but Boomers may need the power of their grown children to get it done.[5]

The harnessed power of students can literally change the world. Today's young people are tired of the cynicism of the previous generation. They believe they can do something that will make a difference. As we harness and focus that attitude toward the Great Commission, the results can change the world.

MOMENTUM

If you apply the principles in this book on a consistent basis in your youth group, you will reach a certain level of evangelistic critical mass. The momentum, once experienced, will catapult your youth group into a mushrooming explosion of evangelistic expansion. The fallout will be felt throughout your community.

The process leading to that evangelistic explosion must be handled with a certain level of patience and persistence. In the initial stages of any philosophical and cultural shift, you can expect some resistance. You can expect students (sometimes key leadership kids) to resist the new focus on evangelism. Some will complain, "All you do is give the gospel every week," or "I go to a Christian school. What lost kids am I going to bring to youth group?" Just remember that such complaints are to be expected. Satan doesn't want to see your youth group go viral. He will use everything and everyone at his disposal to squelch the virus. But as you continue to put together a high quality program, teach your students rock solid truth from God's Word, and give your kids a bigger "Yes!" about the Great Commission, momentum will build, and the complainers will eventually blend in or back out.

YOUTH LEADER INHIBITION

"Evangelism is not my gift."
"We are more concerned about discipleship than evangelism."
"We teach our kids to live the message, not so much give it."
"My kids aren't ready for that step yet."

I am absolutely convinced that the number-one reason most youth groups aren't actively, aggressively, and effectively sharing their faith is not because of church leader hesitation or student intimidation. It is because of youth leader inhibition. Those hesitations are sometimes philosophical, theological, or political. But more often than not they are personal.

What are you afraid of?

Close your eyes and ask yourself what you are most afraid of about evangelism. Are you afraid of personal rejection? Of being stumped by a skeptic's question? Is it the fear of bringing an unknown element into your youth group culture or the possibility of facing an inquisition from wary parents and board members? Whatever your fear, remember this—God is greater. You too need a bigger "Yes!" to plow through the smaller "Nos."

Most of those reading this book have a distinct advantage over me when it comes to energizing and equipping their students in evangelism. You see, I have the gift of evangelism, and I do evangelism training conferences for a living. Most students expect me to have cool stories of powerful proclamation encounters where souls have been radically transformed. Your advantage, especially if you are not naturally gifted in evangelism, is this: you are a fellow struggler with your students. When teenagers realize that you are just as afraid as they are but are sharing the gospel anyway, they will be even more motivated in their own outreach efforts. They will garner strength from your weakness.

GETTING PAST YOUR PAST

Some youth leaders need to get past their past when it comes to evangelism. Perhaps you come from a background where evangelism was thrust upon you like an unwelcome telemarketing call during dinner. You got tired of the model of hit and run, cram and slam evangelism, so you rebelled against evangelism itself. You threw the baby out with the bathwater because you got tired of the screaming, ranting, and raving. Maybe you had a bad experience yourself with an inexperienced evangelist. It's that bad aftertaste that makes you wince at the thought of evangelism.

Getting past your past requires a couple of balancing thoughts. First of all, remember that evangelism is not optional. There are no loopholes. It is a mandate. Second, understand that Scripture is filled with beautiful examples of evangelism that were a perfect blend of love and boldness. True evangelism requires both. Third, realize that there is no right or wrong style of evangelism. God uses the confrontational and the relational, the lifestyle and the verbal. As long as you are lovingly initiating conversations about Christ in some way, you are fulfilling the command to share your faith. Finally, remember that your natural apprehension about sharing your faith is a tremendous advantage. When youth leaders who are not naturally gifted in evangelism witness anyway, they communicate to their students this message: "If I can do it, you can do it too!"

MAXIMIZE YOUR STRENGTHS

God has blessed me with a wife who is totally different from me in almost every way. We tested off opposite ends of the chart on the Meyers-Brigg personality profile test. She comes from a nice suburban upbringing in a solid Christian home. I was reared in a tough urban family that came to Christ over the years. She likes shopping. I loathe it. She is extremely relational. I am extremely visionary. She is loving, patient, and kind. I am extremely volatile, passionate, and focused.

When it comes to evangelism we are two extremes as well. I tend to look at evangelism as a competitive sport. When I meet somebody, I immediately begin plotting how to turn the conversation toward the cross. My goal is to take the fork in the road of the conversation and turn that conversation toward the gospel. If there is no fork, I will make one. That is how God has wired me. It's who I am. Over the years God has used my wife to temper me and teach me more tact and wisdom in my approach, but I will always be bold and aggressive when it comes to sharing my faith.

Debbie is totally opposite. She is equally concerned about the spiritual condition of her lost friends, but she is much more patient than I. She methodically moves into relationships over the long haul, develops deep ties to those friends, and, at the right time, turns the conversation toward spiritual topics. As a public schoolteacher, my wife has had the opportunity to lead several of her students to Christ outside the context of the classroom through the relationships that she has built. She has had a tremendous spiritual influence on the teachers and parents with whom she interacts on a daily basis. I have had evangelistic success in different ways. The key is that, although we are different in our styles, we have both learned to maximize our strengths and minimize our weaknesses.

For the first few years of our marriage I viewed her patience as a weakness. I was constantly challenging her to "close the deal" with her friends. Just as she challenged me to be more loving, I challenged her to be bolder. And now she is. That is one of the beautiful things about marriage—you both rub off on each other.

I thank God for a wife who showed me the beauty of other styles of evangelism. The lesson is this: God made you special, unique, and potent. He wants to use you and every peculiarity about you to advance His kingdom through you.

LEAD THE WAY

In the first chapter of his two-volume book on the life of George Whitefield, Arnold Dallimore writes these words:

 This book goes forth with a mission. It is written with the profound conviction that the paramount need of the twentieth century is a mighty evangelical revival such as that which was experienced two hundred years ago. . . . This book is written in the desire—perhaps in a measure of inner certainty—that we shall see the great Head of the Church once more bring into being His special instruments of revival, that He will again raise up unto Himself certain young men whom He may use in this glorious employ. And what manner of men will they be? Men mighty in the Scriptures, their lives dominated by a sense of the greatness, the majesty and holiness of God, and their minds and hearts aglow with the great truths of the doctrines of grace. They will be men who have learned what it is to die to self, to human aims and personal ambitions; men who are willing to be "fools for Christ's sake," who will bear reproach and falsehood, who will labour and suffer, and whose supreme desire will be, not to gain earth's accolades, but to win the Master's approbation when they appear before His awesome judgment seat. They will be men who will preach with broken hearts and tear-filled eyes, and upon whose ministries God will grant an extraordinary effusion of the Holy Spirit, and who will witness "signs and wonders following" in the transformation of multitudes of human lives. Indeed, this book goes forth with the earnest prayers that, amidst the rampant iniquity and glaring apostasy of the twentieth century God will use it toward the raising up of such men and toward the granting of a mighty revival such as was witnessed two hundred years ago.[6]

This book goes forth with the same mission. Men and women of God are needed to lead the way for viral revival in the twenty-first century. Will you be one of them?

Whether it is church member hesitation, student intimidation, or youth leader inhibition, evangelism antibiotics create an immunity within us to the outbreak of awakening. Don't take them, no matter what anybody says. ✖

THROW OUT THE GEL CAPS:
HESITATION, INHIBITION, AND INTIMIDATION!

MANDATE #1
Identify your biggest
excuse against viral evangelism in your own life and
ministry.

MANDATE #2
List three practical ways
you will start fighting
against that excuse.

S STAFF
INFECTION
QUESTIONS

#1. As leaders, what are our personal evangelistic inhibitions?

#2. Which of the three main antibodies stand the strongest
against viral evangelism in
our youth group?

#3. What are some strategies we
can employ to overcome this
antibody right away?

WATCH OUT FOR TAINTED STRAINS!

A pure virus is unstoppable. Tainted strains, however, are less effective. The same is true of the gospel of Jesus Christ. When the pure message of God's grace is doctored in any way, the results are less than optimal. Many gospel presentations are delivered with vagueness and confusion instead of with clarity and power. Using Scripture as a viral handbook, this chapter will show the importance of keeping the message of grace clear, simple, and untainted.

LEGALISM . . . A VIRUS KILLER

One sure way to stop the spread of the virus through your youth group is to unleash the ultimate virus killer: legalism. What is legalism? It is the refusal to make room for grace. It is the manipulation of God's grace that adds human stipulations. It is taking what was free and adding a fee. It is the arrogant belief that we can do something to earn God's free gift. It is the ultimate slap in God's face. It is humanism. Francis Schaeffer wrote about the tendency of people to try to add works to the free gift of God's grace:

 Man always tries to sneak a humanistic element into salvation. But in the area of individual salvation Scripture rejects all humanism. Man is justified freely "through the redemption that is in Christ Jesus, whom God hath set forth to be a propitiation through faith in his blood, to declare his righteousness for the remission of sins that are past, through the forbearance of God, at this time his righteousness, that he might be just, and the justifier of him who believeth in Jesus." Talk about the atom bomb! This is totally explosive—into the midst of the humanism of any age and expressly into the humanism of the twentieth century.[1]

The explosive doctrine of grace blew away the legalists in Jesus' day and continues to do so today. It is vitally important that we share the undiluted message of grace with our teens. When we do, we will witness explosive growth, both spiritually and numerically.

In the early New Testament, Jewish legalists were trying to run the show among the churches in the Roman province of Galatia. They were spreading the virus killer of legalism by adding prerequisites to the free gift of God's grace. The one predominant prerequisite was circumcision. The false teachers claimed that if you were a Gentile male and wanted to be a part of the *in crowd* of God's acceptance, you had to get circumcised.

Circumcision was of huge importance to the Jewish community. What baptism represented to the Christian, circumcision represented to the Jew. It was an outward sign of internal belief. When God initiated the rite of circumcision with Abraham and Isaac, it became the physical mark that represented a spiritual belief system that was superior to the "uncut" Canaanites around them. It set the Jews apart as God's people.

As the centuries gave way to millennia, circumcision became a symbol of Jewish pride and Gentile disdain. Eventually Gentiles were nicknamed "dogs" by legalistic Jews. When a Gentile converted to Judaism, circumcision was part of the deal. The slice was part of the price.

So when Christianity began sweeping the world and Gentiles started coming to Christ in droves, the Jewish legalists were irked that circumcision was no longer mandatory. They hatched a plan to require the converted Gentiles in Galatia to be circumcised. In their viral-stopping strategy, the grace of God was not enough to fully convert the soul—a knife was needed as well. "How dare these uncircumcised dogs worship by the side of a circumcised Jew in the same church service? Blasphemy!" they argued. As a result, the power of the message of God's grace came to a screeching halt. The virus killer had been unleashed. A tainted strain was being preached.

That demonic deception even affected Peter and Barnabas. They refused to eat ham sandwiches with their Gentile brothers at the local bar and grill. Instead, they were pounding down lox and bagels with their Jewish brothers at the local deli. Why? Because the legalists were watching and waiting, lurking and luring, pointing and prying. They frightened Peter and others as well so much that they backed off from their freedom in Christ and in so doing tainted the strain.

Paul responded with a scathing letter that rips not only those false teachers and the churches of Galatia for buying into their false doctrine but Peter and Barnabas as well. Paul makes the clear case for grace. Look at his rebukes in his letter to the churches in Galatia:

You foolish Galatians! Who has bewitched you? Before your very eyes Jesus Christ was clearly portrayed as crucified. I would like to learn just one thing from you: Did you receive the Spirit by observing the law, or by believing what you heard? Are you so foolish? After beginning with the Spirit, are you now trying to attain your goal by human effort? (3:1–3)

Formerly, when you did not know God, you were slaves to those who by nature are not gods. But now that you know God—or rather are known by God—how is it that you are turning back to those weak and miserable principles? Do you wish to be enslaved by them all over again? You are observing special days and months and seasons and years! I fear for you, that somehow I have wasted my efforts on you. (4:8–11)

You who are trying to be justified by law have been alienated from Christ; you have fallen away from grace. (5:4)

As for those agitators, I wish they would go the whole way and emasculate themselves! (5:12)

Does Paul, the mighty man of God, the esteemed apostle of Christ, the writer of much of the New Testament, sound a little angry? He was infuriated! Why? Because the gospel message of God's free grace had been attacked head-on by the virus-killing threat of legalism. He knew that a little legalism could do a lot of damage. He knew that "a little yeast works through the whole batch of dough" (Galatians 5:9). He knew that the awakening of God's grace in the churches of Galatia had lost its groove. So he wrote a letter that dripped with sarcasm to those who had bought into the message of legalism.

Every Christian culture has had its own versions of that virus killer. A generation after Paul, water baptism became a prerequisite of salvation in many circles. Centuries later Martin Luther took a stand against legalism in the Roman Catholic Church. Today we have several strains of the virus killer of legalism on the loose.

What does that have to do with your youth group?

Everything. If legalism has infected your culture, your message, and your mind-set, the outbreak will never have maximum impact. The purer the virus, the bigger the outbreak. The weaker the strain, the smaller the epidemic.

Think about the legalism that has seeped into much of the Christian culture today. The requirements and conditions that stand in the way of the viral power of the gospel message are many. Let's look at some of the different strains of this virus killer called legalism.

THE "WELCOME TO THE FAMILY, NOW HERE'S THE LIST" STRAIN

In many churches where the grace of God is preached freely to the lost, the law is preached to the saved. To such believers, service to God means living by a list: "Don't drink. Don't smoke. Don't chew. Read your Bible every day. Witness all the time. Go to church every Sunday. Give 10 percent of your income to God." If you live by the list, then you are a good Christian. If you don't, you're not. In the words of Chuck Swindoll, those who preach the list are grace killers:

 There are killers on the loose today. The problem is that you can't tell by looking. They don't wear little buttons that give away their identity, nor do they carry signs warning everybody to stay away. On the contrary, a lot of them carry Bibles and appear to be clean-living, nice-looking, law-abiding citizens. Most of them spend a lot of time in churches, some in places of religious leadership. Many are so respected in the community, their neighbors would never guess they are living next door to killers. They kill freedom, spontaneity, and creativity; they kill joy as well as productivity. They kill with their words and their pens and their looks. They kill with their attitudes far more often than with their behavior. There is hardly a church or Christian organization or Christian school or missionary group or media ministry where such danger does not lurk. The amazing thing is that they get away with it, day in and day out, without being confronted or exposed. Strangely, the same ministries that would not tolerate heresy for ten minutes will step aside and allow these killers all the space they need to maneuver and manipulate others in the most insidious manner imaginable. Their intolerance is tolerated. Their judgmental spirits remain unjudged. Their bullying tactics continue unchecked. And their narrow-mindedness is either explained away or quickly defended. The bondage that results would be criminal were it not so subtle and wrapped in such spiritual-sounding garb.[2]

Those virus-murdering grace killers may be residing in a congregation near you. Those who are driven by the list are unleashing spiritual oppression in lethal amounts into their surroundings.

The list never made anybody more spiritual, just more arrogant. The proof is in the pudding and in the book of Colossians, where Paul gives the ultimate litmus test of legalism. "Such regulations indeed have an appearance of wisdom, with their self-imposed worship, their false humility and their harsh treatment of the body, but they lack any value in restraining sensual indulgence" (2:23). In other words, the list can't remove lust. Some of the most sensual people I know are legalistic. Why? Because the list can't remove the lust. It actually stimulates it. The "thou shalt not" is a turn-on.

What does that mean for your youth group? Simple. If you are teaching them that Christianity is obedience to a list of dos and don'ts, then you are sparking the fire of immoral desire in their hearts. The more they buy into legalism, the more they will struggle with lust.

How do I know? I experienced it firsthand. I went to a strict Christian school that preached the message of grace to the unbeliever and the message of legalism to the believer. The list was firmly placed in my hands, and I tried to obey every rule. They told me that if I wanted to be spiritual, I should read my Bible every day. So I did. They told me that I needed to memorize Bible verses, so I did. As a matter of fact, I memorized entire books of the Bible. They told me to witness, so I did. I estimate conservatively that I witnessed to more than five thousand people by the time I graduated from high school, mostly one or two at a time in local malls and parks. They told me to become a leader, so I became student body president. They told me to study hard, so I graduated with a 4.0. They told me a bunch of stuff, and I tried to do my best to do it all to the letter . . . and I was absolutely miserable inside. Lust became my arch-nemesis. I could do all the external stuff. That was easy compared to conquering the monster of lust.

During my freshman year of college, God introduced me to grace. For the first time since my salvation experience, I felt the power and freedom of God's pure grace. For years I had known and defended the message of God's grace to the unsaved world. But I had sold God's grace short when it came to the Christian life. I had infused human-ism into my Christian walk.

After experiencing God's grace in college, I learned the power of a day-by-day declaration of dependence on the Spirit of God. There were still struggles. But God's "[grace] teaches us to say 'No' to ungodliness and worldly passions, and to live self-controlled, upright and godly lives in this present age" (Titus 2:12).

The key is to teach teens to walk in freedom and serve with passion. Grace elicits that response. When we taste His grace, we want to serve Him. No longer is serving Him a list—it is a longing. It is relational, not religious. It is a response, not a requirement. It is grace, not law. However, the "Welcome to the family, now here's the list" strain is not the only viral hybrid that will lessen the impact of the gospel in your youth group.

THE "DADDY MAY LEAVE YOU SOMEDAY" STRAIN

This virus killer is based on an escape clause in the fine print of many gospel presentations. It is the "Daddy may leave you someday" strain. It is the message of grace that leaves the back door unlocked just in case you or the Father wants to get out. It is the message that says that salvation is only eternal if you stay faithful and keep serving.

Many years ago a young man named Tony was a preacher in the fire-and-brimstone tradition. But as his preaching career was just getting started, he was recruited to fight for his country in the Korean War. He fought, and he was captured. During his captivity, he was tortured for his faith in God and his patriotism toward his country. When he was finally released, that POW came back to America as a celebrated war hero.

Tony had proved himself well on the battlefield, but soon after his return to the States, his spiritual life took a turn for the worse. Slowly, he began to drift into a life of sin. His Bible was replaced with a bottle. He began to pursue a lifestyle that was contrary to his religious roots. As the years passed, that lifestyle spiraled down the road of depravity.

One day he met a girl. They partied. She got pregnant. He left town. A few years later Tony died. The only thing he had left to show for his life was an old, dusty Bible he used to preach from, a few rusty medals from the war, and a son he never met.

That son whom Tony forsook was me. My father abandoned my mother and me before I was even born. I am a bastard child of a deadbeat dad. But one thing has given me hope since my childhood—I have another Father. He will never leave me or forsake me. He will not leave my hopes crushed. I may mess up again and again. But He is always there, waiting patiently, disciplining lovingly, and caring infinitely. I may leave Him (and I do leave Him every time I blatantly sin against Him), but He will never leave me. When I think about that, I can't help but join with Paul in his worshipful refrain:

What, then, shall we say in response to this? If God is for us, who can be against us? He who did not spare his own Son, but gave him up for us all—how will he not also, along with him, graciously give us all things? Who will bring any charge against those whom God has chosen? It is God who justifies. Who is he that condemns? Christ Jesus, who died—more than that, who was raised to life—is at the right hand of God and is also interceding for us. Who shall separate us from the love of Christ? Shall trouble or hardship or persecution or famine or nakedness or danger or sword? As it is written: "For your sake we face death all day long; we are considered as sheep to be slaughtered." No, in all these things we are more than conquerors through him who loved us. For I am convinced that neither death nor life, neither angels nor demons, neither the present nor the future, nor any powers, neither height nor depth, nor anything else in all creation, will be able to separate us from the love of God that is in Christ Jesus our Lord. (Romans 8:31–39)

I have a Daddy who will never leave. So do you, and so do your teenagers. There is no escape clause. There are no "What if?" scenarios. There is no way out of God's unstoppable, unimaginable, and unfathomable love. That freaks me out! It makes me want to serve

Him all the more. It motivates me to serve Him with all my heart and soul and mind and strength. Nothing can separate me from His love, not even me.

It is vitally important for your students to understand that truth. Imagine the psychological effects of having a human father who threatened to leave you every time you really messed up. The results would be devastating. Insecurity would be your lot in life. *Dysfunction* would be the word written on your case file. Having a father who is loving and present is a crucial factor in adolescent development. However, the statistics show what's happening to the contrary:

- Twenty-four million children (34 percent) live in homes without their biological fathers.

- About 40 percent of children in father-absent homes have not seen their father within the past year; and 50 percent of father-absent children have never set foot in their father's home.

- Fatherless boys are 63 percent more likely to run away and 37 percent more likely to abuse drugs, and fatherless girls are twice as likely to get pregnant and 53 percent more likely to commit suicide. Fatherless children are twice as likely to drop out of high school and twice as likely to end up in jail.[3]

The knowledge that a father is present as a role model, a coach, a mentor, and a hero gives children the psychological comfort they need to grow up healthy and well balanced. Without it, the odds are against them. Don't underestimate the power of the father—especially the heavenly Father.

Knowing that there is a Daddy in heaven that loves me, no matter what, gave me the strength to make it through the broken, dysfunctional, inner-city family struggles that I endured. I could easily have taken another path. But the love of the Father drew me in and compelled me to serve Him. Nothing can separate me from His love.

When we share a message infected with the "Daddy may leave you someday" strain, we are taking away the unshakable assurance that flows from an unconditional love. Is it so unbelievable that God cares about His children so much that He would never let them out His grip?

JEREMY AND KAILEY

God has blessed my wife and me with two wonderful children. Jeremy is my rambunctious five-year-old boy, and Kailey is my adorable eighteen month old daughter. I love those two kids with all of my heart. I would die for them without thinking or blinking. If that is the love I as a human father can feel for my son and daughter, what kind of love is in the heart of God Himself for us? If it is even a remote possibility that I as a human dad could love Jeremy and Kailey even if they grew up to turn their backs on me, how remarkable is it to believe that our heavenly Daddy still loves us when we turn our backs on Him? God's love for us is unfathomable, unimaginable, and unending.

Are you infecting your students with a tainted strain? Do you use the threat of abandonment by their heavenly Father as a motivation for them to serve Christ? Do you leave even the slightest escape clause in your gospel presentations? If you do, you have lessened the impact of the virus. The outbreak will not have its full effect. If there is any escape clause in the fine print of your gospel presentations, the impact of the virus is limited. There is no fine print in the free gift of salvation.

THE "YOU MEAN TO TELL ME . . ." STRAIN

"You mean to tell me that all someone has to do is trust in Christ as Savior, and that's all there is to it?"

"You mean to tell me that it doesn't matter how good or bad a person is as long as he trusts in Christ as his Savior?"

"You mean to tell me that a murderer on death row who believes in Jesus is going to heaven, but not my sweet Aunt Alice who just happens to be an agnostic?"

"You mean to tell me . . . ?"

Whenever the message of God's grace is preached freely and clearly, the "You mean to tell me . . ." people show up. That is exactly how you know that you are preaching the grace message in all of its glory.

Paul knew that as soon as he started preaching grace the legalists would try to contaminate his message with the "You mean to tell me . . ." strain.

"You mean to tell me that all these dirty Gentiles have to do is believe and they are forgiven?"

"You mean to tell me that a believing, uncircumcised Gentile is going to heaven before a certified, circumcised Jew?"

"You mean that these Gentile 'dogs' are making it into the kingdom before the chosen people of God?"

Paul called it "the offense of the cross." He says in Galatians 5:11, "Brothers, if I am still preaching circumcision [as a prerequisite to salvation], why am I still being persecuted? In that case the offense of the cross has been abolished." What is the offense of the cross, and why was Paul persecuted for it? The offense of the cross is the anger that burns in those who require conditions to the free gift of God's grace. That offense may be fueled by the fear that God's grace will be abused or misused. It may be tripped by the trigger of logic—it seems too good to be true; therefore, it must be. It may be fanned by the flames of pride—I must do something to deserve it. Whatever the reason, humans have a hard time with grace. It does seem too good to be true. It is a slap in the face of religious self-righteousness. It is illogical. It is shocking. It is truly amazing.

The deadly "You mean to tell me . . ." strain was around during Jesus' ministry as well. His message infuriated the Pharisees and teachers of the law. He preached a message of free grace to all those who would simply believe. He said to the Pharisees, "I tell you the truth, the tax collectors and the prostitutes are entering the kingdom of God ahead of you. For John came to you to show you the way of righteousness, and you did not believe him, but the tax collectors and the prostitutes did. And even after you saw this, you did not repent and believe him" (Matthew 21:31–32).

"You mean to tell me, Jesus, that a prostitute is going to heaven before me, a teacher of the law for all of my life?"

"You mean to tell me, Jesus, that a double-crossing, money-loving tax collector is going to heaven before me, a nationally recognized leader of Judaism?"

Yep. That's exactly what He was telling them. The message of God's free grace angered the legalists and welcomed the sinners.

The offense of the cross is the offense of grace without conditions. Jesus paid the price completely. We have nothing to bring to the table. We simply receive it. We simply believe it.

That may seem risky. To preach a message that is truly by faith alone could lead to rampant disobedience and unruly living.

It could also lead to revival.

Grace is risky. It is downright dangerous—to the kingdom of darkness, that is. The great preacher Martin Lloyd-Jones shared the power of this dangerous grace with his listeners when he dropped this dangerous bombshell on them:

 The true preaching of the gospel of salvation by grace alone always leads to the possibility of this charge being brought against it. There is no better test as to whether a man is really preaching the New Testament gospel of salvation than this, that some people might misunderstand it and misinterpret it to mean that it really amounts to this, that because you are saved by grace alone it does not matter at all what you do; you can go on sinning as much as you like because it will redound all the more to the glory of grace. That is a very good test of gospel preaching. If my preaching and presentation of the gospel of salvation does not expose it to that misunderstanding, then it is not the gospel.[4]

What a statement! Is your gospel message accused of being a license to sin? Do the "You mean to tell me . . ." people attack you for preaching a message that seems way too easy? If not, you have failed to preach the true gospel. You are preaching a cheap grace that lessens the impact of the gospel message. Your virus has been tainted.

THE TIME I WAS ALMOST
THROWN OUT OF THE RESCUE MISSION

I will never forget preaching at the Denver Rescue Mission as a young, wet-behind-the ears, nineteen-year-old "preacher boy." I knew that I had a captive audience. If those men and women wanted to eat and sleep at the rescue mission, they had to listen to my sermon. I also knew that they were used to hearing typical, downtown turn-or-burn sermons. If they hadn't heard them at the rescue mission, they had heard them in the streets of Denver where curbside preachers wield their pointy fingers and push their pointed sermons. So I decided to try something different.

As I stood behind the pulpit and looked at the room filled with the dysfunctional and the drunk, I noticed that the rescue mission staff was sitting off to my left in some chairs along the wall. They too were used to hearing sermons as well. But they weren't prepared for what I was going to say.

"How many of you in this room have ever heard a preacher tell you that if you want to go to heaven, you have to give up your drinking, your smoking, your cussing, your chewing, your drugs, and your sexual immorality?" I asked.

They all kind of looked up at me with groggy looks of acknowledgment. Many raised their hands in affirmation and grunted, "I have."

I went on, "Well, I want to tell you something a little different tonight." I will never forget that moment. Everybody looked up in confusion at once, including the rescue mission staff. "Here's what I want to tell you," I continued. "If you want to go to heaven, keep your alcohol, cigarettes, cuss words, tobacco chew, drugs, and sexual sins." Talk about a cup of coffee to sober up the audience! Their eyes were wide open. Their jaws dropped. By now the rescue mission staff was standing, apparently getting ready to remove me from the pulpit. One of the disheveled men in the audience yelled out a hearty "amen!"

Now that I had their full attention, I went on, "You keep every single one of your sins, and you come to the cross of Jesus Christ. You simply believe that He died for those sins. You simply place your trust in Him to forgive you for those sins. Not only will He forgive you, but He will come to live inside of you, and He will give you the power and desire to turn from those sins. But you cannot turn from your sins until you have the power to do so. And you cannot have the power to do so until you are forgiven. And you cannot be forgiven until you believe."

The rescue mission staff sat back down. Seven people were infected that night with the pure, untainted viral message of God's grace.

From too many pulpits the gospel is presented with conditions. In the process, the grace of God is cheapened by a focus on what we do rather than on what Christ has done. The offense of the cross is abolished when the grace of God is diminished.

Are you infecting your youth group with the "You mean to tell me . . ." strain? Has your message lost the offense of the cross by infusing some subtle human works into the gospel message?

Your gospel presentation to your students must be clear, simple, and untainted. The book of John is a great example of a gospel presentation. The beloved apostle tells us why he wrote the book in John 20:31: "But these are written that you may believe that Jesus is the Christ, the Son of God, and that by believing you may have life in his name." The book of John was written to convert the unconverted. He builds the book around a handful of amazing miracles that Jesus did. He fills in the blanks with a chronology of Christ's ministry and teaching, especially the last week before His crucifixion. One word comes up again and again: *believe*. He uses the word again and again to describe the sole pathway to eternal life.

In his powerful presentation of the gospel, not once does John lay out any requirement for salvation other than faith alone. His message is offensive to the human mind. Simple faith in Jesus Christ is the only prerequisite to salvation given in the whole book of John. Nothing more, nothing less. Some people think that way of salvation is too easy. But how easy is it to stake your eternity on Him whom you have never met? How easy is it to trust fully in Him whom you have never seen? It is so easy that a child can do it, and it is so difficult a religious person can choke on it.

WATCH YOUR MOUTH!

Think about the terms that you use to communicate the gospel. Do they lessen the impact of the gospel message? I believe that a huge number of youth pastors, senior pastors, evangelists, and children's workers unwittingly limit the effectiveness of their outreach because of the terms they use to communicate the gospel.

"ASK JESUS INTO YOUR HEART."

That is probably the most overused, unbiblical phrase used in gospel presentations. Many of us probably remember the Sunday school teacher pointing to the picture of Jesus standing at a door and knocking. "That is the door to your heart, and Jesus wants to come in," they would say. Then they'd quote Revelation 3:20: "Here I am! I stand at the door and knock. If anyone hears my voice and opens the door, I will come in and eat with him, and he with me." The problem is that that verse was not written for unbelievers. John was writing to Christians in the church of Laodicea. The passage is not about salvation but about service and communion with God. Not one passage in Scripture says we must "ask Jesus into our hearts" to be saved.

I remember as a child hearing my Sunday school teacher use this term almost every week. I did not get it. Sitting there in Sunday school as a seven-year-old boy, I wondered, What if I get a heart transplant? Will I go to hell? If I cough too hard will Jesus escape through my mouth? How do I really know He is in my heart? OK, I was a neurotic little kid, but don't miss the point. Unclear gospel presentations limit the impact of the virus.

It was not until Pastor Claude Pettit finally explained the cross to me that I got it. On June 23, 1974, I trusted in Christ as my Savior, thanks to the Spirit of God and a clear presentation of the gospel message. Be clear with your terms.

"JUST SAY THIS PRAYER."

I cringe when I hear youth pastors say this to unsaved kids. Saying a prayer never saved anyone. Faith in Christ alone is the only way. Saying a prayer after the moment of salvation is a great way for the new believer to thank God for the free gift of salvation. But making it a prerequisite to salvation is adding work. I am convinced that there will be people in hell who said the sinner's prayer but never truly believed in the finished work of Christ.

"YOU MUST TURN FROM YOUR SIN."

We hear this one all the time. But stop for a moment and think about the feasibility of that statement. We are asking unbelievers to do something they are unable to do until they become believers!

In one of my favorite books, *The Grace Awakening*, Chuck Swindoll writes:

A sinner cannot commit to anything. He or she is spiritually dead, remember? There is no capacity for commitment in an unregenerate heart. Becoming an obedient, submissive disciple of Christ follows believing in Christ. Works follow faith. Behavior follows belief. Fruit comes after the tree is well-rooted.[5]

After our students believe, the real work begins. Salvation is indeed simple. It is a free gift through faith alone. But it cost Christ everything. And discipleship is difficult. It costs us everything. When we blend the ingredients of salvation and sanctification, we get a "heresy shake." That mixture is the same kind of blending of faith and works that Mormons and Jehovah's Witnesses have concocted. As a matter of fact, one of the last Mormons I talked to on my doorstep said, "We believe that salvation is by faith alone, but you have to turn from your sins." Jehovah's Witnesses say basically the same thing. They have no problem with the turn-or-burn message. But I have a problem with any message that has lost the offensiveness of the cross.

I think the reason that many of us share these tainted strains is that we are afraid of God's grace. We want to ensure spiritual growth in our students so we add conditions to the wonderfully free gift of grace. But when we add to the gospel, we subtract from the impact of the message of grace.

"MAKE JESUS LORD OF YOUR LIFE."

Let's not flatter ourselves. We don't make Jesus Lord of anything. He is Lord! When we come to a saving knowledge of Jesus Christ, we simply acknowledge Him as Lord. In other words, we acknowledge that Jesus is God Himself.

"Jesus is Lord" was the earliest confession of faith. When early believers recognized Jesus as Lord they were recognizing that He was Yahweh. As a matter of fact, the Greek word for Lord (*kyrios*) "is used over 6,000 times in the Septuagint (the Greek translation of the OT) to translate the name of Israel's God (Yahweh)."[6]

When people said "Jesus is Lord" in that culture, they were saying, "Jesus is the God of Abraham, Isaac, and Jacob. Jesus is the I AM. Jesus is God Himself." That was a radical and catalytic statement.

When we speak carelessly in our gospel presentations, the gospel of grace is cheapened. The focus is taken off of Jesus and put onto us. The priority is removed from what Christ has done and diverted to what we must do. Swindoll writes:

 I suggest we openly declare our own spiritual bankruptcy and accept God's free gift of grace. "Why?" you ask. "Why not emphasize how much I do for God instead of what He does for me?" Because that is heresy, plain and simple. How? By exalting my own effort and striving for my own accomplishments, I insult His grace and steal the credit that belongs to Him alone.[7]

The terms we use make a difference. They unleash either a pure virus or a tainted strain. There is no middle ground.

WHAT TERMS SHOULD YOU USE?

Use the terms that God uses again and again throughout the New Testament. *Faith*, *trust*, and *believe* are the words used in Scripture to point the sole way of salvation. "Close to 200 times in the New Testament salvation is said to be by faith alone—with no works in sight."[8]

When asked by the Philippian jailer, "What must I do to be saved?" Paul didn't tell him to say a prayer, surrender all, walk an aisle, or turn from his sins. He simply said, "Believe in the Lord Jesus, and you will be saved." Did Paul preach an incomplete gospel? Of course not. Salvation is that simple. It's not turn or burn, try or fry, forsake or bake. It's believe and receive. We trust in what Jesus did for us on the cross for the forgiveness of our sins and we are saved, period. Then God begins the never-ending work of sanctification and doesn't let up.

As I talk with thousands of youth and youth workers across the nation, I have come to the sobering realization that many are afraid of grace. The simple message of grace seems too dangerous and risky. But therein lies the secret to its power. It is so simple that it offends the self-centered pride of the legalist.

Don't get me wrong. It is dangerous to the kingdom of Satan. It is risky to the status quo. Satan hates this message and will do everything in his power to stop it. He is plotting to keep the virus contained and your youth group quarantined.

Remember, the essence of the grace message is that it is undeserved, not just before we receive it but always. Grace with conditions is not grace. Grace with small print is not grace. Grace with a P.S. is not grace. Grace is grace all by itself. When Paul writes in Romans 5:20, "But where sin increased, grace increased all the more," he is really telling us that for every cupful of sin in our lives God has an ocean of grace to wash it away.

Maybe as a youth leader you have a sin in your past that you think

God will never forgive. Just know that if you have put your faith in Jesus, you are already forgiven! He has separated it from you "as far as the east is from the west." It is gone. Does that exhilarating truth make you feel like going out and committing that sin again? Of course not! It humbles and excites. It makes you feel like serving Him all the more. That's what grace does for us. That's what it will do for our youth groups.

Yes, some will abuse grace. God will discipline them to the point of repentance (Hebrews 12:6) or take them home like He did some of the Corinthian believers (1 Corinthians 11:30). But for most people the message will become a powerful catalyst to fully surrendered service to a fully forgiving Savior. It will cause an outbreak of biblical proportions in your youth group. ✖

RED·DOT REVIEW

TAINTED STRAINS KILL EVANGELISTIC GAINS!

MONKEY MANDATE

MANDATE

Write the answers to these questions on a sheet of paper:

- Have I put the emphasis more on rules than relationship when it comes to motivating my students to serve Christ?

- In what ways have I communicated personal preferences in my life (movie, music, devotional, church attendance) as nonnegotiable standards that every student in my group should live by?

- Am I focusing on external appearances of godliness more than the internal reality?

- Have I taught my students the difference between grace living and legalism?

- Am I presenting a clear gospel presentation that has no hint of works?

S STAFF
INFECTION
QUESTIONS

#1. Identify potential legalistic expectations that exist in our youth ministry culture or philosophy.

#2. In what three ways can we prevent an infusion of legalism in our youth ministry?

#3. How can we better equip our students to walk in grace?

#4. How can we better equip our e-team and youth group to share the pure gospel of grace?

INFECTING POSTMODERN STUDENTS
WITH THE AGE-OLD VIRUS

News flash, 1977—"Smallpox wiped out!" After centuries of wreaking havoc, the monster virus was once and for all defanged and declawed. The world needed no longer cower in its deadly shadow. The disease had been beaten.

News flash, 2006—"The power of the gospel wiped out!" That's the headline that some so-called experts are chiseling onto what they perceive to be the tombstone of truth. Although I acknowledge the truth of the statistics and stories about the ineffectiveness of our outdated methods in reaching this postmodern generation, we must be careful not to throw the virus out just because some of the vials that carry it are cracked. There is no doubt that we need a new approach and a new strategy. But it is that same old-time gospel message that is the key to transforming life. The gospel is not smallpox. It will never be stopped.

The timeless message of truth should never be confused with

ineffective methods. Although many cultural statisticians are dead-on when it comes to evaluating some of the tired strategies of outreach, some are way off when it comes to the solution. The solution is not to move away from the gospel message to more "sophisticated" ways of transforming this generation. The answer is to move back to the heart of the gospel message and learn how to share the story of Christianity in a way that fully infects the soul of today's teenager.

Many methods of evangelism today are too long, too boring, or too weak to make a difference in the postmodern mind. The ones that are too long take the listener way past the two-minute attention span of today's typical teenager. The ones that are too boring fail to capture the full attention of the typical teenager right from the start. The ones that are too weak don't focus on the basic elements that make the gospel message the gospel.

The methods we use to reach teens today must be concise, relevant, and strong, just like the gospel presentations of the New Testament. They must resonate and relate while being convicting and convincing at the same time.

WHAT IS A POSTMODERN TEENAGER?

One specific encounter changed my life and the way I presented the gospel. Mike Metzger was the speaker that day. I was in a room with about thirty presidents and executive directors of other parachurch organizations in Washington, D.C. The purpose of the meeting was to provide a time of prayer, strategy, and networking. Mike Metzger gave the final talk about reaching postmodern students for Christ. We all gathered in a large room and took our seats. Little did I know that a few hours later I would have a transformed perspective and a revolutionized method of sharing the gospel.

Metzger began by explaining the term *postmodern*. He showed us the differences between the worldviews of modernism and postmodernism. He identified modernism as being characterized by knowledge gained by reason, conquest, certainty, progress in life, choice, and Western superiority. In contrast, postmodernism is characterized by knowledge gained by indwelling, skepticism, purposelessness in life, and truth through story. He went on to tell us that it was our job as leaders in youth ministry to help teenagers learn how to communicate the gospel in a culturally relevant way. In other words, we must not use modernist approaches to the postmodern mind or vice versa. We must "become all things to all men" without compromising the core of the gospel message.[1]

At first I was pretty uncomfortable with some of the things Metzger was saying. They went against the grain of the way I had been taught. But the more he spoke, the more I was convinced that his arguments were not only logical, but also biblical. As a result of those few hours, our methodology and strategy for evangelism at Dare 2 Share changed completely. Methods and strategies may change, but the gospel never does.

The typical student today is steeped in a popularized postmodern worldview. They are not impressed primarily with the fluidity of thought and logic of our gospel presentations as much as with the story of the gospel and how it makes them feel. That doesn't mean that we throw out doctrine, truth, and logic. It does mean that we must seize their hearts and their minds with the true and exciting story of Christianity.

ASSUMPTIONS WE MUST ACCEPT

What methodologies can we use to reach the typical postmodern teen? How do we effectively infect today's students with the age-old virus? Before we seek to answer that question, we must address a few necessary assumptions.

1. THE GOSPEL WORKS IN ANY CULTURE

"I am not ashamed of the gospel, because it is the power of God for the salvation of everyone who believes: first for the Jew, then for the Gentile" (Romans 1:16).

The gospel message is inherently transformational in any culture.

It works for the Jew as well as the Gentile. The postmodern teen, as well as the modern adult, can be transformed by its awesome power.

Sometimes when analysts of contemporary student culture start sharing statistics and facts, youth leaders freak out. Many of them are intimidated and tentative about reaching out to them. They are not sure how to do it in this mosaic culture of multitasking, truth-questioning, easily distracted teenagers. So they don't. That is a huge mistake.

The one assumption, the most important assumption, you as a youth worker must accept is that the gospel works in any culture, even this one—especially this one. Throughout church history the gospel message has been effective in virtually every single part of the world. Of course, some groups have been more difficult to reach because of ingrained belief systems that are unbiblical. Yet even then, the gospel eventually penetrates hardened hearts and made-up minds. Why? Because the message of the gospel is not just a competing belief system. It is not merely one of the many horses to bet on at the race-track of worldviews. It is the truth supported by hard facts, energized by the Holy Spirit, and confirmed by the sinner's conscience. It is not a truth devoid of feeling. It's ablaze with feeling, passion, and power. Its logic can transform the mind. Its heat can warm the cold heart.

When you share the gospel message in this postmodern student culture, share it with the internal confidence that it is a dynamic and explosive force that can penetrate the hardest of walls with the shrapnel of truth. Speak that message of hope knowing that it is living and active and hungry. It will not stop until it has caught its prey. Speak with the absolute assurance that God in His sovereignty will bring those whom He has called when He has called them in spite of the cultural nuances that seem to be roadblocks to belief. Don't hesitate to share the gospel with teens of today.

2. THE GOSPEL DOESN'T CHANGE, BUT OUR TACTICS SHOULD

The second assumption is that although the gospel doesn't change, our tactics should, depending on our audience. As we will see later,

Paul used a vastly different technique when he spoke to the Greeks on Mars Hill from the one he used with the Jews in the synagogue.

For example, if you go to an unreached tribe in Papua New Guinea and begin with the *Four Spiritual Laws* right off the bat, the responses might vary. But most likely you'd be beaten or eaten. Missiologists complete years of study in order to identify belief systems in other cultures and to find common ground. Then they develop a strategy based on that research. It is then tried and tweaked until the most effective methodology is uncovered. Today's student culture is no different.

You probably wouldn't approach a student with a Jewish background the same way you would approach a student from a Wiccan belief system. The entry points are different. One has a monotheistic worldview. The other is polytheistic or atheistic. One accepts the Old Testament as authoritative. The other rejects Scripture as absolute truth.

How do we become skilled at bringing the good news to this culture of students? We become students of the students. We study them. We discover what makes them tick and what gets them ticked. We find out what they value. In other words, we listen.

That means not passive listening but aggressively paying attention. We listen to find entry points into their worlds. We ask questions that open doors and initiate conversations about the gospel. We try to tweak until we find an effective method. In other words, we look for an infection portal.

Infection is the "state or condition in which a pathogenic agent invades the body."[2] Those pathogenic agents invade and infect through "portals of entry." For the human body the mouth and nasal passages are two major portals of entry. For the human soul it is the mouth and ears. If we listen when our students speak, they will listen when we speak. The message we share is infectious and can break down the barriers of spiritual immunity to transform the soul of the postmodern teenager completely.

3. SCRIPTURE PROVIDES A TEMPLATE
FOR REACHING POSTMODERN TEENAGERS

The third and final assumption in reaching postmodern students with the gospel message is that God's Word gives us a template for that very goal. This template is found in Acts 17 where Paul speaks to the men on Mars Hill.

WHAT PLANET ARE YOU FROM?

It's a whole new world compared to when veteran youth leaders and parents of teenagers were in high school themselves. Rent *Back to the Future* at your local video store. In it you can watch two generations of teenagers. The early eighties teen versus the mid-fifties teen. Then pop in *Mean Girls* or another of the vast array of more current high school flicks. Study the comparisons. Three different generations. Three completely different value systems. Three different planets. I know one thing. Today's teenagers are from Mars.

Mars Hill was the first-century equivalent of postmodern thought. It was truly the marketplace of ideas. It was also the place where Paul the apostle tangled with the best minds of his day. It is where he made the case for Christianity with the mental giants who represented the eclectic worldviews of the first century. But that audience was totally different from his Jewish audience. And they required a different strategy.

In the first century there were two broad categories of belief systems—monotheism and polytheism. There were those who believed in one God (the Jews) and those who believed in many gods (just about everyone else). Most of the evangelism examples in the book of Acts are focused on reaching the monotheistic Jews with the message that Jesus was the Christ. Because most Jews viewed the Scriptures as truth, the early apostles wielded the passages with precision and persuasion.

But what about those instances where the apostles were addressing the polytheistic Gentiles instead of the monotheistic Jews? The apostle Paul was a master at reaching both Jews and Gentiles with the timeless message of the gospel. But his technique changed when he spoke to each group. Why? Because one group accepted the Scriptures, believed in a promised Messiah, and feared God. The other group did not.

Paul used the special revelation of God's Word and biblical arguments to convince the Jews that Jesus was the Christ, and he used the natural revelation of creation and logic to convince the Gentiles. Acts 17 gives two examples of evangelistic outreach—one to the Jews and one to the Gentiles. In the first part of Acts 17 Paul's consistent strategy and technique for reaching the Jews is clearly demonstrated. It is built around Scripture texts and solid arguments. "As his custom was, Paul went into the synagogue, and on three Sabbath days he reasoned with them from the Scriptures, explaining and proving that the Christ had to suffer and rise from the dead" (Acts 17:2–3).

In Acts 17:18–21 we see Paul's strategy for reaching the Greeks with the message of the gospel:

> *A group of Epicurean and Stoic philosophers began to dispute with him. Some of them asked, "What is this babbler trying to say?" Others remarked, "He seems to be advocating foreign gods." They said this because Paul was preaching the good news about Jesus and the resurrection. Then they took him and brought him to a meeting of the Areopagus, where they said to him, "May we know what this new teaching is that you are presenting? You are bringing some strange ideas to our ears, and we want to know what they mean." (All the Athenians and the foreigners who lived there spent their time doing nothing but talking about and listening to the latest ideas.)*

The technique Paul used in reaching that audience of philosophers with the message of the gospel was a totally different and unique strategy from the one he used to reach the Jews. We will explore the parallels between how Paul reached the Athenians and how we can reach our students. But first let's look at something surprising.

THE ADVANTAGES OF EVANGELIZING
A POSTMODERN GENERATION

Advantages? That's hard to believe especially when we hear forecasts that our efforts will be futile among a relativist generation. Yet in spite of what the naysayers say, there are some definite advantages in reaching out to this postmodern generation.

ADVANTAGE #1—POSTMODERN TEENS
ARE MORE EXPERIENTIAL THAN LOGICAL

"The challenge lies before us to reach a generation that hears with its eyes and thinks with its feelings."[3]

Postmodern teens feel more than they think. How is that an advantage? Easy! Christianity is both experiential and logical. We have the tools to capture both the mind and the heart of the typical teenager today. Sometimes we forget that Christianity is meant to be experienced and felt as well as thought through and contemplated. It reaches both mind and heart. The historical books of the New Testament (Matthew through Acts) swell with emotion and experiential Christianity. Doctrine was the backbone of the early church, but emotions were the heart of it, ranging from unquenchable fury to unbelievable joy. Jesus weeps over disobedient Jerusalem, and then rages in the temple over religious rip-offs. The disciples flee the garden of Gethsemane in absolute terror, and then experience absolute shock and gladness over the resurrected Christ.

Those are just a few of the many emotional outbursts of the early church as recorded in the text. God is the maker of emotions. We can use that fact to reach students, or we can complain that teens today just don't care about truth. One boxer used to defend his body punching versus head-hunting style of pugilism by saying, "Kill the body and the head will die." Seize the heart of the teenager, and the head will follow. The question is, *Are you seizing the hearts of the visiting teenagers in your youth group?*

When visitors come to your youth group, do they feel the presence of God? I don't mean this in the incantation fashion. You know what I mean—those services where Christians try to conjure Him up by end-less repetitions of emotional worship songs until God finally "comes down" upon the auditorium. We need to be careful of becoming like the prophets of Baal on Mount Carmel. There is danger in singing and yelling and dancing—everything short of cutting ourselves—until there is an emotional response from the audience. Some worship lead-ers won't stop until the sacrifice is consumed by the fire of God. Unfortunately, the only thing burned is the newcomer who walks away thinking that Christianity is more smoke and mirrors than spir-it and truth.

So what am I talking about when I refer to visitors feeling the presence of God? I mean the unveiling of His person. He is already here. He is always here. Whether we feel Him or not, He is here. Truly effective worship leaders and teachers unveil His ever-present pres-ence. And when His presence is unveiled, everybody knows it.

God does not primarily work through the earthquake or hurricane or firestorm; rather, He is in the gentle whisper of the dusty details of everyday life. Do your visitors hear the whisper in your youth group? Is it too faint to be heard above the music or the teaching or the games? Or do they hear something gentle and quiet, powerful yet restrained? Do they sense something genuine and real? Do they feel something different?

That kind of atmosphere cannot be faked. It must be cultivated. It must flow from the heart of the leader into the heart of the youth group climate. It starts with you. It continues with your kids. It cul-minates with the visitor. The best way for your visitors to begin expe-riencing Christ is for you to experience Him every day. When they look at you, they will experience Him. You can't fake that.

ADVANTAGE #2—POSTMODERN TEENS ARE MORE OPEN TO SPIRITUAL IDEAS

Have you noticed that teens today are more open to talking about spiritual things than ever? If you haven't, go to your local teen hang-out and strike up some spiritual conversations. I have been initiating spiritual conversations with teenagers since I was a teenager in the late seventies and early eighties. I have never found teenagers more open to talk about "God and stuff" than right now. Kids are open to spiritual truth. The problem is that they are open to all types of spiritual input. We Christians have the better case! We must get in there and make that case for Christianity to them.

Although it is great to have a clever opening line or question, you don't have to be clever. You can just bring it up. If you share the gospel with a loving heart and a listening ear, you most likely have an audience with today's typical teenager. These teens can handle bluntness. What they can't handle is unwillingness to listen.

I want you to notice this phrasing in Acts 17:21: "All the Athenians and the foreigners who lived there spent their time doing nothing but talking about and listening to the latest ideas." That gives us an insight into the culture that Paul was talking to. They loved to talk about belief systems, philosophies, and religions. The philosophers on Mars Hill jawed about all sorts of ideas. And they were open to new ones. Starbucks may be the Mars Hill for one teenager, and for another it may be an Internet chat room. The point is that kids are open to hearing and sharing new ideas.

ADVANTAGE #3—POSTMODERN TEENAGERS LOVE A GOOD STORY

The fact that today's teens love stories is great news for youth leaders, senior pastors, evangelists, and Christian teens. Why? Because God's story is the greatest story ever told! We need to learn how to tell it in all of its fascinating glory. Like a great novel, it is full of twists and turns and intrigue. But unlike a novel, it is not fiction. It is a love story that just happens to be true.

Mike Metzger wrote, "If one reads carefully through the Bible, the reader will notice that the book follows the outline of great narrative. It has a beginning, a setting, characters and plot, conflict, and plot resolutions."[4] The story needs to be told with passion, excitement, and clarity to the postmodern mind.

PAUL'S TACTICS ON MARS HILL

With those advantages in mind, let's discover the tactics Paul used to reach his hillside audience with the gospel of Jesus Christ.

STRATEGY #1—HE USES AN ATTENTION GETTING OPENER THAT IS CULTURALLY RELEVANT.

In Acts 17:2–3 Paul is focused on reaching Jews in the synagogue, so his attention-grabbing introduction is probably, "Open your scrolls to . . ." But Paul doesn't start out that way with this audience. Why? Because this group opposes the Jews, and they don't accept the Scriptures as absolute truth. So instead of starting with the Scriptures, he starts with a great opening line: "Men of Athens! I see that in every way you are very religious. For as I walked around and looked carefully at your objects of worship, I even found an altar with this inscription: TO AN UNKNOWN GOD. Now what you worship as something unknown I am going to proclaim to you" (vv. 22–23).

Reaching kids in this culture for Christ is no different. It takes a great opening line . . . an attention grabber. The problem is that Christians are notoriously boring with their witnessing approaches. Your approach could be Socratic (focus on asking questions). It could be provocative (saying something hair-raising). It could be narrative (sharing a story or modern-day parable). But it must be creative.

Are you creative when you present students with the message of the gospel? That doesn't mean that you have to come up with something new every week. But it does mean that you are always aware of what is happening around you. Paul paid attention. As he made his way to Mars Hill, he noticed the many altars to false gods. Then he saw one with the unknown god inscription. *Aha! What a great opener!* he must have thought.

Those "Aha" experiences can happen when you are reading a newspaper or watching a movie. They can take place in the middle of a conversation or as you listen to the radio in the car. Always look for and pray for creative ways to bring up the subject of the gospel in an attention-getting way.

If you can't think of something new, there are some proven openers that seem to be timeless. The Evangelism Explosion opening question has been around for decades: "If you were to die tonight, do you know for sure that you would be in heaven?" Why does that question work so well? Because most postmodern people still believe in heaven, and the fact is that everybody is going to die someday.

Another question that gets the attention of today's teenagers is, "Do you have any spiritual beliefs?" Then let them talk. Ask them what they think about God, about Jesus, about heaven, about what happens after they die. When they are finished sharing their beliefs, then you can share yours.

The need for creativity applies to gospel tracts as well. How many times have you picked up a gospel tract that has bad artwork on the outside and outdated print on the inside? Some tracts make Christianity look bad. If the church were a marketing firm, we would go bust. If you choose to use gospel tracts, make sure they are sharp, clear, concise, and conversational. Too many tracts are too long and too boring. May the gospel presentations we give in verbal and written form reflect the God we serve in their creativity and excellence!

In our one-on-one evangelism with teenagers, sometimes we need to become better fielders than pitchers. Mike Metzger has some profound insights on pitching versus fielding in evangelism:

 In baseball, the pitcher pretty much controls the tempo of the game. . . . In the game of baseball, the pitcher dictates what kinds of pitches are delivered to the batter. When one observes most of the current training and approaches to evangelism the materials make a similar assumption—that Christian evangelists are the "pitchers" in the ongoing conversations in culture. Evangelism is often portrayed as being a presentation—a "pitch" if you will—with training in how to respond to the listener's questions. . . . By and large, postmodern people are not inclined to come and hear a Christian presentation. They long for conversation. Few want to play in the Christian ballpark anymore. Many of the well-intentioned evangelistic events don't make sense to the postmodern mind any-more—they are unintelligible. Evangelicals make the pitch—but no one is up to bat.

Evangelism in a postmodern world means that Christians are going to have to become better listeners. . . . In other words, evan-gelists need to become great listeners—able to "catch" whatever comes out to them, and turn it toward the story of the Gospel.[5]

It is easy to turn conversations with teenagers toward the gospel. It takes a few questions, a lot of listening, and the willingness to seize that magic moment. For some, responding to the gospel is a short jump, and for others, it is a long journey. Sometimes the process of evangelism and conversion can take place in a few minutes. Many times it is a long journey over the course of days, weeks, months, even years. But our responsibility is to verbally share the gospel with a lov-ing heart and listening ears.

STRATEGY #2—HE TELLS THE WHOLE STORY OF CHRISTIANITY, STARTING WITH CREATION.

Paul makes no assumptions about his audience. He starts at the very beginning: "The God who made the world and everything in it is the Lord of heaven and earth" (Acts 7:24).

He starts with Genesis 1, not Genesis 3. He doesn't begin with sin. He begins with the creation. Paul knows that unless his audience understands the beginning of the story, they won't get the end of the story. In Paul's day, a lot of theories were floating around about how life began. Paul clarifies that question up front. The same clarification must be made today.

Kids must understand that they are the result not of random chance but of divine design. The message of Christianity is that God made humanity unique and special, set apart from the rest of creation. When we share the gospel with students today, we must share the story, the whole story, and nothing but the story with them. The story doesn't start with sin. It starts with creation.

When presenting the gospel message, most Christians use the bad news/good news approach. The bad news is that we are sinners. The good news is that Christ died for our sins. But on Mars Hill, Paul used the good news/bad news/good news approach. He started with the good news of creation, continued with the bad news about sin, and finished with the good news about Jesus.

At Dare 2 Share Ministries we use a template for sharing the message of Jesus called the GOSPEL. Journey. It is not so much a method but a way of chronologically telling the whole story of the gospel message as it unfolds throughout the entire Bible!

God created us to be with Him.
Our sins separate us from God.
Sins cannot be removed by good deeds.
Paying the price for sin, Jesus died and rose again.
Everyone who trusts in Him alone has eternal life.
Life that is eternal means we will be with Jesus forever.

G: tells the story of Genesis 1 and 2.
O: tells the story of Genesis 3.
S: sums up the Israelites failure to achieve a relationship with God through good deeds, the Ten Commandments, and sacrificial system. We see this from Genesis 4 through Malachi 4.
P: tells the story of Matthew, Mark, and Luke.
E: is most of the New Testament from John through the book of Jude.
L: is found in Revelation as all of God's children will rule and reign with him forever!

This simple GOSPEL acrostic tells the whole story of Christianity from creation to sin to redemption and beyond. Whatever strategy you use to share the gospel with teens today, make sure it tells the whole story of Christianity.

STRATEGY #3—PAUL PAINTS THE
PICTURE OF A LOVING YET HOLY GOD.

The thrust of Paul's presentation is a benevolent God patiently waiting for humankind to come to Christ. "From one man he made every nation of men, that they should inhabit the whole earth; and he determined the times set for them and the exact places where they should live. God did this so that men would seek him and perhaps reach out for him and find him" (Acts 17:26–27).

Paul paints the gospel as a love story. He preaches a loving God who is patiently waiting for humanity to return to Him. That is why I like the GOSPEL acronym so much. It paints the same picture of a loving romance between God and the people He created. It is like a love story in six scenes (see chart below).

When sharing the gospel with students, we must keep in mind that the Bible is a love story, filled with all the elements of a good novel . . . romance, tragedy, broken hearts, sacrifice, second chances, and happily ever afters. The difference is this: the Bible is nonfiction.

Are you sharing the gospel as the good news that it is? For kids who often feel lonely, depressed, and unloved, it is especially vital that they hear the message for what it truly is—good news.

There is a downside that must be communicated as well. Paul communicates that downside clearly to his philosophizing audience: "For he has set a day when he will judge the world" (v. 31).

The Ultimate Love Story

SCENES	SCRIPT	CHARACTERS	SETTING	POINT
SCENE 1 The Sacred Romance	Genesis 1,2	Adam, Eve, Jesus	Garden of Eden	God created us to be with Him.
SCENE 2 The Broken Heart	Genesis 3	Adam, Eve, Jesus, Satan	Garden of Eden	Our sin separates us from God.
SCENE 3 The Devastating Separation	Genesis 4-Malachi 4	Jesus, Humanity, Satan	The World	Sins cannot be removed by our good deeds.
SCENE 4 The Climactic Sacrifice	Matthew-John	Jesus	Calvary	Paying the price for sin, Jesus died and rose again.
SCENE 5 The Second Chance	Acts-Revelation 20	Jesus, Humanity, Satan	The World	Everyone who trusts in Him alone has eternal life.
SCENE 6 The Happy Ending	Revelation 21, 22	Jesus and His Church	Heaven	Life that's eternal means we will be with Jesus forever.

To paraphrase the cliché, all good news and no bad news makes Jack a dull boy. The bad news is that sin separates us from God, in some cases eternally. When sin entered the picture, death was holding its hand. Those who die in sin without Christ awaken in hell without hope.

Don't forget the bad news. It makes the good news that much better.

STRATEGY #4—HE USES RELEVANT EXAMPLES.

Paul quotes secular poets to make spiritual points. "'For in him we live and move and have our being.' As some of your own poets have said, 'We are his offspring'" (Acts 17:28).

If Paul did that, why can't we? Why can't we show clips of secular movies to make spiritual points? Why can't we use music, television, and technology to pound home the truth? I am not talking about showing or quoting anything inappropriate. I am talking about lighting a candle instead of cursing the darkness. If we don't understand where our teens are at, we may miss them altogether. As George Barna observed:

 The pet peeve of the younger generation is irrelevance: they quickly abandon anything that is not wholly germane to their personal passions. They have significantly altered expectations and lifestyles through their demand that things foster shared experience and be "real," adventuresome, and memorable. They have little patience for anything based on tradition, customs, ease, or social acceptability. If they do not immediately sense the relevance of something, they dismiss it out of hand and move on to the next alternative.[6]

It is our responsibility as proclaimers of the good news to live in two worlds—the biblical world of truth and the secular world. In his powerful book *Between Two Worlds*, John Stott wrote, "A true sermon bridges the gulf between the biblical and the modern worlds, and must be equally earthed in both."[7] That is true for youth leaders as well.

STRATEGY #5—HE USES APOLOGETICS AS A P.S. TO THE LOVE LETTER OF THE GOSPEL.

At the end of his talk, Paul gives the ultimate apologetic—the resurrection of Jesus Christ from the dead. "He has given proof of this to all men by raising him from the dead" (Acts 17:31).

The resurrection is undeniably powerful proof that Jesus was who He claimed to be. More than five hundred witnesses saw Him over the course of forty days. Many of those witnesses died for their assertion that Jesus had risen from the dead. Paul hammers home his sermon with that powerful evidence.

Notice that Paul waits until the very end of his talk to make this apologetic point. Up to that point he is simply sharing a story. Then he says in essence, "Oh, by the way, guys, this story I just shared with you is absolutely true, and here is the proof. . . ." That's when he got a reaction from his hearers: "When they heard about the resurrection of the dead, some of them sneered, but others said, 'We want to hear you again on this subject'" (v. 32). In the minds of most of the philosophers on Mars Hill, the word proof was anathema, and the concept of resurrection was ludicrous. Paul was no longer talking in philosophical generalities. He was being dogmatic. That was as catalytic then as it is today.

In sharing the message of the gospel with postmodern students, we must be very careful how we use apologetics. We must not start out arguing. If we do, we will lose our audience right up front. We must start by sharing the story of the gospel persuasively and powerfully. At the right time we should say, "Oh, by the way, here's how we know it's true. . . ." That's when we will get the reaction—either positive or negative.

The gospel should be shared like a love letter. Apologetics should be tacked on like a P.S. Why? Because apologetics have never saved anyone. The gospel does that. Well-thought-out arguments support at best. But they do not save. They are important. But they are not as important as the gospel message.

When you use words like *proof* to the postmodern mind, you will often be met with a raised eyebrow. That's OK. Use it anyway. But use it as an epilogue, not as an introduction. Use it the way Paul used it on Mars Hill. Some will balk and others will believe.

As we present the love story of the gospel to students, we must never forget to present the catalytic reality that Jesus called Himself "the way," not "a way." Christianity is inclusive in the fact that everyone is welcome to believe. It is exclusive in the sense that those who don't are condemned to an eternity separated from the love of God.

The key is to share the gospel story as the better story that just happens to be true. We must be loving. We must learn to listen. But we must share the story as truth. Because it is true.

ULTIMATE REALITY

Just a few weeks ago I was in the mountains filming what I believe is the ultimate reality show. We had seven young people ranging in age from 16 to 20 in the rugged mountains of Colorado for six days. Why? To film a project called "GOSPEL Journey . . . the Ultimate Adventure."

These were not actors, and before this trip I had never met any of these young people. And they were, shall we say, an eclectic group. There was Andy the atheistic jock. There was Ashley, ex-Jehovah's Witness current party girl. In addition, we had an urban girl named Tasondra, an evangelical named Ben, a Hispanic Episcopalian named Eric, and a minister's daughter named Tiffany. Last, but certainly not least, we had Stephen, the loud and proud Wiccan who had something to prove.

Over the course of six days we went through the six parts of the GOSPEL Journey point by point. We tied in extreme challenges (rock climbing, repelling, rope courses, etc.) to be visual examples of these spiritual truths. Every day I shared with them a twenty to twenty-five minute talk on at least one of the points of the GOSPEL and then opened it up for discussion. And boy did we ever "discuss." There were questions, arguments, tears, and transformation.

Two of these young people put their faith and trust in Christ at the end of the week (you'll have to see the DVDs to find out who!).

What amazed me about this week is that these were teenagers whom I had absolutely no relationship with beforehand. We created a relationship around a dialogue about truth, theology, God, salvation, redemption, and sin. And these teens did more than just sit there. They engaged! As a matter of fact, long after the lessons and official interaction times were over, these teenagers initiated the conversations on their own! One of the best conversations took place in a hot tub. The talk was as hot and brisk as the water they were sitting in. The camera crew rushed to set up the cameras to catch the moments like these that were totally spontaneous.

At the end of it all I talked to one of our producers who was there the whole time. She told me that she had assumed that these teenagers would put up with my talks about God and then change the conversation to other more "relevant" subjects as soon as the cameras stopped rolling. But this week changed her thinking. She told me that what she saw this week was that the actual gospel message spurred these teens to conversations totally on their own. That's almost all they talked about, sometimes up to two or three in the morning when all the cameramen were in bed. She was shocked and rocked at how these postmodern, mostly unchurched teens were longing to talk, to *really* talk, about these truths.

What does all this mean for you and your teens? Simple. Life is a reality show. Don't miss it. Don't let your teens miss it. Get them to engage their friends in loving and compelling ways with the overarching story of God. The simple gospel truth is compelling enough to launch a conversation, build a relationship, and transform a life.

What did I learn from my adventure in the mountains? I learned that the principles that Paul used on Mars Hill with a group of Greek philosophers work just as well 2,000 years later in the Rocky Mountains with a group of postmodern teenagers. I learned that these twenty-first century teens aren't just open to engage about spiritual subjects, they are longing to connect spiritually on the deepest level. I learned that much of the prevailing thought about reaching this generation is way too convoluted, complicated, and confusing. It comes down to the simple reality that the gospel "is the power of God for the salvation of everyone who believes" Romans 1:16. The simple gospel is enough, enough to convert the soul, any soul, especially the soul of the postmodern teenager. ✖

RED·DOT REVIEW

THE OLD-TIME GOSPEL CAN
STILL INFECT A POSTMODERN WORLD!

MONKEY MANDATE

STAFF
INFECTION
QUESTIONS

MANDATE

Write out the gospel in a letter to a typical postmodern teenager using the five strategies utilized by Paul in Acts 17.

1. Use an attention-getting opener that is culturally relevant.

2. Tell the whole story of Christianity starting with creation.

3. Paint a picture of a loving, yet holy, God.

4. Use relevant examples.

5. Use apologetics as the P.S.

#1. How would you defend the concept that the gospel is still relevant in this postmodern world?

#2. Read each others letters from the Monkey Mandate. What do you think of each letter and how well it communicates the gospel to a typical postmodern student?

#3. What movies, songs, and media could we review to better understand the postmodern mind-set?

#4. How could we create our own GOSPEL Journey experience for the teenagers in our youth group and their unreached friends?

HOW TO GIVE
AN INFECTIOUS INVITATION

What do dirty syringes and dirty sex have in common? You guessed it. They are two of the primary ways that the devastating HIV virus spreads from victim to victim. If the HIV virus were a bullet, those would be its two biggest guns.

HIV by itself is powerless. It must have someone to infect and some way to infect him or her. That's where needles and naughtiness come into the picture. They spread death from victim to victim without regard to race, religion, or gender. A virus is looking for a warm host, and any potential corpse will do.

The major reason that the AIDS epidemic infected the sex and drug cultures so thoroughly is because each of those groups has a vehicle to carry the virus from victim to victim . . . sex and syringes. Viruses need vehicles. Without them, outbreaks and epidemics would never take place.

The same is true of spiritual epidemics. There must be a vehicle to transport the virus to the "victim." In the youth group setting that vehicle is the invitation. Listen to the apostle Peter's invitation: "With many other words he warned them; and he pleaded with them, 'Save yourselves from this corrupt generation'" (Acts 2:40).

If an evangelistic epidemic is going to spread through your youth group, you must learn not only to present the gospel clearly but also to give an infectious invitation. Youth leaders who are effectively unleashing the virus through their youth groups have mastered the invitation process.

Every great evangelist knows the value of the invitation. For five decades Billy Graham traveled the world preaching the message of the gospel. I am sure it is safe to say that in every crusade he has ever done he has given an invitation to the lost to trust in Christ as their Savior. Now Franklin Graham has picked up his father's awesome mantle and over the next several decades as, God willing, Franklin continues his dad's work, there will continue to be invitations given at those powerful outreach events.

An invitation is a sacred moment. In that moment there is a hush in both heaven and hell. All of the angels in heaven are looking down, and all the demons in hell are looking up in breathless anticipation. In that holy moment, an individual chooses whether to accept or reject Christ's finished work on the cross. It is that blessed and momentous occasion where a sinner is invited to become a saint. When that decision is made, all of heaven breaks out in a party, and all of the fallen angels break out in tears.

Some people discount invitations as relics of the past. They consider them to be emotional and manipulative rantings of insecure preachers who need to measure their preaching power by the sheer number of people who respond. Unfortunately, sometimes they are right. We have all seen invitations abused. But that abuse shouldn't make us unbalanced in our approach to evangelism. An invitation tempered by the proper amounts of wisdom, persuasion, and love can be a powerful and effective tool to bring people into the kingdom of God.

The invitation process involves a certain urgency that is unmistakable. More than a century ago, D. L. Moody was doing a Sunday night preaching series on the life of Christ.

 On the fifth Sunday night, October 8th, he preached to the largest congregation that he had ever addressed in that city, having taken for his text, "What then shall I do with Jesus which is called Christ?" After preaching . . . he said, "I wish you would take this text home with you and turn it over in your minds during the week, and next Sabbath we will come to Calvary and the cross, and we will decide what to do with Jesus of Nazareth."

Later, Moody lamented:

What a mistake! I have never dared to give an audience a week to think of their salvation since. If they were lost they might rise up in judgment against me. . . . I have never seen that congregation since. I have worked hard to keep back the tears today. . . . I want to tell you one lesson I learned that night, which I have never forgotten, and that is, when I preach, to press Christ upon the people then and there, and try to bring them to a decision on the spot. I would rather have my right hand cut off than to give an audience now a week to decide what to do with Jesus.[1]

What happened to traumatize the great evangelist so deeply that he determined never to preach again without giving a direct and bold invitation? The great Chicago fire of 1871. As he preached that night, Chicago was burning. In just a few hours the building where he had been preaching was reduced to ashes. He never saw those people again. He had missed his opportunity to invite them to Christ. But he would never miss such an opportunity again.

You may be thinking that is fine for the evangelist in a crusade setting, but what does it have to do with you? The answer is simple: Every youth group meeting should be a crusade.

Paul told Timothy, who wasn't naturally gifted as an evangelist, to "do the work of an evangelist" (2 Timothy 4:5). I am begging you to do the same thing. Use your weekly youth group meeting as your crusade setting. At the end of every youth group meeting, give the gospel and give an invitation.

What does an effective invitation look like? Once again the book of Acts holds the answer.

> *"Therefore let all Israel be assured of this: God has made this Jesus, whom you crucified, both Lord and Christ." When the people heard this, they were cut to the heart and said to Peter and the other apostles, "Brothers, what shall we do?" Peter replied, "Repent and be baptized, every one of you, in the name of Jesus Christ for the forgiveness of your sins. And you will receive the gift of the Holy Spirit. The promise is for you and your children and for all who are far off—for all whom the Lord our God will call." With many other words he warned them; and he pleaded with them, "Save yourselves from this corrupt generation." Those who accepted his message were baptized, and about three thousand were added to their number that day. (Acts 2:36–41)*

A contagious invitation has three elements:

1. It is preceded by a clear presentation of the gospel.
2. It continues with a simple invitation to believe.
3. It culminates with an opportunity to respond publicly.

Each of those elements is essential to the contagious invitation. On the birthday of the church all three were used to initiate the first viral event of the body of Christ. In response, more than three thousand men (and probably thousands more women and children) were added to the church that day. Let's examine the three elements of an infectious invitation.

1. IT IS PRECEDED BY A CLEAR PRESENTATION OF THE GOSPEL.

Peter pulled no punches with the Jews who were gathered at the temple for the celebration of Pentecost. He quickly and effectively wielded the Old Testament Scriptures and then plunged the sharp blade deep into the souls of his hearers.

As Peter fired off verse after verse to his Jewish audience, he made his case with astonishing precision and power. Within just a few minutes he had clearly presented the gospel to thousands of Jews who had come from all over the early world.

Peter proved that Jesus was not only the Christ, the Messiah Himself, but also God the Son. Peter bellowed in his climactic closing argument, "God has made this Jesus, whom you crucified, both Lord and Christ" (Acts 2:36). The Messiah who had come to deliver them from the tyranny of the Romans had been murdered by the treachery of the Jews. What was the crowd's response? "They were cut to the heart" (v. 37). That crowd was shaken and shocked. The church exploded that day from a small group Bible study into a megachurch.

Peter made three truths crystal clear to his deluded Jewish audience: who Jesus was, why Jesus came, and what Jesus offered. Those are the same three truths that every clear presentation of the gospel contains.

WHO JESUS WAS

Jesus hit the crux of the issue with His disciples in Matthew 16:13: "Who do people say the Son of man is?" They responded, "Some say John the Baptist; others say Elijah; and still others, Jeremiah or one of the prophets" (v. 14). Jesus then asked who they thought He was. Peter nailed it, "You are the Christ, the Son of the living God" (v. 16).

Entrance into heaven is only possible through Jesus Christ Himself. That may not sell well in this free-for-all culture of have-it-your-way religion. But that's the way that it is. Our students must understand that in this culture of "tolerance," such a proclamation will not be tolerated. As they share the gospel with their friends, they will be accused of being intolerant and closed minded. That is inevitable because Jesus made Christianity exclusive when He proclaimed, "I am the way and the truth and the life. No one comes to the Father except through me" (John 14:6). God does not tolerate any other pathway to Him than His Son.

As you prepare your teenagers to be outbreak evangelists, you must constantly enable them to walk the tightrope of balance between the two poles of boldness and love. As they share the message of Jesus Christ, they must be authoritative without being arrogant, they must be confident without being condescending, they must be daring without being demeaning. Each word must be drenched in love and empowered by the Spirit. They must learn to listen first and speak later. But when they do speak, they must speak without flinching, having utter confidence in the absolute truth of God's Word.

Equipping our students to share the gospel begins with helping them to share who Jesus is to their audience. He is God Himself.

WHY JESUS CAME

Peter makes clear in his Acts 2 sermon that Jesus came to die. Although his Jewish audience knew that they were the ones who had initiated the execution, Peter shows that it was all part of God's eternal plan.

> *"Men of Israel, listen to this: Jesus of Nazareth was a man accredited by God to you by miracles, wonders and signs, which God did among you through him, as you yourselves know. This man was handed over to you by God's set purpose and foreknowledge; and you, with the help of wicked men, put him to death by nailing him to the cross. But God raised him from the dead, freeing him from the agony of death, because it was impossible for death to keep its hold on him." (Acts 2:22–24)*

Peter is saying in essence, "Make no mistake about it: Jesus came to die." Why? Later Peter makes it clear: "For the forgiveness of your sins" (v. 38). Most of the Jews were looking for (and still are looking for) the Christ to deliver them from the oppression of tyranny, while establishing His kingdom. But they somehow missed the Old Testament passages that spoke clearly of a suffering Messiah (Psalm 22; Isaiah 53; etc.).

Once they understood who Jesus was and why He came, the response was dramatic and traumatic: "When the people heard this, they were cut to the heart" (v. 37). After realizing that they had killed the Messiah who came to deliver them, their consciences were shredded with conviction. Now they were ready for the third component of the gospel message.

WHAT JESUS OFFERS

Jesus offers the forgiveness of sins. What the law of God could not do, the Son of God could. The law offered judgment. It represented the righteousness of God, the unattainable standard, and the demanding qualifications for entrance into heaven. The Son offers forgiveness. He represents the righteousness of God imputed, the unattainable standard reached, and the demanding qualifications satisfied. There is only one requirement . . . repentance.

Once you have made a clear presentation of the gospel, you are ready for the second component of effective invitations.

2. IT CONTINUES WITH A SIMPLE INVITATION TO BELIEVE.

In Acts 2:38 Peter gives his audience a simple invitation to believe. He makes clear that the road to heaven is paved with repentance. In many ways repentance and faith are synonyms. When you believe, you repent; and when you repent, you believe. In Scripture they are often used as synonyms. When God commands you to believe, He is commanding you to repent and vice versa. Repentance is not separate from belief. In the context of presenting the gospel, repentance is belief. If they were two separate acts or steps, they would each be identified explicitly throughout Scripture as the way of salvation. Yet the words are used separately and interchangeably. "Repentance and faith can be used in some passages as synonyms. This is easy to explain because any time one shifts his trust from himself to God and believes that Jesus is God, he has changed his perspective; he has repented."[2]

The word *repent* simply means "to change your mind." The context in which it is used in the New Testament determines what the change of mind is about. For the Jews in Peter's audience, it was a change of mind about who Jesus was. They had viewed Him as some renegade rabbi. But Peter makes clear that He was much, much more. "'Therefore let all Israel be assured of this: God has made this Jesus, whom you crucified, both Lord and Christ.' When the people heard this, they were cut to the heart and said to Peter and the other apostles, 'Brothers, what shall we do?'" (Acts 2:36–37).

Peter's response is simple: Repent. In essence, he is saying to his audience, "Change your mind about who Jesus is, why Jesus came, and what Jesus offers!" Isn't that what belief is? Isn't that the essence of faith?

Our charge in youth ministry is to get students to repent. We must call them to change their minds about who Jesus is. The students out there who are trusting in Allah instead of Jesus must repent. They must see Christ as the only way and trust in Him alone. We must get them to repent of their view of why Jesus came. He didn't come to live a good life and show a good example. He came to die for our sins, be buried, and rise again. We must challenge them to repent of what they are trusting in to get them into heaven. Jesus offers salvation through faith alone in the finished work of the cross. The teens who accept Mormonism as the way of salvation must repent and see the true Jesus of the Bible as the only way to eternal forgiveness. Those who are trusting in their good deeds must change their minds from a trying mentality to a trusting mentality. The reception of salvation requires an absolutely different way of thinking. It demands dependence in a world that respects independence. It demands believing in a world that respects achieving.

When students repent (change their minds about who Jesus is, why Jesus came, and what Jesus offers), they believe (trust in what Jesus did on the cross). As a result, they receive the free gift of eternal life. That is a simple message. It is the message that Peter preached on the day of Pentecost. It is the message that we must preach every week in our youth group meetings.

BE PERSUASIVE

"With many other words he warned them; and he pleaded with them, 'Save yourselves from this corrupt generation'" (Acts 2:40).

Peter wasn't passive. He was persuasive. He warned his audience of the consequences of not believing. Another way of saying that is that he showed them the drawbacks. Or another way is to say that he scared them. Now we must be careful with this, but the invitation is a great time to talk about the drawbacks of rejection of Jesus Christ. Loneliness is a drawback. Hopelessness is a drawback. Hell is a pretty big drawback too.

"He pleaded with them." Peter begged his audience to believe. And guess what? He was passionate and emotional.

Sometimes people complain that invitations are manipulative and emotional. They should never be manipulative, but they should always be emotional. To reach postmodern students we must seize their hearts. There are some things that we should be emotional about. The eternal destiny of the kids in our youth group is one of them. How emotional do you think we will be on the day of the great white throne judgment when every unbeliever is condemned to the unquenchable flames of an inescapable hell? We need to preach now the way we will feel then. We need to preach with fire so that they won't feel the flame. We should be at least as passionate and persuasive as we would be if we were trying to talk a suicidal person down from a ledge. Why? Because in this instance the ledge is indecision and the landing is the abyss.

3. IT CULMINATES WITH AN
OPPORTUNITY TO RESPOND PUBLICLY.

Let's play some word association. When I say the words *respond publicly*, what comes to mind? Let me guess. "Altar call" or "raised hands" or something like that? When we think of responding publicly in the context of youth group or a church service, we get visions of a Billy Graham outreach meeting—new converts flooding the aisles as "Just As I Am" plays in the background.

If you were to play this same word association game with the early church, the results would have been a little different. Say the words *respond publicly* to one of those Christians, and the words *water baptism* were their first response. Why? To them water baptism was the first step toward discipleship. It was the public proclamation of the inward transformation. It was a way of saying to the watching world, "Hey! I am a Christian now, and I am not ashamed! Watch! As I am being immersed into this river, it symbolizes my being immersed into this new group and this new lifestyle."

We have formalized baptism now that we have taken it out of the river and brought it into the church. Once upon a time when a non-Christian became a Christian, the response was immediate, dramatic, and public. But we have turned it from an immediate act of obedience after salvation into the culmination of a four-week class on baptism long after a person has become a Christian.

Maybe that's one of the reasons we don't have more committed believers earlier in the game. If more new believers made this public proclamation earlier in the process, perhaps surrender to Christ would occur sooner, bigger, and stronger.

The only case we see in Scripture of believers who did not make a public proclamation of their faith and trust in Jesus Christ is in John 12:42–43. "Yet at the same time many even among the leaders believed in him. But because of the Pharisees they would not confess their faith for fear they would be put out of the synagogue; for they loved praise from men more than praise of God." The apostle John says that the leaders believed in Christ. But they didn't publicly identify with Him.

As a result, they didn't mature as quickly because they "loved praise from men more than praise of God."

Today the call to the altar has replaced the call to baptism in many churches and in many youth groups. In some churches there is neither call at all.

Baptism doesn't save, but it does brand. Think about how important branding is in the business world. It is that symbol that strikes recognition in the minds of potential customers. When you see the swoosh, you think of Nike. When you see a big yellow M, you think of McDonald's. When you see the trusty green emblem, you think of Starbucks (where I am typing these words right now).

What does that have to do with you and your invitation? A lot. Peter asked his audience to "repent and be baptized." Change your mind (repentance), and then change your affiliations (baptism). Make the internal decision (repentance) and then the public proclamation (baptism). Get saved, and then get branded. Baptism is the Nike swoosh of Christianity. It is the symbol that represents the substance.

Are there any steps in between the internal decision and the external ordinance? Yes. Even for the early disciples there was a walk down the aisle, so to speak, not to the altar but to the river or lake where they were being baptized. That walk from the place of internal decision to the place of water baptism was their personal walk of death. As their friends and family watched them walk toward the water, they knew there would be a new priority in the life of the new believer. Baptism was the symbol of their death to their old lifestyle and their rebirth in newness of life.

That walk of death is vitally important in their new life. I am convinced that the more public the walk of death is, the more likely it is that the new believer will make a long-term commitment that will stick. The walk from repentance to baptism can be the most important decision the new believer makes. Perhaps part of that walk includes having them raise their hands or walk an aisle after they have trusted in Jesus Christ as their Savior.

THE BOWED HEADS/CLOSED EYES/
RAISED HANDS APPROACH

I like to use the bowed heads/closed eyes/raised hands approach because it allows a student to make an internal decision without having to worry about being singled out. Often a request for an immediate public response such as walking up an aisle turns a student from thinking about the message of the gospel to thinking about standing up in front of his or her peers. Although I believe it is vital that new believers make a public proclamation soon after they believe, I also am convinced that we must be sure that the public response does not short circuit their true conversion.

Warning! Many churches make new believers walk an aisle before they explain how to get to heaven. Pastors and youth pastors say something like, "If you want to get saved today, then come down to the altar and one of counselors will tell you how." I disagree with this approach because it puts the focus on a decision to walk an aisle rather than on the finished work of Christ and our inability to save ourselves. "The altar call has become the climax and culmination of the entire meeting. Many stanzas of a hymn are sung, during which time all kinds of appeals are made to the sinner to walk the aisle, and the clear impression is given to the sinner that his eternal destiny hangs on this movement of his feet."[3] We must be sure that we don't mistake walking an aisle with coming to Christ. There will be people in hell who made their way forward to the altar but never found Jesus.

Usually after sharing the gospel I say something like this:

Can you please bow your heads and close your eyes? If today, in the quietness of your heart, you have put your faith and trust in Jesus Christ as your Savior, I would like to pray for you. In just a minute, with all heads bowed and eyes closed, I am going to ask those of you who understood that message for the very first time to let me know who you are by simply raising your hand and putting it back down quickly. Now, raising your hand doesn't get you to heaven, it just lets me know who you are so I can pray for you. So with your heads bowed and eyes closed, if what I said made sense and you are putting your faith and trust in Jesus Christ for the very first time today, will you simply raise your hand and put it back down?

I then acknowledge those who raise their hands by saying, "God bless you." Often I will ask them to look at me while everybody else's head is bowed with their eyes closed. In those precious few moments I welcome them into God's family and let them know that I want to help them grow in their newfound faith. That connects them with me and makes follow-up an easier process. After preaching for more than a decade at the same church, I found that to be the most effective way of identifying new believers. It is simple. It is nonthreatening. But it gives the new believer a practical way to begin the process of public response.

It also has some benefits for the rest of the believers who have their heads bowed and their eyes closed. For one, it allows them to enter into the celebration. When they hear the words "God bless you" acknowledging someone who is coming to Christ, they get pumped about what God is up to in their midst. Furthermore, they can enter into the battle of spiritual warfare. It reminds them to pray for unbelievers to respond in faith to the invitation. It causes the whole body of Christ in that youth group to call out to God for His sovereign hand to move in the hearts of the unbelievers. Finally, it enables them to know that something is happening in their youth group. It reminds them to bring their friends who don't know Christ so that they can hear and believe the message of the gospel of Jesus Christ.

Once again, it is very important to follow up every public gospel presentation with a public opportunity to respond. That public response is a baby step toward the baptismal, the public branding of the new believer as part of the team.

THE HIDDEN BENEFITS OF BAPTISM

When someone comes to Christ, baptism should follow as quickly as possible. As long as the new believer understands that baptism is not a requirement for salvation, it is vitally important that he or she be branded as part of the body of Christ. One of the results of baptism is that it causes the entire congregation to celebrate. It celebrates a changed life and a newfound faith. It is the birthday party for the new believer. But others outside the spiritual family should be invited as well. Unbelieving family and friends should be cordially invited to witness and celebrate the baptism. It is a testimony to the watching world that the new Christian believes that Jesus is Lord!

I will never forget baptizing some teenagers at a reservoir in Wyoming. As we stood in the water, I noticed that several people on the shore were watching the celebration. After the baptism, I walked out of the water with the teenagers, and one family waved me over. They asked me what was going on. So I told them. Over the next several minutes I was able to share with them the good news of the gospel of Jesus Christ. They were very receptive. As I walked away, I couldn't help but think that kind of scenario was probably a common occurrence with the first-century Christians. As new believers were baptized publicly in the local river or lake or sea (as opposed to a baptismal tucked away in a church building), people would talk. The gospel would be presented, and more people would "walk the aisle" to take the next step of baptism.

The goal is to get each student who comes to your youth group to take the steps between repentance and baptism as soon as possible. Each step is increasingly public and powerful. Each step takes them one step closer to spiritual maturity. But it all starts with the invitation.

Never underestimate the power of an infectious invitation. Peter didn't. ✖

RED•DOT REVIEW

AN EFFECTIVE INVITATION IS
FOUNDATIONAL TO VIRAL EVANGELISM!

MONKEY MANDATE

STAFF INFECTION QUESTIONS

MANDATE
Commit yourself to give an effective invitation every time you share the gospel.

#1. Why is it important to give an invitation every time we give the gospel?

#2. How can we be more effective at taking students from decision to discipleship in the youth group setting?

#3. What tools and training do we need to make available to our e-team to help in the discipleship process?

VIRAL FAILURES

When we think of plagues, we think of AIDS, Ebola, anthrax spores, and, of course, the Black Death. But in 1918 the Great Flu Epidemic killed an estimated 40 million people virtually overnight. If such a plague returned today, taking a comparable percentage of the U.S. population with it, 1.5 million Americans would die.[1]

I t was quick. It was deadly. Then it was gone. "It swept the globe in months, ending when the war did. It went away as mysteriously as it appeared. And when it was over, humanity had been struck by a disease that killed more people in a few months' time than any other illness in the history of the world."[2] That killer flu was so deadly that the average life expectancy dropped by twelve years in 1918. But by 1919, the average life expectancy was almost back to normal. Even today, scientists are perplexed by that quick-moving epidemic that claimed so much and then, almost magically, disappeared.

In evaluating the great flu epidemic of 1918, I am reminded of the fast and furious pace of the viral spread of Christianity in the first century. I am also reminded of how much of the mysterious momentum of exponential evangelism seemed to suddenly disappear by the second century. Like the epidemic of influenza in 1918, it was gone almost as fast as it came.

By the end of his life, the apostle John was the sole survivor among the early apostles. He had lived through beatings and torture. He was broken and boiled in oil. He had seen the glory days of the church in its inception. He had also witnessed the slow cooling of much of the spiritual awakening that characterized the early church. Now an old man sentenced by Rome to spend the rest of his days in exile on the island of Patmos, John received an apocalyptic vision that we call the book of Revelation.

Typically when Christians think of the book of Revelation, they ponder the seven seals, the Antichrist, and the beast. You know, *Left Behind* end-times stuff. But that focus causes us to miss the power of the beginning of this amazing book. Whereas the last nineteen chapters of Revelation give us a glimpse of our future as humans, chapters 2–3 give us a glimpse of our past as a church.

Fifty-one verses chronicle the fall of the early church from viral revival to contained Christianity. The seven churches that were scattered throughout the province of Asia were once ablaze with the power and presence of Christ, but most of them had faltered. The blaze of praise had turned to a flicker of faith. The hurricane of holiness had become the whisper of worldliness. John wrote to remind them of the holy epidemic that had been squelched by their sin and indifference.

Five out of seven churches that were once on fire were in danger of having their candles snuffed out altogether. Jesus warned one congregation, "If you do not repent, I will come to you and remove your lampstand from its place" (Revelation 2:5). Jesus was telling them that they were in danger of losing the power of His presence in their midst. Somehow those five churches had digressed from the awakening we see in the book of Acts to the point where they were involved with immoral practices, false doctrine, or, worst of all, lukewarm Christianity.

Those five churches were viral failures. As a result, the message of the gospel was quenched, and the manifest power of the Lord was thwarted. John, the apostle who had rested his head upon the chest of Christ at the Last Supper, the one who had witnessed the gruesome crucifixion of Christ firsthand, the first apostle to witness the empty tomb, the one who had witnessed Christ's ascension into the skies and the descent of Christ's Spirit upon each of the disciples on the day of Pentecost, the one who had seen the movement of awakening that started in Jerusalem and spread like an epidemic across the globe— now he was witnessing something else: the institutionalization of the church.

These passages have contemporary application. "Many of the evils and shortcomings which exist in the church today are a direct outgrowth of neglect of the solemn instruction given to these seven churches."[3] Each of the five failing churches had characteristics that we see in youth groups that have lost their spiritual energy and are in danger of losing power. Those ancient churches bring practical lessons to the modern movement of youth ministry.

As we discuss each of these viral failures, ask yourself one question, "Which of these churches describes my youth group?" For the last several chapters we have constantly referred to the success stories in the book of Acts to guide us in building and reshaping our youth ministries. Now let's look at some examples of what not to do.

THEY LEFT THEIR FIRST LOVE

"To the angel of the church in Ephesus write: These are the words of him who holds the seven stars in his right hand and walks among the seven golden lampstands: I know your deeds, your hard work and your perseverance. I know that you cannot tolerate wicked men, that you have tested those who claim to be apostles but are not, and have found them false. You have persevered and have endured hardships for my name, and have not grown weary. Yet I hold this against you: You have forsaken your first love." (Revelation 2:1–4)

The Ephesian church started with a bang and was ending with a whimper. In the beginning, the Ephesian believers, many of whom were led to Christ during Paul's third missionary journey, were on fire for Christ. They were the ones who were trained in Paul's two-year training stint at the school of Tyrannus. They were the ones who in two short years reached "all the Jews and Greeks who lived in the province of Asia" (Acts 19:10) with the message of the gospel of Jesus Christ. The Ephesian believers became the prototype for revival and awakening. They were viral in their Christianity . . . in the beginning. Now they were viral failures. What happened?

Spiritual movements tend to become institutionalized. The movement John Wesley helped to launch is a clear example of that. Methodism started as a kind of holy rebellion against the staunch legalism of the Church of England. Although Wesley himself was an Anglican priest, he was often prevented from speaking in Anglican pulpits. So he took to the fields. Thousands would gather in city after city and town after town to hear the cantankerous open-air communicator who preached the strange doctrine of salvation by faith alone in the finished work of Christ. Although Wesley's desire was to reform the Anglican Church, he ended up unintentionally leading a quasi-rebellion against it. Thus the Methodist movement was born.

Methodism attracted an intense group of followers. They met in small groups of five to ten people called "bands." Bands did not meet in local churches, and people from different religious backgrounds could attend as long as they were Christian. "Band members were expected to abstain from doing evil, to be zealous in good works, including giving to the poor and to use all means of grace."[4] In addition, members were expected to meet at least once per week in their band meeting, to be on time to that meeting, to confess their specific sins to each other, and to pray for each other.

Wesley established a small army of lay preachers who traveled the countryside to preach the gospel and minister to those involved with the bands. Those itinerant preachers "were taught to manage difficulties in the societies [a group of bands], to face mobs, to brave any weather, to subsist without means, except such as might casually occur on their routes, to rise at four and preach at five o'clock, to scatter books and tracts, to live by rule and to die without fear."[5] And they did! Wesley recruited and trained thousands of tough-minded, blue-collar itinerate preachers to fan the flames of revival all across England

and much of America during his lifetime. Under Wesley, the Methodist movement was evangelistic, on fire, and passionate.

Under his leadership, Methodism was also advancing and adventurous (although somewhat legalistic). It was driven by a Great Commission mind-set. Its members were rebelling against the religious system that stifled the spiritual passions of the people of God. But as the years gave way to decades and the decades to centuries, Methodism began to look more like the church it once rebelled against than Wesley's brand of spiritual revolution. Generally speaking, Methodists of the twenty-first century are totally unlike their eighteenth-century counterparts. No longer are they the rebels outside the system; now they are the typical church attendees within the system. Evangelism is no longer the driving force behind Methodism. Although I know firsthand of many Methodist churches across the country that are serious about sharing their faith and advancing the kingdom (and they are probably much more balanced in their approach than Wesley was), generally speaking, the fires of revival are now smoldering embers. Institutionalization is the fire extinguisher of spiritual movements, not only on a denominational level but also on a typical youth group level.

YOUTH PASTOR MIKE

Mike started his quest into youth ministry about twenty-five years ago. He is a lifer. Two decades ago he made a lifelong commitment to youth ministry. By God's grace he plans to retire as a youth pastor.

When Mike began his trek into youth ministry in the mid-seventies, it was at the apex of the Jesus Movement. Larry Norman and Keith Green burst onto the fledgling Christian music scene with a message behind their music. Tens of thousands of young, happy hippies who were tired of the drug scene came to Christ in droves. These "Jesus people" had a new kind of drug. They no longer needed the needle or the pill or the bottle. They had the Lord. And, as the song goes, Jesus was "just all right with them."

Back then youth ministry seemed simpler. It wasn't about programs and policies, schedules, or annual retreats. It was about loving Jesus. All that other stuff just happened.

Innocent and idealistic nineteen-year-old Mike arrived at his first youth pastorate armed with a love for Jesus and a one-year certificate from a local unaccredited Bible college. He didn't care that the church that had hired him didn't have enough budget for a full salary. He was going to lead the Jesus revolution in his city, whatever it took.

Soon he had weekly meetings that numbered well over one hundred students in attendance. Kids were coming to Christ in droves. They had Communion every week and baptisms every month during the youth meeting itself.

Some parents started complaining. They didn't view Mike as a real pastor. They didn't think he should be baptizing kids or serving Communion. And the kids that came to Christ in droves seemed to be leaving the youth group almost as fast as they came. There was a lot of fallout, a lot of complaints, and a lot of conversions. Eventually, the senior pastor started to chime in. He pulled Mike aside again and again and warned him against "letting things get out of hand."

To address those growing complaints, Mike decided to enroll in a local, accredited Christian college and take night school classes until he could graduate with a real degree. It took six years, but he finally achieved his goal.

During that six-year stint, he read everything he could find about organizing and administrating youth ministry. He diligently applied and tweaked those principles until his youth group was a well-oiled machine. His ministry became so effective that he started getting offers from all across the nation.

By that time the Jesus Movement had died out, but youth ministry was in a growth mode. Now seminars were being offered and idea books were available. But in spite of the programization of his youth ministry, Mike still loved Jesus with all of his heart and so did most of his kids. Newly ordained with six years of hard work under his belt, he had earned the respect of his pastor, his peers, and the parents of his youth group teens.

He finally accepted an offer from one of the big churches that was courting him. He took on the new job with a flurry of fire. Big churches need big organization. The last youth pastor was a great guy but a lousy administrator. Under the former regime, the youth ministry had dwindled in attendance. It was time for a change. Mike was the guy for the job.

In no time, he turned things around. The midweek meeting surged in attendance and Sunday school was at an all-time high. But in the midst of all the change one thing got left in the dust—his passion for God. He forgot the fundamental building block of an effective youth ministry—modeling and multiplying a love for God.

Today Mike runs his youth ministry with an exacting schedule. Next summer's junior high and senior high camps are already planned. A top-notch youth speaker and musician have already been recruited. Wednesday night youth meetings, Sunday morning teaching schedule, and youth leadership staff meetings have been planned for the next two quarters. For Mike, youth ministry has become a science. Add the ingredients of fun games, great worship, quality teaching, yearly missions trips, and the right amount of adult sponsors and a successful youth ministry is born. Or is it?

What we don't see behind the flash of a large youth ministry budget and an externally successful youth ministry program is the true spiritual condition of the teenagers. Many of them are going through the motions of attending youth ministry because Mom and Dad make them go or because their friends are going or because it's fun. Mike has made the mistake of putting his primary focus on building a youth ministry structure instead of starting a spiritual movement. Like the church of Ephesus, all the external actions are fine. But the heart is gone—the heart of passion for Christ, the heart of brokenness over the lost, the heart of servanthood toward the body.

Most of Mike's kids will leave the church completely after they graduate from high school. They will forsake their roots because they were never that deep to begin with. In the midst of tight schedules, fun games, and the latest and greatest in youth ministry paradigms, Mike has forgotten the fundamental rule of youth ministry: give them a love for Jesus first, and everything else will fall into place.

Mike is a great youth leader from an external standpoint but a viral failure from God's. He has left his first love. Please allow me take a little liberty with the first few verses of 1 Corinthians 13:

> *If I speak like Louie Giglio and Doug Fields, but have not love, I am only a resounding gong or a clanging cymbal. If I have the gift of administration and can organize any youth ministry to be pur-pose-driven and if I have a faith that can move stubborn elder boards to action, but have not love I am nothing. If I give all my time to my youth group and surrender my body to the rigors of youth ministry, but have not love, I gain nothing.*

Youth leader, have you left your first love? Has your youth group? Is the undercurrent that drives your youth ministry a true passion for the Lord Jesus Christ? Or are you so busy organizing that you have for-gotten that your foremost job is to fan the embers of love for Christ in the hearts of your students into an unquenchable inferno?

It starts with you. You are the youth leader, the leader of youth. Get back to your first love. Those around you will catch fire, get infected, and never be the same.

THEY TOLERATED FALSE DOCTRINE

> *"To the angel of the church in Pergamum write: These are the words of him who has the sharp, double-edged sword. I know where you live—where Satan has his throne. Yet you remain true to my name. You did not renounce your faith in me, even in the days of Antipas, my faithful witness, who was put to death in your city—where Satan lives. Nevertheless, I have a few things against you: You have people there who hold to the teaching of Balaam, who taught Balak to entice the Israelites to sin by eating food sacrificed to idols and by committing sexual immorality. Likewise you also have those who hold to the teaching of the Nicolaitans. Repent therefore! Otherwise, I will soon come to you and will fight against them with the sword of my mouth."* (Revelation 2:12–16)

The tried and tested believers in the church of Pergamum had endured persecution from the unbelieving community and had not faltered in their profession of faith. When the Roman authorities asked them to recognize the emperor as divine, they refused. They were willing to die for their belief that Jesus is Lord.

Where they choked, however, was not in the face of deadly persecution but in the slow and steady onslaught of spiritual erosion. Although they had stood toe-to-toe with the scowling Roman who demanded that they bow the knee and burn the incense to the emperor or risk certain death, they had failed to stand against those in their own community who were teaching false doctrine. They had given in to the subtle sin of tolerance.

Those early Christians had allowed others into their fellowship who held to another spiritual belief system. Those false teachers were not passive spectators but active recruiters. They were out to win others in the church service to their spiritual perspective. They proselytized freely with no repercussions from the leaders of the church of Pergamum. Jesus reminded them that if they didn't deal with the false teachers swiftly and completely, He would sharpen His sword and visit their church Himself. That visit would be a thorough cleansing.

If we fail to discipline false teachers in our youth groups, Jesus will do it for us—and it will get ugly. The toleration of false doctrine in a church or a youth group setting is like putting a bottle of arsenic between the salad dressing and ketchup bottle in our refrigerators. One bad grab on a late-night feeding binge, and you are suddenly snacking at the deli in heaven.

CHERYL THE ADULT SPONSOR

Maybe it all started with those new age, self-help books, but somehow Cheryl, the once reliable adult volunteer, has begun to steer some of her high school girls in a different direction. She talks with them about the Bible, but she is also teaching the girls meditation as part of their spiritual disciplines. At first it sounded harmless, but this kind of meditation is more Hare Krishna than wholly Christian. She has also begun to question whether or not Jesus is the only way. She says things like, "Christianity is fine for us, but we need to be tolerant of other belief systems as well. As Jesus said, we must love and accept everyone." She takes a dab of mysticism, a hunk of Hinduism, and a few green leaves of Christianity, mixes it together with the bottle between the ketchup and the salad dressing and puts together a chef salad from hell. What's worse, she is serving it to the kids around her.

The problem is that Cheryl is the wife of a key board member in the church who happens to finance a large portion of the annual budget. She and her husband live in a huge house and open it freely to the youth of the church. If the youth leader attacks her false teaching, he will incur the wrath of an angry husband. If the angry husband suspends donations, the youth leader may incur the wrath of his pastor. He could actually be fired for his stance against false doctrine. So instead of taking that risk, the youth pastor turns a deaf ear to Cheryl's whisperings. He decides to let it go, so he won't be let go.

Perhaps that is an extreme example of tolerating false doctrine. But I have seen youth leaders tolerate all sorts of teachings in their youth groups for the sake of convenience. What's even worse is the passive attitude of many youth leaders when it comes to training their own students.

Do your students know what they believe and why they believe it? Have you trained them to master the basics of Christianity? Are you actively encouraging them to question their faith and pointing them back to the preponderance of evidence that Scripture holds? Are you making disciples who are able to spot false teachers a mile away? Are you tolerating pieces of New Age thought, Eastern mysticism, worldliness, and false doctrine in the belief systems of your students?

Students who don't know what they believe or why they believe don't see the need to witness. Evangelism at its root is seeking to convince people that they are wrong about what they believe, that what the Bible says is true, and then getting them to change their minds. Your kids won't risk sharing their faith if they are not convinced their faith is the absolute truth.

This is probably a good time to tell you about about a free resource called *Soul Fuel* available on www.dare2share.org. *Soul Fuel* is a free online training resource that provides teens with an interesting, relevant way to know and own what they believe. Dare 2 Share's goal is to capture the heart of every teenager in America for Christ, starting with the teens in our own homes and churches. *Soul Fuel* is one of the tools developed to accomplish that goal. Visit us online to sign up your teens, their parents, and yourself for the free *Soul Fuel* resources.

Shepherds, protect your lambs from the wolves, no matter what the cost—even if you lose your job. (You probably don't get paid that well anyway!) And you don't want Jesus knocking on your youth group door ready to wield the sword in His hand. Believe me, it will get ugly. The virus will stop infecting, and the Spirit will stop empowering.

THEY TOLERATED SEXUAL IMMORALITY

"To the angel of the church in Thyatira write: These are the words of the Son of God, whose eyes are like blazing fire and whose feet are like burnished bronze. I know your deeds, your love and faith, your service and perseverance, and that you are now doing more than you did at first. Nevertheless, I have this against you: You tolerate that woman Jezebel, who calls herself a prophetess. By her teaching she misleads my servants into sexual immorality and the eating of food sacrificed to idols. I have given her time to repent of her immorality, but she is unwilling. So I will cast her on a bed of suffering, and I will make those who commit adultery with her suffer intensely, unless they repent of her ways. I will strike her children dead. Then all the churches will know that I am he who searches hearts and minds, and I will repay each of you according to your deeds." (Revelation 2:18–23)

A sensual cloud hung over the church of Thyatira. It rained down lewd and crude drops of sexual promiscuity on the members. A false prophetess nicknamed Jezebel was the one doing the rain dance, calling together the clouds of compromise into a thunderstorm of sin. As a result, that body of believers was drenched in the stench of impurity.

Like trying to light wet wood, the church of Thyatira became unusable to God. In a last-ditch effort, He calls them to instant purity or swift judgment.

At first glance, this passage may seem to have little relevance to your youth group. Most of us don't have false prophets named Jezebel running around wreaking unholy havoc on our students. But if we use Jezebel as an analogy of worldliness among our Christian teenagers, that passage takes on a whole new significance.

Students and adults alike have been desensitized to Jezebel's constant, unblushing flirtations. From movies that blur the line, to Internet sites that cross the line, to relationships that erase the line, the steady allure of sensuality has all but captured the souls of Generation Next.

BRIAN THE KID

He has been going to First Baptist all of his life. He knows the Bible stories and the memory verses. He even did some time in a Christian school. Brian knows the ropes of Christianity and is making a noose of them.

One Sunday morning he is genuinely interested in the lesson. It is on prophecy and future stuff and sounds pretty cool. For once he is learning something from his youth leader that he didn't know already. But just ten hours before, he was in his room surfing websites that nobody, let alone a fifteen-year-old church boy, should be surfing. And what's worse, he doesn't even give it a second thought during the youth leader's talk. Even when the youth leader gives the final warning, "So be careful what you are doing, because Jesus could come back at any time," it doesn't register.

What is truly sad is that Brian represents to a greater or lesser degree the vast majority of students in his youth group. Some are hooked on more than just cybersex. They are fully engaged with a member of the opposite or same sex. They too sit in youth group singing, yawning, and praying without the slightest tinge of remorse about their actions from the night before. How can that be? They have gone to bed with Jezebel and have somehow been able to justify it to themselves.

It's what I call "the God stuff/my stuff" myth. That is the myth that segregates their religion from their routine, the sacred from the secular. Until our teenagers see that it's all "God stuff," that will continue to be a problem. Enabling them to accept the lordship of Christ over every area of their existence will erase the line between their stuff and God's and merge them into one singular song of praise and purity.

THEY FAILED TO FOLLOW THROUGH

"To the angel of the church in Sardis write: These are the words of him who holds the seven spirits of God and the seven stars. I know your deeds; you have a reputation of being alive, but you are dead. Wake up! Strengthen what remains and is about to die, for I have not found your deeds complete in the sight of my God. Remember, therefore, what you have received and heard; obey it, and repent. But if you do not wake up, I will come like a thief, and you will not know at what time I will come to you." (Revelation 3:1–3)

The members of the church of Sardis were the first off the starting block but the last to cross the finish line. Their sprint gave them a reputation of being championship level Christians, but God knew that over the long haul they were lagging behind.

The text doesn't get specific about what the church in Sardis failed to complete. Perhaps it was a failure to follow through on instructing the congregation in the basics of Christianity. Maybe it was a short-circuited emphasis on the sign gifts without focusing on the "greater gifts" of prophecy, preaching, and teaching. Perhaps this strong rebuke had to do with being a body that focused on evangelism to the exclusion of discipleship. Whatever the specifics, God has a low tolerance for good starts and bad finishes.

CHRIS THE YOUTH PASTOR/EVANGELIST

He is dynamic, passionate, and popular. Through his winsome leadership, the youth group at his church has grown from twenty to more than two hundred. A large percentage of his kids are new believers who came to a saving knowledge of Christ at his youth group. He has poured almost all of the youth budget into making his Wednesday night youth meeting the most popular place to be. It is fun, friendly, and fast. Every week kids come to Christ.

Chris's teaching is heavy on humor and light on truth. But at the end of every talk Chris gives the gospel. And every week kids come to Christ . . . in droves.

The problem is that most of them sooner or later leave the youth group. Why? It's not because it suddenly got boring. It is definitely fun. But most students who are fun junkies have a short attention span. They start looking for their fun somewhere else.

Chris has failed to follow through. He puts all of his efforts into creating a fun environment on Wednesday night that will hook students, but he has little time, money, or desire to follow up. As a result, Jesus is in their hearts, but His Word is not in their brains. Chris has given a deadbeat dad to hundreds of spiritual orphans. His youth group has a reputation of being alive due to the massive numbers of new converts, but in God's economy it is about to die.

Win, build, train, send . . . that is the Great Commission. And that final mandate of Jesus comes full circle. In other words, it begins with and ends with evangelism. A person comes to Christ through evangelism, is taught, trained, and turned loose to begin the whole process on someone else.

Let's see how Chris scores on his Great Commission report card. In winning others to Christ he gets an A+. He is a master evangelist and knows how to get them to respond. In building up believers who know the basic truths of God's Word, however, he scores an abysmal D-. His touchy-feely chats on Wednesday nights are the only growth vehicle for his students. In training them to live and give their faith, Chris gets an F. He does all of the evangelism in the youth group himself. All his kids do is invite their lost friends to come on Wednesday nights. Finally, in sending them to tell others Chris fails again.

Youth leader, how do you score? We must reproduce producers who reproduce. We must aggressively evangelize, aggressively teach, aggressively train, and aggressively send. And when I use the word *aggressively* please don't mistake it for *abrasively*. Every effort we make from evangelism to discipleship should be drenched in a Spirit-empowered love.

Many youth leaders have a problem opposite to Chris's. They focus heavily on discipleship but never see kids come to Christ. Their kids are growing deep in their faith but have become stagnant at the same time. They are more like the Dead Sea than the Sea of Galilee.

The Dead Sea is dead because there is an inlet but no outlet. If you go fishing in the Dead Sea at night, the only thing you will catch is a cold. Why? It receives but never gives. It gets filled up but never gets poured out. On the other hand, the Sea of Galilee is teeming with life because it has an inlet and an outlet. Chances are that if you cast your net on its waters, you will be eating fish sticks for dinner.

Dead Sea youth groups hear the truth, experience worship, play games, and go to retreats, camps, and all-nighters. They may grow deep in their faith. But they are dead. They spend all of their time getting filled up with truth and fun and nachos but never pour out the cool water of grace to others. Sea of Galilee youth ministries receive and reciprocate. They get filled up with all the same things, but they have an outlet . . . evangelism.

This kind of discipleship is hard work. It requires a commitment to evangelize and disciple. It demands strategic planning, adult staffing, and passionate praying. But it's worth the sweat. Yes, there will be fallout among students. There always is. Some students will make an initial decision for Christ in your youth group and then drop out of sight for months at a time. Others will grow for a while and then disappear. Does that mean that they weren't legitimate decisions? Sometimes. Other times they are genuine believers whom God will take out to the woodshed of trial in order to steer them back to Himself. Yes, some will fall out. Some will burn out. And some will fade away. But those that hang in and grow strong can change the world.

THEY BECAME COMPLACENT

"To the angel of the church in Laodicea write: These are the words of the Amen, the faithful and true witness, the ruler of God's creation. I know your deeds, that you are neither cold nor hot. I wish you were either one or the other! So, because you are lukewarm—neither hot nor cold—I am about to spit you out of my mouth. You say, 'I am rich; I have acquired wealth and do not need a thing.' But you do not realize that you are wretched, pitiful, poor, blind and naked. I counsel you to buy from me gold refined in the fire, so you can become rich; and white clothes to wear, so you can cover your shameful nakedness; and salve to put on your eyes, so you can see." (Revelation 3:14–18)

When we think of the church of Laodicea, we tend to think of lukewarm mediocrity. That church was so tepid spiritually that it made God gag. But sometimes we fail to look further in the passage to discover why they were lukewarm.

The church of Laodicea was wealthy and proud. They thought they had everything they needed. But they were wrong—dead wrong. As one commentator writes, "Their lack of economic need seems to have blinded their eyes to their dire need of spiritual riches."[6]

Spoiled rich kids. Who can stand them? Not you. Not me. Not God. The church of Laodicea was filled with them. Because of their financial status and rotten attitudes, their once sizzling sprint for God had slowed down to a lukewarm limp. Money can do that. It can make a church indifferent about God's presence and independent of God's provision. God uses money—or the lack thereof—to teach us valuable lessons. But if we give in to its many temptations, we will become just like the Laodiceans . . . fat and sassy.

LISA THE YOUTH PASTOR

BMWs, Mercedeses, and Lexuses fill the church parking lot every Sunday morning. Spoiled rich kids fill the youth group every Wednesday night. The abundance of money has its advantages. Youth group fund-raisers are unheard of at this church. In her four-year tenure here, Lisa has never had to raise a dime for any camp or retreat. The budget is big enough to provide scholarships for the handful of blue-collar kids who attend their white-collar meetings.

The pretty kids go here. It's fun. The music is great. The lessons are short. The youth group is exciting. Lisa knows how to pull it all off. There is a team of in-house counselors for students who struggle and enough ministry opportunity for any flavor of kid to fit in. The kids here don't love God with all their heart, soul, mind, and might as much as they enjoy Him. They enjoy Him on Wednesday night and Sunday morning. The rest of their time is theirs.

The teens in Lisa's group, like the church of Laodicea, don't desperately need God. How can they when they have everything else? They have the trendiest fashions to clothe their bodies, the best games to engage their minds, the hippest music to tickle their ears, the latest movies to dazzle their eyes, the strongest drugs to numb their senses, and the coolest cars to impress their friends. If they could see themselves as God sees them, they would be singing a different tune. "But you do not realize that you are wretched, pitiful, poor, blind and naked" (Revelation 3:17).

Helping our students to see their true spiritual condition is part of the responsibility of the truly successful youth leader. Before a viral event can take place, the sneezers must be infected themselves.

LEARNING FROM FAILURE

Jesus gave each of those viral failures the charge to change. There is a simple pattern in each of the warning passages that runs like a current through Revelation 2–3.

RECOGNIZE THE IMPORTANCE OF YOUR LEADERSHIP IN TRANSFORMING YOUR YOUTH GROUP

Each of the warning passages in the book of Revelation starts with the phrase "To the angel of the church in _____ write. . . ." The question is, "Who is that angel?" Is there an angel appointed to each of the churches? Why would Jesus tell John to write letters to an angel?

Whereas some interpreters believe that the angels in these passages refer to celestial beings, others say they represent human messengers. The word *angel* can refer to a human or heavenly preacher. In my opinion, the most logical interpretation of these passages is that the messengers are the primary preachers in each congregation. Jesus commands John to deliver the warnings to those who were preaching to those congregations. It is almost as though Jesus is saying, "Hey, here is a sermon for you to preach to your congregations, gentlemen. It's already outlined, illustrated, and ready to go."

The primary preacher in a congregation of adults or students is in a tremendous position of responsibility. In other words, God holds that person responsible for the spiritual maturation of those under his or her leadership.

I hear this all the time: "Well, I am just a junior high guy," or "I am not a full-time, paid youth pastor," or "I just teach senior high Sunday school." It doesn't matter. You are responsible. You are the angel of the teenagers under your care. Take it seriously. God does. The old statement is true, "Everything rises or falls on leadership."

ELICIT HONEST FEEDBACK FROM THOSE YOU TRUST

That is exactly what all of these passages are . . . feedback. God is giving these churches His evaluation of them. He grades them on heart, performance, endurance, purity, and perspective. And He doesn't grade on a curve.

What if God were to grade your youth group on those issues? How would you do? What would He say about their penchant for purity, pursuit of truth, and passion for Him? What would He say about yours?

Those churches had a rare privilege—they got to hear God's perspective of them. We don't have that same opportunity today. In lieu of that great privilege, I believe that our only viable alternative is to elicit honest feedback from those we trust.

It can hurt. But when we ask the question, "In your honest opinion, how can I improve my youth ministry?" God does some great things. Ask parents of teenagers. Ask teenagers. Ask pastors. Ask mentors. Ask friends. Ask people who will give you honest and valid input.

I am constantly seeking input from students and from youth leaders about Dare 2 Share Ministries. Throughout the years, their evaluations, suggestions, ideas, and criticisms have driven the program. Of course we don't put into effect every suggestion we receive. But we look for patterns. If we hear a consistent criticism or suggestion that is biblical and fits within our core values, we act upon it as soon as possible. As you do the same, your youth ministry will become an upward spiral of shared ideas and transformational flux.

Criticism can be the youth minister's best friend. When it comes to programming, training, outreach, discipleship, leadership, or just about anything else, failure can show us what not to do again. Focus groups and honest feedback are vital to the process of learning from your wipeouts. Humility is the key. To receive proper criticism and reject improper criticism takes wisdom, prayer, and patience. But if youth leaders can master the process, they will maximize their youth ministry efforts and minimize their failures over the long haul.

CONTEMPLATE THE CONSEQUENCES OF YOUR CURRENT APPROACH TO MINISTRY

Every one of the warning passages contains a punishment and a reward. If the church failed to act on the warning, there was punitive action. If they obeyed, there was a divine reward. The same is true in our youth ministries.

Your youth ministry is no less in the economy of God than any of the churches in the New Testament. Although the warnings in Revelation 2–3 were written to specific bodies of believers, they were written for our benefit as well. Think about the consequences of your current approach to youth ministry. If you continue down the same path you are walking right now, what will be the long-term results in the lives of your students? Are they being trained, equipped, and transformed by the mission and message of Jesus Christ? Or are they simply being entertained by one of His messengers?

Ponder these sobering words from Mark Senter in his instant classic *The Coming Revolution of Youth Ministry* about current approaches to youth ministry: "Strategies have become flawed. There is no way in which the tactics currently being used will stem the tidal wave of spiritual, moral, and psychosocial problems faced by the current and coming generations of adolescents."[7]

The road less traveled is unpaved and dangerous. But it leads those who dare walk its rocky path to transformation. So before you merge onto the highway of typical youth ministry paradigms and programs, get out the map of God's Word and make sure you are headed in the right direction.

BE WILLING TO MAKE RADICAL CHANGES

According to Stephen Covey, every significant break*through* started as a break *with*. From Martin Luther nailing his ninety-five theses to the Wittenberg door in the sixteenth century, to the Puritans breaking with conventional Christianity in the seventeenth century, to George Whitefield busting out of the institutionalized church to preach in the fields in the eighteenth century, to Hudson Taylor adapting the dress and customs of the Chinese in the nineteenth century, to Billy Graham filling stadiums in the twentieth century, every breakthrough started as a break with. Luther broke with Catholic theology. Knox broke with Catholic politics and power. Whitefield broke with the notion that the gospel had to be preached in a church building. Taylor broke with conventional missionary mind-sets of his day by becoming like the Chinese in dress and customs instead of asking them to become like him.

Graham broke with sectarian, nonecumenical evangelistic approaches by seeking to unite all Christian churches in cities for crusades.

Jesus commanded five of the churches in the book of Revelation to break with something as well. He ordered them to make immediate and radical changes. He may be asking you to do the same thing. Are you willing to do what He tells you? The operative word is *do*. Don't talk about it. Don't put it to a committee meeting for review. Do it. That's why I love Charles Spurgeon's manly mandate to his preacher boys:

 Brethren, do something; do something; do something. While committees waste their time over resolutions, do something. While Societies and Unions are making constitutions, let us win souls. Too often we discuss, and discuss, and discuss, and Satan laughs in his sleeve. It is time we had done planning and sought something to plan. I pray you, be men of action all of you. Get to work and quit yourselves like men.[8]

Going viral takes action. Make no mistake—real revival takes hard work. Flip through the pages of church history. Whether it be the tens of thousands of miles covered by Wesley on horseback across the eastern United States to preach or Moody's almost ceaseless energy as he set up an evangelistic empire, true awakening is preceded by hard work. Awakening always comes in the context of active waiting. The men and women of God didn't lock themselves in a room until "God came down." They acted as if He were already here and plunged themselves into evangelistic efforts, all the while begging God to sanctify their efforts and anoint their mission with a touch of His sovereign hand.

Spurgeon told his students to "do something." While everybody else sits in brainstorming sessions or the latest seminar to unveil the latest plan about the latest youth ministry paradigm, we are called to do something viral!

Youth leader, let me ask you a series of questions:

1. When is the last time you shared your faith (outside of an outreach meeting)?
2. Do you spend more time talking about evangelism than doing it?
3. Have you filled your schedule with so many meetings that you don't have time for actual ministry?
4. Are you so consumed with the latest youth ministry paradigms (conferences, seminars, books, CDs, and so on) that you have ignored the oldest youth ministry paradigm (the book of Acts)?
5. Do you measure your effectiveness by what you are doing rather than by what is getting done?
6. Have you lost your drive to reach every student in your community with the gospel of Jesus Christ?
7. Do your actions line up with this drive?

Talk is cheap in battle. Imagine being in a wartime situation that requires you to lead a small group of soldiers on a specialized and dangerous mission across enemy lines. You plan your strategy. You consult with your superiors. You arrange all of the equipment and weaponry that you will need. Everything is in place. So what do you do now? You go for it!

Twenty-first century Christianity tends to focus on the strategizing and planning of the invasion. First-century Christianity simply invaded. They had a plan. They executed the plan. They made adjustments on the fly. They learned from their mistakes and conquered a world for Christ.

The great strategist General George S. Patton said, "A good plan violently executed now is better than a perfect plan next week."[9] What is true on the battlefield is true in youth ministry as well. Don't be a viral failure! Many early churches started with a bang and ended with a whimper. What started out as an epidemic was contained by the Devil himself. Refuse to let him quarantine your vision and passion for true awakening.

"He who has an ear, let him hear what the Spirit says to the churches" (Revelation 2:29). ✖

DON'T LET THE VIRAL REVIVAL COME TO A SCREECHING HALT!

MANDATE

Write a letter from Jesus' perspective to yourself and your youth ministry. Share what you perceive would be His commendations and His condemnations to you, your youth staff, and your youth group.

S STAFF INFECTION QUESTIONS

#1. Share the letter the youth leader wrote, and discuss it.

#2. What are some specific ways we can guard against viral failure as a youth ministry?

#3. How well do we recognize the importance of the youth pastor's leadership in transforming our youth group?

#4. Who can give us honest feedback as to our effectiveness in our quest for spiritual awakening?

#5. What are the consequences of our current approach to youth ministry (both good and bad)?

#6. What five to ten radical changes could we make in our youth ministry to foster viral revival?

GO VIRAL!

*Independent of host cells viruses cannot
replicate. Rather, they invade a host cell and
stimulate it to participate in the formation
of additional virus particles.*[1]

Viruses only can multiply through invasion of a host cell. Once
lodged within the host, the virus can then reproduce itself. The
newly formed virus particles can escape and invade other host
cells where more virus particles will be formed. That exponential
process is what initiates a full-blown infection. The nature of a virus
is to invade a host cell and then multiply itself in others. The same is
true of the gospel message.

By itself, the gospel cannot reproduce itself. It needs a host. Once
lodged within an individual's heart, its nature is to seek to invade and
multiply. It does not exist only to lie dormant and passive, but its purpose is to aggressively spread to others.

In the early New Testament that is exactly what took place. The
gospel invaded and multiplied again and again until the whole world
was infected. For the gospel to go viral again, carriers and sneezers are

desperately needed. The question is whether you will choose to be used by God to go viral in your community of young believers.

Reread the book of Acts, and see if you don't get a chill. Underline all of the keys to revival, and you will be astounded by the simplicity of the early church's approach. They were fiercely focused, shockingly strategic, and amazingly resilient.

This final chapter is designed to help you successfully go viral. It is built around principles found primarily in Matthew 10, where Jesus sends out His disciples to invade the cities, towns, and villages of Galilee with the gospel of the kingdom. I think you will find the principles eerily applicable as you seek to launch this paradigm for proclamation in your youth group.

TAKE A DAY AWAY TO PRAY

"Jesus went out to a mountainside to pray, and spent the night praying to God. When morning came, he called his disciples to him and chose twelve of them, whom he also designated apostles" (Luke 6:12–13).

The first principle comes from Luke's gospel. Before the first apostles were chosen, before the first mandate was given, before the first soul was saved, Jesus got away to pray. He chose a mountainside as His prayer closet. He snuck away in the darkness of night to commune in secret with His Father.

A mission of biblical proportions was about to begin. He needed the Father's wisdom to choose the right men. He drew from the Father's strength to courageously lead the charge. This God-man lived as a perfect man fully dependent on the Father. In so doing He gave us a pattern to live by. If the Creator of the universe took a night to pray for the courage and wisdom to choose and lead His e-team, how much more do we need to do the same thing?

Prayer is the best brainstorming session you will ever have. The Father, Son, and Holy Spirit are around the table with you in the conference room of intercession. As you lean on God, listen to His Word and lay out your requests. The results will be a spiritual business plan for your ministry that is indestructible.

The best plans are hatched in prayer, because the incubator is the warmth of God's presence. When we are under the lights of His glory, we can't help but think in a whole new way. So my challenge to you is take a day away to pray.

One of the disciplines that I began when I was in my early teens was to journal my prayers to God. Every once in a while I review my old prayer journals to see how God used that precious time with Him to prepare the way for every landmark in my spiritual journey.

When I planted a church with one of my best friends in 1989, those days away to pray prepared me for the long, difficult, yet rewarding job as a preaching pastor of a fledgling, then growing, then exploding body of believers. Those days away to pray often meant renting a hotel room somewhere in town or going to a cabin in the mountains by myself. That decade of pastoring was paralleled by a decade of journaling and praying. It sank my roots deep in Christ. As a twenty-three-year-old church planter without any formal church-planting training, I knew that God's strategic plan would be hammered out in the closet of prayer.

By 1999, a different kind of journaling began to take place. It no longer centered on the pains of pastoring a church. Now the focus was on the prospect of launching into Dare 2 Share as a full-time occupation. It was one of the hardest times in my life. The church was wildly successful. More than a thousand people considered Grace Church their home and me their preaching pastor. I loved sharing the Word with them every week and shepherding that exciting and passionate spiritual flock.

But deep inside me something was stirring. I had always told friends that I planned to preach at Grace Church and do Dare 2 Share simultaneously for the rest of my life. When I took those days away to pray, however, it was almost as though I could hear the gentle whisper of God's voice telling me that it was time to make a decision. It was exactly what I didn't want to hear. Finally, after the Columbine tragedy, the whisper became a scream. That final day away to pray was the hardest I have ever experienced. God was clearly leading me to resign from Grace Church and pursue His calling of training teenagers for the rest of my life. So I did. Reading that resignation letter before a church that I loved was the hardest thing I have ever had to do. But I knew that God had led me to it through hours and hours of prayer.

Maybe it's time for you to rent a hotel room.

DEVELOP YOUR E-TEAM

"He called his twelve disciples to him and gave them authority to drive out evil spirits and to heal every disease and sickness" (Matthew 10:1).

Jesus had an e-team. He trained them. He equipped them. He turned them loose. In Matthew 10, He gives them a mission, a message, and a mandate. He turns His disciples loose to evangelize the towns, villages, and countryside. His plan was systematic and strategic.

Jesus handpicked twelve men from all of Israel and poured His life into theirs. For more than three years He prepared them, taught them, equipped them, rebuked them, and loved them. Their outreach mission in the book of Matthew is just one chapter in their spiritual development. Jesus was preparing them to conquer the world with His message of hope.

He didn't choose the brightest, the richest, or the most popular to be His followers. He chose those with a heart for Him, a passion for His kingdom, and a capacity to change. Those men shook the world after He left in bodily form and invaded their souls with His Spirit.

The disciples were so influenced by Jesus that the Pharisees, shocked at their blue-collar boldness, proclaimed, "When they saw the courage of Peter and John and realized that they were unschooled, ordinary men, they were astonished and they took note that these men had been with Jesus" (Acts 4:13). There was only one explanation for Peter and John's courageousness in the face of danger: they had been around Jesus a little too long.

That's the kind of impact God wants you to have on a handful of students in your youth group. Too many youth leaders spend too much time on the problem kids in their youth group. Meanwhile, the ones who have the most capacity to make an eternal difference for the kingdom are underchallenged. As a result, many of our most spiritually potent teens become bored with youth group. No one ever pulls the pin on their grenade, so the evangelism explosion never takes place.

Jesus encouraged His disciples with the parable of the sower. He reminded them that as they ministered, some seeds would grow and others would not. The point? Go with the growers and pray for the others.

The Pareto Principle applies here. "Every leader needs to understand the Pareto Principle in the area of people oversight and leadership. For example, 20 percent of the people in an organization will be responsible for 80 percent of the company's success."[2] That principle is true in the business world. It is also true in the world of discipleship. Why not spend 80 percent of our time with the 20 percent of our kids who have more capacity for spiritual growth and evangelism explosion? Isn't that exactly what Jesus did? Long after the crowds were gone, Jesus was hanging out with His spiritual posse.

Jesus had an e-team. They were the ones who unleashed the epidemic of evangelism long after Jesus was sitting at the right hand of the Father. They were the ones who took the truths from the life of Jesus and radically applied them all across the early world. Their message was simple. Their dedication was unmatched. The results were amazing.

Amidst the herds of nerds and flocks of jocks in your youth group is a handful of students waiting to be commissioned. This e-team can lead the charge and shake the world. They have the same Spirit dwelling in them as the first apostles did. The question is, Will you choose them, invest in them, train them, and unleash them?

MAKE A GOOD PLAN

These twelve Jesus sent out with the following instructions: "Do not go among the Gentiles or enter any town of the Samaritans.

Go rather to the lost sheep of Israel. As you go, preach this message: 'The kingdom of heaven is near.' Heal the sick, raise the dead, cleanse those who have leprosy, drive out demons. Freely you have received, freely give. Do not take along any gold or silver or copper in your belts; take no bag for the journey, or extra tunic, or sandals or a staff; for the worker is worth his keep."
(Matthew 10:5–10)

Jesus had a plan. His strategy was simple. It centered on unleashing His disciples two by two across the cities of Galilee with a succinct message: "The kingdom of heaven is near."

The plan of Jesus was focused. The message was to be preached, not among the Gentiles or the Samaritans but to the Jews in Galilee.

The plan of Jesus was powerful. His disciples were empowered to do the miraculous. When the crowds gathered as a result of the divine display of signs and wonders, a singular sentence about the proximity of God's kingdom was to be proclaimed to the astonished throng.

The plan of Jesus demanded risk. There was no backup plan. His followers were called to go out in absolute faith. The disciples were turned loose with no money in their wallets or extra clothes in their backpacks. That was because Jesus understood that the ultimate preparation for their journey was an attitude of dependence on God.

Youth leader, do you have a plan? Are you systematically preparing your students to be unleashed in a journey of risk, power, and focus with a simple message of hope?

I encourage you to take the principles that you have learned in this book and make a plan that fits your youth ministry culture. Make it your own. In fact, I want to encourage you to share your insights and ideas with us at Dare 2 Share Ministries. Almost all of our training materials available on- and off-line are the result of youth leader input and ideas. Visit www.dare2share.org on a regular basis to get and give strategic resources.

Our goal is that Dare 2 Share become a conduit for youth ministries around the world to build a template for youth awakening—a Great Commission execution strategy on a grassroots level. One of the quickest and most effective ways to do that is through the Internet.

Whether it be through chat rooms or data exchange, the information superhighway is without speed limits.

One of the reasons that Doug Field's *Purpose Driven Youth Ministry* has worked so effectively is that he has taken ideas that he successfully implemented in his own youth group and has shared them with everybody who wanted them. What if everybody were sharing with everybody else? The best ideas from youth groups, both big and small, would create an upward spiral of shared information that every youth ministry could benefit from in a powerful way. That is the opportunity that the Web creates.

As you make your plan, remember that every youth ministry culture is unique. So become a pirate. Pillage this book, and steal ideas from successful youth ministries. Some you'll take; others you'll tweak. And others you may trash. But keep working and reworking until it fits your unique culture. Then share the results with us at www.dare2share.org, so that others can pirate your stuff.

EXPECT TROUBLE!

"Be on your guard against men; they will hand you over to the local councils and flog you in their synagogues. On my account you will be brought before governors and kings as witnesses to them and to the Gentiles" (Matthew 10:17–18).

Jesus told His followers to expect trouble. He guaranteed them persecution and problems. As ambassadors of the catalytic Christ, they could expect revival and rebellion in every town they visited on their Galilean evangelistic outreach tour.

The pattern of revival and rebellion is evident throughout the book of Acts. The gospel is preached in a new city. Initially there is an overwhelming response. Dissenting religious leaders stir the crowd against the visiting preachers. The crowd turns on the Christians. Riot, imprisonment, flogging, or excommunication ensues.

It is no different today. Trouble and trial follow evangelism and epidemics. Why? Because Satan will do everything in his power to stop you from going viral. Sometimes he will use parents, peers, and other pastors to discourage or distract you. Other times he will use secret sins to bring you down and drain you of your power and potential. He has a vast arsenal of weapons to use against you. If he can't get you through the front door of persecution, he will get you through the back door of lust, compromise, bitterness, busyness, or discouragement.

Jesus also warned His disciples, "Brother will betray brother to death, and a father his child; children will rebel against their parents and have them put to death. All men will hate you because of me" (Matthew 10:21–22). When the message of Jesus is proclaimed, some get saved and others get mad. Those who get mad will make it their goal to keep you quiet. I have talked to many youth leaders from liberal church backgrounds who have experienced this problem after bringing their teenagers to a Dare 2 Share conference. When student-led evangelism disrupts the applecart of the status quo, somebody will pay. Usually it is the youth leader.

Your students will also encounter resistance on their campuses as they seek to reach their friends with the good news of the gospel. Teachers and administrators in the public school system often try to keep Christian students quiet about their Christianity both in and out of the classroom. Armed with the misused mantra of "separation of church and state," they will do their best to quell the swell of evangelism in your students.

Evangelism is not politically correct. It swims against the tide of have-it-your-way religion. At its raw roots evangelism is telling people they are wrong about what they believe and asking them to change their minds. No matter how nicely we put it, the gospel will be met with resistance. In the words of Jesus, "A student is not above his teacher, nor a servant above his master. It is enough for the student to be like his teacher, and the servant like his master. If the head of the house has been called Beelzebub, how much more the members of his household!" (Matthew 10:24–25). In other words, if they persecuted Jesus, they will persecute His students—and ours.

Expect trouble, but don't be afraid of it. Jesus told His followers, "So do not be afraid of them. . . . Do not be afraid of those who kill the body but cannot kill the soul. Rather, be afraid of the One who can destroy both soul and body in hell" (Matthew 10:26, 28). We should not be afraid of what others think of us. The One we should fear is God Himself.

BE CONTAGIOUS YOURSELF

"Anyone who loves his father or mother more than me is not worthy of me; anyone who loves his son or daughter more than me is not worthy of me; and anyone who does not take his cross and follow me is not worthy of me" (Matthew 10:37–38).

Infectious Christianity starts with discipleship. We must not merely be believers. We must be followers. The church of the twenty-first century is filled with believers. The church of the first century was filled with disciples. Maybe that's why we don't see the same spirit of sweeping revival of Acts today. We have big buildings, large budgets, wonderful programs, and lazy Christians.

The way of Christ is the way of the cross. The way of the cross is the pathway of self-denial and sacrifice. The cross demands loss. We must lose our desires and dreams in the shadow of its crossbeams. Otherwise, we are calling our kids to a synthetic religion instead of authentic Christianity.

It starts with us. If we want our kids to be disciples of Christ, we must be His disciples first. You can't infect if you are not contagious. That means that if God is going to unleash a viral event through your youth group, you yourself must be infected enough to sneeze, scratch, and bite. (Remember the monkey?)

How do we stay contagious enough to start an epidemic? First of all, it takes spiritual cultivation on a moment-by-moment basis. I am not talking about simply reading the Bible every day with some prayer time thrown in for good measure. I am talking about the constant current of God's power flowing through us via His Holy Spirit. It is a daily declaration of dependence on God that will give us the strength we need. Jesus put it this way: "I am the vine; you are the branches. If a man remains in me and I in him, he will bear much fruit; apart from me you can do nothing" (John 15:5).

That simple analogy of a branch gaining nourishment from the vine gives us the key to truly contagious Christianity. It is not through some artificial methodology or strategy. It is not by some mystical discipline or formal ritual. It is simply through realizing and relying. We realize that apart from Christ we have no power to live victoriously or to infect virally. Then we rely on Him to live through us and infect others through us. It is all about Him—His power and His strength. We simply must be connected to Him.

From my legalistic background I came kicking and screaming to this humbling realization. It was hard for me to put aside my prideful ambitions of world conquest in the name of the gospel and realize that apart from Christ I could do nothing. Through my college years God used a series of devastating circumstances to put my self-sufficient attitude in the shredder of trial. I finally came to the conclusion that the Christian life was not about conquering the world for the sake of Christ but about allowing Him to conquer me for the sake of His glory. Only then could that message truly go viral through this broken vessel. The more He has broken me over the years, the more He has used me. I look forward to the trials of tomorrow for the viral Christianity they will produce.

Paul wrote to the Corinthians: "We have this treasure in jars of clay to show that this all-surpassing power is from God and not from us" (2 Corinthians 4:7). Once the jars are broken, the hidden treasures spill out for everyone to see and enjoy. The same is true of us. Once God breaks us, the life of Christ spills out. It's then, and only then, that we can't help but be contagious.

In their book *When God Weeps*, Joni Eareckson Tada and Steven Estes write, "Suffering is the tool he uses to help us need him more."[3] When we need Him more, He uses us more. When He uses us more, people get infected.

What better testimony of viral Christianity than a woman whose paralysis serves as a catalyst of contagion for everyone she touches. Joni Eareckson Tada is a remarkable woman who knows the value of brokenness. Having been paralyzed in a wheelchair for more than thirty years, she knows better than most the immense value of brokenness. As a result of her shattered vertebrae, God crushed her self-dependence and caused her to trust in Him alone. She has been infecting others with her unique brand of contagious Christianity ever since.

Maybe it's not a bone that God needs to break for you; perhaps it is a dream, a relationship, a habit, or a bank account. Whatever it is, God will use the shattering of the vessel of your life to infect others around you with the viral power of the gospel unleashed.

When we pick up our cross and follow Jesus, we are dying to ourselves and choosing to become infected by His Spirit. We are saying no to our dreams, desires, and aspirations and saying yes to His dream for us (godliness), His desire for us (servanthood), and His aspiration for us (fruitfulness).

Jesus called His disciples to come and die. He is calling us to do the same. It is when we die to ourselves and He lives through us that we truly become contagious in our Christianity.

Are you infected?

LEAD THE CHARGE

"After Jesus had finished instructing his twelve disciples, he went on from there to teach and preach in the towns of Galilee" (Matthew 11:1).

Jesus didn't just command His disciples to go out and share their faith. He gave them instructions in chapter 10 and then led the charge in chapter 11.

In the history of humanity there has never been a better leader than Jesus Christ. If you could dream up the ultimate leader, he would be only a tiny fraction of the leader that Jesus Christ was and is. The Son of God so inspired His followers that they literally changed the course of human history without ever firing a shot. Jesus took twelve young raggedy men and turned them into world-changers. His training technique was centered on action. Show-and-tell was not a game to Him. He showed them how after He told them why.

That kind of leadership is rare today. It is much easier to condense our lessons into twenty minutes on Sunday morning or Wednesday night and spend the rest of our time playing games. But if you want to go viral as a youth group, you must be a Jesus kind of leader. You must show and tell. You must lead the charge.

When I think of leadership, I think of war. True leaders are revealed under fire. Maybe that's why I love a good war movie. Whether it be a classic like *Tora! Tora! Tora!* or something like *Saving Private Ryan* or *Pearl Harbor*, I am enthralled by stories of courageous leadership in the face of overwhelming odds. Maybe that's why my all-time favorite movie is *Sergeant York*.

The movie was nominated for an astounding eleven Oscar awards in 1941. It is a dramatic and powerful story of a rebellious young man in the back hills of Tennessee who is radically converted to Christ right before World War I. Because of his newfound Christian convictions, he hesitates to enlist in the army and decides instead to appeal for exemption. He becomes a conscientious objector. In the innocence of his walk with Christ, he couldn't reconcile "Thou shalt not kill" with fighting for one's country.

The army denied Alvin York's application for exemption. He had to fight. Being a conscientious objector in a boot camp full of gung ho battle boys was no easy thing. He was constantly scrutinized and criticized, partly because of his backwoods hillbilly drawl but mostly because of his pacifism. A pacifist couldn't be a patriot in his world of red-blooded Americanism.

But Alvin York excelled in boot camp in spite of the furrowed brows. An avid hunter, he excelled at marksmanship and soon became known as the pacifist who could shoot.

In a last-ditch effort to solve the internal dissension that was rattling the conscience of this godly young man, his commanding officer gave him a book on American history to read. The book chronicled how the founders of America had purchased with their own blood the freedom Alvin now enjoyed. The officer gave Alvin some time off to go back to the woods of Tennessee and read that book and his Bible to see if he could resolve his conflict of loyalties. The officer assured him that if he still felt that he couldn't fight for his country when he came back, he would recommend an exemption for Alvin.

Those few days in the hill country of Tennessee weren't spent with his family. They were spent with the Bible and a book on American history. He read amazing stories of patriots, like his hero and fellow Tennessee native Daniel Boone, as they spilled blood for the freedom he enjoyed as an American. Phrases like "obey your God" and "serve your country" rattled around in his brain as he prayed and thought and read and studied.

Finally, he stumbled across a tiny verse in the Gospels: "Give to Caesar what is Caesar's, and to God what is God's" (Matthew 22:21). Thunderstruck, Alvin York knew his dilemma was solved. It wasn't God or country. It was God and country, in that order.

Alvin York returned to his base and expressed his desire to fight for his country. He still had some questions, but the big ones had been answered.

It was in the field that Alvin York showed his leadership. His courage and love for his fellow soldiers, together with his down-home common sense and excellent marksmanship, made him a formidable foe for the Germans. In a crucial battle at Argonne, the Americans were pinned down by German machine-gun nests. Alvin York made his way up a hill through a barrage of enemy fire to flank the gunners. One by one he picked them off. He single-handedly caused the Germans on that hill to surrender. By the end of the day, he had taken 132 German soldiers prisoner by himself.

In one day Sergeant York became a national hero. What's amazing about his story is that it is absolutely true. Sergeant Alvin York became an icon of heroism in the free world and was the most highly decorated soldier of World War I. Never proud of the fact that he had killed Germans, he chose to focus on the American lives that had been saved by his actions that fateful day.

Courage under fire—that's exactly what it takes. Believe me, when you start to put into practice the principles in this book, you will come under fire. There will be students, parents, and pastors who don't like the change of focus. Satan will do everything in his evil power to deceive, distract, discourage, and destroy you. But it is in such situations that heroes emerge.

You must lead the way. When everybody else is cowering in foxholes, you must climb the hill in spite of the danger and flank the enemy. You must stand in the power of the Spirit, refuse to stop shooting, and the enemy will surrender.

Leadership requires risk. If you are not risking, you are not leading. I am not talking about reckless abandon. I am talking about strategic courage in the face of overwhelming odds. The voices of doubt from within and the critics from without must be quieted by an overwhelming passion to proclaim Christ. The war for the Great Commission culture in your youth group is won or lost with you, the youth leader. Fight!

THREE FINAL WARNINGS

My first warning is this: if you apply the principles in this book, you will become the hunted. Just as Rene Russo and Dustin Hoffman hunted down and destroyed the deadly strain of the Ebola virus in the movie *Outbreak*, Satan will do what he can to hunt you down and kill the epidemic of evangelism in your youth group.

The last thing the Devil wants to see is a resurrection of the revival that ran rampant in the first-century Mediterranean world. The kingdom of darkness never quite recovered from the first run of this truth virus. So much momentum was unleashed in the first hundred years of Christianity that the aftershocks are still felt today.

So Satan will be busier than you are. He will align all of the resources of his dark kingdom to stop the flicker from turning into a flame and the flame into an inferno. He will ask God for permission to sift you like wheat and cut you like butter. He will beg God to break down the hedge of protection so that he can bring you to your knees in defeat.

He may do that through major catastrophic crises. But Satan, like God, usually doesn't make counterattacks through the earthquake, windstorm, or firestorm. His modus operandi is the dusty details of day-to-day life: the cumulative complaints from irritated parents over the new Great Commission focus, the whining of students who are tired of hearing you give the gospel every single week, and the internal doubts that plague you when nobody comes to Christ over a long period of time. It's usually the little irritations that sideswipe our effectiveness.

Job remained steadfast under the barrage of Satan's biggest blows. Lost riches, destroyed home, dead family, devastating disease. Job kept his eyes riveted on God and refused to doubt Him. So Satan sent three friends to "comfort" him. Enter accusation. Exit integrity. In defending himself to his judgmental friends, Job accused God. Satan didn't win through the frontal assault. He won through covert operatives whom Job thought were his buddies.

Satan will try to do the same to you. He will do what it takes to keep the virus locked away in the pages of Acts and not turned loose through the lives of your students. Unleashing a viral revival through your teenagers is not a blissful journey through a wonderland of problem-free Christianity. It is raw and real. Major awakenings and big trouble are brother and sister, not distant cousins. So prepare yourself.

My second warning to you is that God will not use dirty vessels. This warning is tucked away in 2 Timothy: "In a large house there are articles not only of gold and silver, but also of wood and clay; some are for noble purposes and some for ignoble. If a man cleanses himself from the latter, he will be an instrument for noble purposes, made holy, useful to the Master and prepared to do any good work" (2:20–21).

What does that mean? If you are harboring secret sin in your life, God will not use you. So if you mess up, 'fess up. He will choose to use you when you choose to be a clean vessel.

Finally, remember that real revival is not just doing more. Techniques, methods, programs, and strategies are all fine and good, but they will never bring about revival. Only when we plug into Jesus Christ as our strength will we have the capacity to be carriers of infectious Christianity. Jesus put it clearly in John 15:5: "Apart from me you can do nothing." Paul put a positive spin on the same truth in

Philippians 4:13: "I can do everything through him who gives me strength." Viral revival is simply Jesus living through us, nothing more, nothing less.

That means that every day we must declare our dependence on Him. The more we learn to become dependent on Him, the more His awakening will be unleashed through us. So make time daily to plunge into His Word. In the midst of the monotony of daily to-do lists, remind yourself to rely on Him. Without His power coursing through our spiritual veins, we are not infected, let alone contagious.

THESE LAST DAYS

I believe that in these last days God is aligning His remnant across the globe. Even now He is preparing to unleash His outbreak through Christian young people in Africa, India, Poland, and Peru. Why not the students of your youth group? Why not you?

D. L. Moody was motivated by this quote, which he heard as a young man: "The world has yet to see what God will do with and for and through and in and by the man who is wholly consecrated to him."[4] Those seventeen words drove him day and night. He worked with all his heart to be that man. In the wake of his legacy, millions have been exposed to the gospel of Jesus Christ. One man changed the lives of millions. If God could use one man that way, what could He do through the Christian young people of this culture? Maybe the quote should go like this: "The world has yet to see what God can do through one generation wholly consecrated to Him."

God loves to use the improbable to accomplish the impossible. He longs to use the unlikely to accomplish the unbelievable. He yearns to use the leftovers to pull off the far out. It brings Him glory to use weak and underestimated vessels. Look at the disciples He chose in the Gospels. Look at the people He has used throughout church history. Look at the kids in your youth group. The raw elements of a viral revival are already there—His people, His Spirit, and His message.

God is searching for a carrier. "I looked for a man among them who would build up the wall and stand before me in the gap on behalf of the land so I would not have to destroy it, but I found none" (Ezekiel 22:30).

The walls were about to come tumbling down in Jerusalem. God had pronounced judgment through His prophets on the City of David. When Abraham bartered with God over the destiny of Sodom and Gomorrah, hundreds upon hundreds of years earlier, God finally concluded that if He could find ten righteous men in those cities, then He would spare them. In Ezekiel, God is saying He is looking for just one righteous man whom He could use to bridge the huge chasm between holy God and rebellious Israel. That one carrier could infect the Israelites with the truth of God's Word and impending judgment. One mediator could intercede on behalf of His chosen people. God was searching for one righteous person to fill the gap. But He found none.

He is still searching today. He is looking for prayer warriors, spiritual leaders, and contagious carriers all wrapped up in one. Will He find one in you?

The choice is yours. The time is now. The message is waiting . . . to go viral! ✖

RED·DOT REVIEW

IF YOU ARE NOT INFECTED YOURSELF, YOU CAN'T INFECT OTHERS

MONKEY MANDATES

MANDATE #1
Take a day away to pray. Go ahead and rent that hotel room!

MANDATE #2
Write a strategic plan for your youth group and your e-team!

MANDATE #3
Go for it!

STAFF INFECTION QUESTIONS

#1. What are the twenty things we could do as a staff to blow the top off of our evangelistic efforts in this youth ministry?

#2. Narrow those down to three.

#3. Choose at least one that you will implement.

#4. How can we make this idea a reality?

#5. How do each of us see ourselves contributing to the e-team success?

NOTES

Chapter 1: Bad Monkey!

1. George Barna, *Revolution* (Wheaton: Tyndale, 2005), 31–32.

2. "Hidden Killers, Deadly Viruses," http://library.thinkquest.org/23054/gather/index.shtml

3. Seth Godin, "Unleash Your Ideavirus," Fast Company, August 2000, 116.

4. Helena Curtis and N. Sue Barnes, *Invitation to Biology* (New York: Worth, 1985), 625.

5. "Hidden Killers, Deadly Viruses," http://library.thinkquest.org/23054/gather/index.shtml

6. Paul Borthwick, "Risky Business," accessed Feb. 2001; www.youthministry.com

7. *The Columbia Encyclopedia*, 6th ed., s.v. "sneeze," www.bartleby.com/65

8. Walter A. Elwell, ed., *Baker's Evangelical Dictionary of Biblical Theology*, s.v. "evangelize" (Grand Rapids: Baker, 1996).

9. Bill Hybels and Mark Mittelberg, *Becoming a Contagious Christian* (Grand Rapids: Zondervan, 1994), 46.

Chapter 2: "It's Gone Airborne!"

1. Michael W. Metzger, "Making Disciples in Postmodern Cultures," (paper presented to staff of Campus Crusade for Christ, Severna Park, Md., December 1998), 5.

2. Ibid., 27.

3. Ibid., 28.

4. Charles R. Swindoll, *Rise and Shine* (Portland, Ore.: Multnomah, 1989), 69.

5. Doug Fields, *Purpose Driven Youth Ministry* (Grand Rapids: Zondervan, 1998), 106.

6. Malcolm Gladwell, *The Tipping Point* (Boston: Little Brown, 2000), 172–73.

Chapter 3: Student Super Sneezers

1. Douglas Hyde, *Dedication and Leadership* (Notre Dame, Ind.: Univ. of Notre Dame, 1966), 17–18.

2. Richard N. Ostling and Joan K. Ostling, *Mormon America: The Power and the Promise* (San Francisco: Harper, 1999), 206–7.

3. Ibid., 156–57.

4. Alvin Reid, "The Zeal of Youth: The Role of Students in the History of Spiritual Awakening," in *Evangelism for a Changing World*, ed. Timothy K. Beougher and Alvin Reid (Wheaton: Harold Shaw, 1995), 233.

5. Jonathan Edwards, "Some Thoughts Concerning the Present Revival of Religion in New England, and the Way in Which It Ought to Be Acknowledged and Promoted, Humbly Offered to the Public, in a Treatise on That Subject," in *The Works of Jonathan Edwards*, ed. Sereno E. Dwight (London: Banner of Truth, 1834), 1:423.

6. Reid, "Zeal of Youth," 237.

7. Centers for Disease Control and Prevention, National Center for Chronic Disease Prevention and Health Promotion, "National Youth Risk Behavior Survey (YRBS)," accessed in *Health, United States, 2005: With Chartbook on Trends in the Health of Americans* (Hyattsville, Md.: 2005), 252.

8. *Child Trends Databank; Percentage of Students in Grades 9-12 Who Report Being in a Physical Fight in the Past Year, Selected Years, 1991-2003*, accessed at www.childtrendsdatabank.org/tables/22_Table_1.htm. *Percentage of High School Students in Grades 9 to 12 Who Have Been Victims of Dating Violence in the Past Year, 2003*, accessed at www. childtrendsdatabank.org/figures/66-figure-1.gif. *Percentage of High School Students Who Carry Weapons, Selected Years, 1991-2003*,

accessed at www.childtrendsdatabank.org/figures/19-figure-2.gif. *Percentage of Students Ages 12-18 Who Reported Being Targets of Hate-Related Words at School During the Previous Six Months.* www.childtrendsdatabank.org/tables/94_Table_1.htm.

9. "Generation Rx: National Study Reveals New Category of Substance Abuse Emerging" (Washington, D.C.: Partnership for a Drug-Free America, 2005.) accessed at www.drugfree.org

10. George Barna, *Third Millennium Teens* (Ventura, Calif.: Barna Research, 2000), 56–57.

Chapter 4: Creating a Contagious Youth Ministry

1. "The Bible Encyclopedia" s.v. "synagogue," www.christiananswers.net/dictionary/synagogue.html

2. George Barna, *Third Millennium* (Ventura, Calif.: Barna Research, 1999), 59.

3. "Teenagers," Barna Research Online, accessed August 2001, www.barna.org.

4. Dave Rahn and Terry Linhart, *Contagious Faith* (Loveland, Colo.: Group, 2000), 68.

5. John C. Maxwell, *Developing the Leader Within You* (Nashville: Thomas Nelson, 1993), 2.

6. Malcolm Gladwell, *The Tipping Point* (New York: Little Brown, 2000), 33.

7. Ibid., 56, 58.

8. Rahn and Linhart, *Contagious Faith*, 44.

Chapter 5: Increasing the Velocity of the Virus

1. Kenneth L. Barker, *NIV Study Bible* (Grand Rapids: Zondervan, 1985), 1646.

2. Dave Rahn and Terry Linhart, *Contagious Faith* (Loveland, Colo.: Group, 2000), 93.

3. Kate McGeown, "China's Christians Suffer for Their Faith," BBC News, 9 Nov. 2004, accessed at http://news.bbc.co.uk/2/hi/asia-pacific/3993857.stm

4. Misty Bernall, *She Said Yes* (Farmington, Pa.: Plough, 1999), 115.

5. Rahn and Linhart, *Contagious Faith*, 51.

6. Dan Hayes, *Fireseeds of Spiritual Awakening* (San Bernardino, Calif.: Here's Life Publishers, 1983), 86.

7. George Barna, *Third Millennium Teens* (Ventura, Calif.: Barna Research, 2000), 59.

8. Philip Yancey, *What's So Amazing About Grace?* (Grand Rapids: Zondervan, 1997), 72.

Chapter 6: Don't Take Your Antibiotics!

1. Rob De Salle, *Epidemic!* (New York: New Press, 1999), 108.

2. Stephen R. Covey, *The 7 Habits of Highly Effective People* (New York: Simon & Schuster, 1989), 255.

3. Ibid., 244, 255.

4. Ridge Burns and Pam Campbell, *No Youth Worker Is an Island* (Wheaton: Victor, 1992), 66–67.

5. Neil Howe and William Strauss, *Millennials Rising* (New York: Vintage, 2000), 366.

6. Arnold Dallimore, *George Whitefield* (Carlisle, Pa.: Banner of Truth, 1970), 15–16.

Chapter 7: Watch Out for Tainted Strains!

1. Francis Schaeffer, *The Church at the End of the Twentieth Century* (Wheaton: Crossway, 1994), 51–52.

2. Charles R. Swindoll, *The Grace Awakening* (Dallas: Word, 1990), 3.

3. Wade Horn, *Father Facts* (Lancaster, Pa.: National Fatherhood Initiative, 2004), accessed at www.fatherhood.org/fatherfacts_t10.asp; Phyllis Schlafly, "Federal Incentives Make Children Fatherless" (Alton, Ill.: Eagle Forum, May 11, 2005), accessed at www.eagleforum.org.

4. Martin Lloyd-Jones, *Romans: The New Man, An Exposition of Chapter 6* (Grand Rapids: Zondervan, 1973), 8–9.

5. Swindoll, *Grace Awakening*, 22–23.

6. Kenneth L. Barker, *NIV Study Bible Text Notes* (Grand Rapids: Zondervan, 1985), 1721.

7. Swindoll, *Grace Awakening*, 44.

8. Ron Rhodes, *The Complete Book of Bible Answers* (Eugene, Ore.: Harvest House Publishers, 1997), 187.

Chapter 8: Infecting Postmodern Students with the Age-Old Virus

1. Michael W. Metzger, "Making Disciples in Postmodern Cultures," (paper presented to staff of Campus Crusade for Christ, Severna Park, Md., December 1998), 5.

2. Rob DeSalle and Marla Jo Brickman, "Infection," in *Epidemic!* ed. Rob DeSalle, 79.

3. Paul Copan, *True for You, but Not for Me* (Minneapolis: Bethany, 1998), 155.

4. Metzger, "Making Disciples," 28.

5. Ibid., 31–32.

6. George Barna, *Revolution* (Wheaton: Tyndale, 2005), 44.

7. John R. W. Stott, *Between Two Worlds: The Art of Preaching in the Twentieth Century* (Grand Rapids: Eerdmans, 1982), 10.

Chapter 9: How to Give an Infectious Invitation

1. William R. Moody, *D. L. Moody* (Murfreesboro, Tenn.: Sword of the Lord), 144–45.

2. Joseph C. Dillow, *The Reign of the Servant Kings* (Hayesville, N.C.: Schoettle, 1993), 32.

3. James E. Adams, "Decisional Regeneration," August 2001, accessed at www.gracesermons.com/hisbygrace.html.

Chapter 10: Viral Failures

1. Gian Kolata, *Flu* (New York: Touchstone Rockefeller, 1999), back cover copy.

2. Ibid., 5.

3. John Walvoord, *The Revelation of Jesus Christ* (Chicago: Moody, 1966), 51.

4. Howard A. Snyder, *The Radical Wesley* (Downers Grove, Ill.: InterVarsity, 1980), 59.

5. Abel Stevens, *The History of the Religious Movement of the Eighteenth Century, Called Methodism, Considered in Its Different Denominational Forms, and Its Relations to British and American Protestantism*, 3 vols. (New York: Carlton and Porter, 1858–61), 11, 461.

6. Walvoord, *Revelation*, 94.

7. Mark Senter III, *The Coming Revolution in Youth Ministry* (Wheaton: Victor, 1992), 16, 26–27.

8. C. H. Spurgeon, *Lectures to My Students* (Lynchburg, Va.: Old-Time Gospel Hour, 1875), 36.

9. Alan Axelrod, *Patton on Leadership* (Old Tappan, N.J.: Prentice-Hall, 1999), 130.

Chapter 11: Go Viral!

1. Donna O. Carpenter, *Professional Guide to Diseases* (Springhouse, Pa.: Springhouse, 2001), 155.

2. John C. Maxwell, *Developing the Leader Within You* (Nashville: Thomas Nelson, 1993), 22.

3. Joni Eareckson Tada and Steven Estes, *When God Weeps* (Grand Rapids: Zondervan, 1997), 21.

4. William R. Moody, *The Life of D. L. Moody* (Murfreesboro, Tenn.: Sword of the Lord, n.d.), 134.